A Guide to Research, Writing and Design on the Internet

CAROLE RICH
UNIVERSITY OF KANSAS

CREATING
ONLINE MEDIA

Web site: http://www.mhhe.com/rich/

McGraw-Hill
College

Boston   Burr Ridge, IL   Dubuque, IA   Madison, WI   New York   San Francisco   St. Louis
Bangkok   Bogotá   Caracas   Lisbon   London   Madrid
Mexico City   Milan   New Delhi   Seoul   Singapore   Sydney   Taipei   Toronto

McGraw-Hill College

A Division of The McGraw·Hill Companies

CREATING ONLINE MEDIA

Copyright © 1999, by The McGraw-Hill Companies, Inc. All rights reserved. Printed in the United States of America. Except as permitted under the United States Copyright Act of 1976, no part of this publication may be reproduced or distributed in any form or by any means, or stored in a database or retrieval system, without the prior written permission of the publisher.

This book is printed on acid-free paper.

3 4 5 6 7 8 9 0 QPD/QPD 3 2 1 0

ISBN 0–07–303415–0

Editorial director: *Phillip A. Butcher*
Sponsoring editor: *Marjorie Byers*
Marketing manager: *Carl Leonard*
Senior project manager: *Denise Santor-Mitzit*
Production supervisor: *Scott M. Hamilton*
Cover design: *Gino Cieslik*
Interior design: *Sophia Kourkouvis/Hughes Design*
Compositor: *Shepherd Inc.*
Typeface: *11/12 Bembo*
Printer: *Quebecor Printing Book Group/Dubuque*

Library of Congress Cataloging-in Publication Data

Rich, Carole.
    Creating online media : a guide to research, writing and design
on the Internet / Carole Rich.
        p.   cm.
    Includes index.
    ISBN 0–07–303415–0 (alk. paper)
    1. Interactive multimedia.   2. Web sites—Design.   I.   Title.
QA76.76.I59R53   1998
005.72—dc21   97–34190
                                                                                CIP

http://www.mhhe.com

BRIEF CONTENTS

Is writing for the Web any different from writing for a print publication? The executive editor of MSNBC News discusses how writing for the Web is changing. You'll learn how to write nonlinear stories in layers and teasers that will make people want to click into your stories. You'll also learn proper style for the Web.

Should you link to hate groups? Should you quote sources from discussion groups without permission? Is your Web site copyrighted if you don't register it with the U.S. Copyright Office? The answers in this chapter may surprise you.

APPENDICES

A brief list of style tips and proper citation formats for research papers with Internet sources.

Scores of sources for reporting, writing, research, design and sites for students and professionals seeking careers in the media.

A list of sources and copyright permission.

A complete list of all the terms mentioned in individual chapters.

CONTENTS

INTRODUCTION

If you have only 20 seconds to make an impression that will entice readers into your Web site, how should you design your home page?

If you find information from a discussion group or Web sites on the Internet, should you use it in a news story?

If you are writing for an online publication, are the techniques different from writing for print?

You'll meet editors, designers and experts in online media who will discuss these issues in this textbook. You'll also learn how to create Web sites and explore the legal and ethical problems emerging in online media.

This book offers instruction in basic skills for producing online media. Every chapter is accompanied by Web sites that provide links to sites mentioned in the text as well as interactive exercises called *Safaris*. It is a book for students and teachers who have no experience in online research, writing or design as well as those who have some experience with this type of media. It does not attempt to teach advanced Web design or theoretical concepts, although issues of how online communications will affect print publications are addressed.

The book can be used for a full course in online media or as a supplemental text in other courses to provide skills for using the Internet in research, reporting and writing.

The chapters in the textbook are organized in a fashion similar to Web sites. If you want to skip to topics within the chapter or start with the interactive quizzes, you can use the Hyperleaps at the beginning of the chapters to find the sections of interest to you.

Every chapter provides definitions of terms related to the content, and a full glossary is included in the appendix and online. To access the McGraw-Hill Web sites for the book, you'll need the password that comes with your textbook. Each chapter begins with a story about online editors or media sites to show you how people in this field do their jobs and why they are excited about online communication. But this book is mainly an interactive text that you *do,* not just one that you read. It is written to be used with a computer; that way you can create Web pages and explore online sites as you read the text. Unlike how-to books that just teach techniques of creating Web sites, all the instruction in this book relates to types of media—newspapers, magazines, broadcast, advertising and public relations. You'll find hundreds of online media sources in the textbook and on our Web site.

The danger of writing this kind of book is that technology changes rapidly. While it is true that Web sites change addresses frequently, we will be updating our links on the book's Web sites.

Many educators are concerned about whether we should be teaching students to use software in academic programs. But to create online media, you need tools. Software is a tool, just as a camera is a tool for photojournalism, and computers are tools for writing stories. Once you learn how to use one Web editor or browser, you can easily adapt to new or different versions. Learning how to create Web pages with software is the easy part. More important is the need to develop critical thinking to create online media. This book offers that kind of instruction.

All directions for creating Web documents are written for Macintosh and Windows platforms. Basic browsing and searching instructions are offered for Netscape Communicator and Microsoft's Internet Explorer because these two browsers are the most popular. I have chosen to use Netscape's Page Composer Web editor for only one reason: It is free to academic users. Many other software programs may be superior, but they cost money. At the time of publication, Microsoft's FrontPage Web editor, another good Web creation tool, was not free. If you prefer other products, you can use them and still read this book to learn concepts of creating online media.

Each chapter is self-contained; you can use the chapters in any order. If you prefer to learn about legal and ethical issues of online media before you create Web pages, start with that chapter at the end of the book. Legal and ethical issues also are discussed in other chapters where the issues are relevant. If you prefer, you could start with the chapters on reporting and writing. I have organized the book to begin with basic skills of creating Web sites because my students in an online media course want to learn those techniques before applying them to online reporting and writing. Several terms are repeated in different chapters to reinforce concepts and to facilitate use of the book in any order.

I wish to express special thanks to the faculty of The Poynter Institute for Media Studies in St. Petersburg, Fla., who offered me training, resources and their expertise. I also thank all the sources who shared their time and knowledge about online media with me. But I especially thank my editor, Marge Byers, who had the vision, enthusiasm and inspiration to encourage me to write this book, and my senior project manager, Denise Santor-Mitzit.

I would also like to thank the professors who reviewed the manuscript: Glen L. Bleske, California State University, Chico; Robert Huesca, Trinity University and Barbara Hipsman, Kent State University.

I hope you enjoy using this book as much as I enjoyed writing it. If you have problems with the instructions or find links that do not work on our Web sites, please contact me, and I will correct them or respond to your concerns. I welcome your feedback. You can reach me via e-mail at (crich@ukans.edu).

Carole Rich

Part

Mastering Basic Skills

Chapter I

GUTENBERG TO GIGABYTES

* To introduce students to an award-winning online media site.

* To learn Internet and computer terms.

* To understand the Internet and the World Wide Web.

* To learn what job skills online media experts consider important.

* To understand the importance of interactivity.

If you want to test your knowledge before reading the Frequently Asked Questions in this chapter, leap over the questions starting on Page 9 to the Safaris at the end of the chapter or take the interactive quiz on our Web site, **http://www.mhhe.com/socscience/comm/rich/ch1/** You'll need the password that comes with your book.

The following Web sites are mentioned in this chapter; you can link to them on our Web site:

The Internet Chicago Tribune:
http://www.chicago.tribune.com
Microsoft's Sidewalk sites:
http://www.sidewalk.com

You'll find more complete explanations of these terms in this chapter. A full glossary is included at the end of the book and on our Web site:

http://www.mhhe.com/socscience/comm/rich/glossary.html

BIT, BYTE A bit is the smallest unit of data transmitted on computers. A byte is a string of eight bits, the unit of data needed to store one character. For example, a byte to make the letter *A* requires the eight digits 01000001.

CLIENT An application on a computer that requests information from another computer that has software to "serve" to you. The computer that delivers the information is the "server."

CYBERSPACE A term coined by science fiction writer William Gibson in his book, *Neuromancer,* to describe a simulated realm on a computer where people experience "virtual reality" by interacting with technology that makes their actions seem real.

DOMAIN The part of an Internet address that identifies the name of the computer serving the information, the organization and the type of site such as *edu* for educational, *gov* for governmental, *org* for organization, or *com* for commercial.

DNS Domain Name Server (or Domain Name System), a standard system of addressing World Wide Web sites; also a synonym for an Internet address.

GIGABYTE One billion bytes of data.

HOME PAGE The entry page to a Web site.

HTML HyperText Markup Language, a coding language for documents on the World Wide Web.

HTTP HyperText Transfer Protocol, a system of rules that computers on the World Wide Web use to transfer HTML documents.

HYPERLINK Also called a *link* in HTML documents, a hyperlink allows you to click and connect to another document on the World Wide Web. Links in text usually are in a different color from the text and often are underlined. Images also can serve as hyperlinks.

INTERNET A global collection of computer networks that are connected through cables, phone lines or satellites to share information.

MEGABYTE One million bytes of data storage.

URL An Internet address, called a *Uniform Resource Locator,* to locate sites on the Internet, much like your street address locates where you live. The *AP Stylebook* refers to it as a

Universal Resource Locator, but that is not the preferred term.

WORLD WIDE WEB A worldwide system of storing and retrieving Internet documents coded in a format that includes links to other documents, graphics and multimedia.

Howard Witt

For 15 years Howard Witt worked in Russia, Africa, Canada and Los Angeles as a reporter for the *Chicago Tribune.* Now he is reaching readers all over the world without leaving his fifth floor office in the newspaper's Chicago headquarters.

Witt is associate managing editor for interactive news at the *Chicago Tribune,* where he supervises the content and production of the company's online news, classified advertising and entertainment products. Many journalists might consider Witt's former career as a foreign correspondent for the *Tribune* rather exciting. But when Witt turned 37, he was worried that he would get bored if he continued doing the same type of work.

"I had to plot a career for another 30 years," he says. "I wondered what I would do." So when Owen Youngman, director of the *Tribune's* Internet operation, offered him the job as associate managing editor, he seized it. "I just figured this [the Internet] is something new and different—an opportunity not to be missed."

He turns to his computer, accesses a homicide package his staff produced and clicks on a searchable map to locate his neighborhood. Then he types in his home address to demonstrate how the database will show the number of homicides in his neighborhood. It also provides links to specific court cases if he wants to find out more about them. These interactive search functions make the database of homicide statistics relevant to users. The package also contains news and feature stories.

Other online *Tribune* packages feature 360-degree angle photographs, called *photo bubbles,* that give viewers the feeling of being on the scene. The *Tribune* is also producing multimedia stories with audio and video. These and other features earned the Internet *Tribune* the award of Best Online Newspaper by the Newspaper Association of America in 1997.

THE INTERNET AND THE WORLD WIDE WEB

Presentations like these on the Internet, a vast global network of computer connections, are changing the nature of mass media. Anyone in the world with an Internet connection can access this information on the online *Chicago Tribune* site in seconds. The Internet has been described as the most significant development in mass media since Johann Gutenberg printed books with moveable type on a mechanical printing press in the mid-1400s. That may be an overstatement because radio and television also had profound influences on mass media, but the Internet now can combine all these media. In fact, many of the terms used in online media sites, such as *channels, producers,* and *netcasts,* derive more from broadcast than print.

The Internet was created in the 1960s by the U.S. Department of Defense, but it contained only text documents and was difficult to use. In 1989 a researcher, Tim Berners-Lee, created a system of linking documents to each other by a coded language called *hypertext.* Documents created with this coding are a part of a storage and retrieval system on the Internet called the *World Wide Web.*

Think of the Internet as your university and the Web as the vast number of courses linked by a common code—grades—to structure them and a common enrollment procedure to retrieve them. Without access to the university (the Internet network), you can't link to (or enroll in) the courses. By 1993 a browser called *Mosaic* made it possible to view documents on the Web with graphics and multimedia, and the Web became the most popular part of the Internet other than electronic mail. The Internet also contains many other text documents and discussion bulletin boards called *newsgroups* that are not part of the Web.

Almost all major media newspapers, magazines and broadcast stations have created sites on the World Wide Web, many with multimedia. Despite the computer skills needed for this new media, Witt stresses that journalists need to master the basic skills of reporting and writing. "We need reporters who know how to think critically, have curiosity and the essential ability to report and write an engaging story," Witt says.

He is not alone. Those convictions are echoed by editors at the online versions of the *New York Times,* the *Los Angeles Times,* MSNBC, CNN, *Time* magazine online, and other new media journalists. You'll read more about Witt and these other journalists in this chapter and throughout the book as they address various skills we will study.

JOB SKILLS

Consider some of these skills that online editors seek in new employees:

* **Leah Gentry,** editorial director of the *Los Angeles Times* Web site: "When I hire, I look for two skills: You have to be a crackerjack journalist, and you have to be flexible. When the industry changes tomorrow, and it will, you can't freak out."

* **Flora Garcia,** production manager for Time Online, the Web site for *Time* magazine: "I want to know how you deal with chaos, how can you problem-solve. What we're looking for is a different type of student, a Renaissance journalist hacker. It requires a different personality. I want to know if this person can deal with whatever we throw at them. News is becoming much more than presenting one type of thing. I look to journalists because I want someone who is careful and who understands what accuracy is and someone who can cast a story. I also want someone who can work with other people."

✳ **Dan Patrinos,** senior editor/electronic services at *The Milwaukee Journal Sentinel:* "I want people who can work as a team, people who are flexible. I'm also looking for people who are not enamored with technology. It's the content that makes a difference. When we hire a sports producer, I want someone who knows sports, who has clippings, who can write. And it helps to know Photoshop. I want people who can help develop revenue streams. We must make money."

✳ **Mitch Lazar,** producer, new business development, CNN Interactive: "When we hire at CNN Interactive, we look for people who can tell stories. Good writing is the foundation of what we do. We want good writing and good people skills."

✳ **Meredith Artley,** producer, *The New York Times* online version: "Creativity. I ask to look at their home page and see what they've done with it. A good writing background. A lot of enthusiasm; someone who is excited about the Internet."

You'll get a chance to create your home page and an online resume with instructions in later chapters. Why should you learn about online journalism? Skeptics question whether online media will survive, and other critics wonder whether print media, especially newspapers, will survive. But all types of media are creating sites on the Internet anyway, so journalists need to master online skills.

CHICAGO TRIBUNE PLANS

The Tribune Company is investing heavily in the Internet, just in case newspapers are jeopardized in the future. In addition to creating Web sites for suburban communities around the Chicago area, the company is a partner with America Online in a $100 million plan to create a network of Digital City local sites throughout the country. These sites will feature news, entertainment and information to serve as virtual guides to the cities.

Digital City sites will compete with Microsoft Corporation's plans to create online "Sidewalk" cities throughout the United States as guides to entertainment, restaurants and other city attractions. Newspaper industry leaders fear that the Sidewalk sites will threaten the advertising base of newspapers. As a result, major media companies such as Knight-Ridder and the Tribune Company are developing their own entertainment guides to cities. Media leaders also worry that their online sites may compete with their print products for advertising and readers.

Howard Witt considers the *Tribune* Internet sites as another option for readers, not as a threat to the print products. "This company has TV stations, newspapers, radio stations, and we own the Chicago Cubs," Witt says. "We don't care how people see our content. It's all *Tribune* content that can make money from advertising. We're taking bets on the future. If people prefer to use the Internet, we intend to be there."

HOW PEOPLE USE ONLINE MEDIA

The Internet *Tribune* statistics show that people aren't using the newspaper's Web sites to read news. "People don't come here to look; they come here to do things," Witt says. "The last thing they want to do is read text. What they want is more information relative to them."

More than 1.5 million users accessed the *Tribune* Web site in one month, but the majority of them searched for homes in the real estate database, for jobs on the *Tribune's* "Careerpath," and for used cars in the online classified advertisements. Software that keeps track of page views, the number of times a Web page was accessed, shows that the search engine page for real estate ads was viewed 334,000 times in one month compared to 38,000 page views for the main *Tribune* news page. The only news-related site that attracted a lot of users was sports.

However, in other online newspaper sites, local news is very popular. A German report compiled by the IFRA Institute in Darmstadt shows that 51 percent of all Web users access local information almost exclusively. The study also showed that in 1997, every day 71,000 new users logged on to the Internet. As the use of the Internet continues to increase, reading news online is expected to become more popular.

News is the primary draw for CNN Interactive. As a result, many local online newspapers don't feature national or international news stories on their sites. And online reading habits vary from one community to another. In the *Idaho State Journal's* Internet site, the most widely read information is the obituaries.

In contrast, when famed columnist Mike Royko died in April 1997, his online obituary in the Internet *Chicago Tribune* didn't draw many readers, possibly because they had read about it in the print *Tribune* or heard about it on television. But within minutes of the news, e-mail messages poured in from people responding to his death.

"We had over 700 messages a week after he died," Witt says. "This is where I understood the power of this medium for the first time. These are poignant, heartfelt messages that can bring a tear to your eye. People from around the world felt this loss. It was absolutely remarkable to see. If he had died five years ago, some people might simply have written a letter to the editor. This (online message board) allows us to let people grieve together and share something like this. This is a pinnacle of what interactivity means."

THE CHANGING NATURE OF JOURNALISM

Andy Beers, executive producer of news at MSNBC, a Web site partnership between Microsoft Corp., NBC and cable CNBC television, says the interactive way people use the Web will change the role of journalists. In the past, journalists controlled what stories people should read or view, but on the Web, people can get the information they want when they want it.

He describes a recent election night when millions of people turned to the Web for results. If you seek election results on TV, you might have to listen to an entire broadcast before you hear the results you want, he says. If you want the results in a newspaper, you have to wait until the paper comes out the next morning or afternoon. But on the Web, you can seek the election results you want at any time, as long as the Web site is providing and updating the information, he says.

In addition, he says, Web users want their information in several ways. They want it in layers. Some people want only headlines, others want a little more information in news briefs, and still others want more depth on a subject, including a full story and links to related information.

"What does all this mean for journalists?" Beers asks. "I think all of us carry a lot of baggage based on some kind of entitlement that we're in a position to decide what people need. The Internet will break through that and force us to examine the way we do our jobs. People will find what they want. I think we have to start thinking of editors as facilitators to help people find the information they want instead of deciding what we think is right for them."

Beers says that core values of journalism won't change. He says values of being factual, unbiased and providing information that makes an impact on society are still important. "The new media has some really exciting and useful capabilities for people. It can change the way people get information. But when you let people get involved in making decisions about what they are interested in, we have to change journalism to be more inclusive. There's a great deal of power in helping people find information."

You will study the skills you need to provide information for new media in forthcoming chapters. In keeping with the interactive spirit that characterizes the

World Wide Web, you can learn more about the Internet in the rest of this chapter by leaping directly to the quiz at the end of the chapter or taking the interactive version on our online site.

http://www.mhhe.com/socscience/comm/rich/ch1/

If you don't know much about the Internet, you can first read the following Frequently Asked Questions, called FAQs, and answers and then take the quiz at the end of the chapter. The use of FAQs is a common method of presenting information on Web sites. You could also check the glossary for answers to many of these questions.

http://www.mhhe.com/socscience/comm/rich/glossary.html

FAQS

WHAT DOES *CYBERSPACE* MEAN?

Cyberspace is a term coined by author William Gibson in a science fiction novel called *Neuromancer.* Not coincidentally, it was published in 1984, a year made famous by George Orwell in his futuristic book of that name. Gibson's view of the future is a pessimistic one dominated by computer technology. His characters, inspired by greed and corruption, mentally travel through a simulated realm called *Cyberspace,* where they experience "virtual reality" by interacting with technology that makes their actions seem real. *Cyberspace* is now used in a broad sense to refer to information in computer networks.

WHAT IS THE INTERNET?

The Internet is an interconnection of computers that spans the globe. This global network is connected via smaller networks called *LANs,* local area networks, that function as relay stations, like airports or train stations. The Internet was started by the U.S. Defense Department in 1969 as a network called ARPANet, Advanced Research Projects Agency Network, to create a communication system in case of nuclear war.

WHAT IS THE WORLD WIDE WEB?

The World Wide Web, also called *WWW* or the *Web,* is a system of storing and retrieving documents on the Internet that share a common coded language, HyperText Markup Language (HTML). Unlike plain text documents, HTML documents can contain graphics, multimedia and clickable links to other documents. The Web was developed in 1989 at the CERN physics laboratory in Geneva, Switzerland, by physicist Tim Berners-Lee as a system of transferring ideas among scientists. It became popular in 1993 when a browser, Mosaic, was developed by the National Center for Supercomputing Applications (NCSA). This software made it possible to view Web documents with graphics. Mosaic has been usurped by more popular browsers, Netscape and Microsoft Internet Explorer. The Web is only a part of the Internet, but it is sometimes mistakenly used as a synonym for the Internet.

WHAT IS THE DIFFERENCE BETWEEN HYPERTEXT AND HYPERMEDIA?

Hypertext is coded (HTML) text that contains links, also called *hyperlinks,* to other documents. Hypermedia is also created with HTML codes but can include graphics, audio and video.

WHAT IS A URL?

A URL is an Internet address, pronounced as individual letters, *U-R-L,* not "earl." It stands for Uniform Resource Locator or Universal Resource Locator, meaning it's a uniform way that computers read addresses, just as the Postal Service reads ZIP codes. You need to write a URL in the location box of your browser to access documents on the Internet. All documents on the World Wide Web have URLs that start with *http://* (for HyperText Transfer Protocol) and end with *htm* or *html*.

WHY DO SOME WEB DOCUMENTS END WITH *HTML* AND OTHERS WITH *HTM*?

Documents created on PCs often end with *htm* because the number of characters you can put in a filename is limited, whereas Macintosh documents have no

10

limits, so those documents can carry the *html* tag. You can rename a document created on a PC if you prefer the more common *html* extension on a Web document.

WHAT DOES *HTTP* MEAN AND WHY DO ALL WORLD WIDE WEB DOCUMENTS START WITH IT IN THEIR ADDRESSES?

HTTP stands for HyperText Transfer Protocol, the rules by which hypertext documents are transferred on the Internet. It's a coded common language that allows computers to communicate with each other and relay information, like a universally understood SOS telegraph code. Major browsers automatically insert the HTTP code so you don't have to type it in when you call up an Internet site.

WHAT IS A PROTOCOL?

A protocol is a rule or set of commands that allows computers to communicate with each other.

WHAT IS TCP/IP?

TCP/IP means Transmission Control Protocol/Internet Protocol, and you need to have it on your computer to connect to the Internet. When you get your Internet account from your service provider, you will receive a TCP/IP number to insert in your computer to set up your Internet connection.

WHAT IS PPP?

PPP stands for Point-to-Point Protocol, a method by which your computer can communicate with a modem and a telephone line to make an Internet connection.

WHAT DOES *MODEM* MEAN?

Modem is a combination word for modulator, demodulator (notice the *mod* and *dem* parts of the two words). It's a device that connects your computer to a phone line so you can transmit information. Modems are sold by the speed with which they transmit data measured in bits per second (bps); the higher the bps number, the faster the modem.

WHAT IS MEANT BY THE *DIGITAL REVOLUTION* AND WHY DO PEOPLE REFER TO DIGITS WHEN THEY ARE TALKING ABOUT THE INTERNET?

The dictionary defines *digits* as fingers and toes or as a number system. Because computers transmit all data in the form of digits—a combination of ones and zeros—the rise of computer transmission, especially on the Internet, has been called the *Digital Revolution*.

WHAT ARE *BITS, BYTES, MEGABYTES* AND *GIGABYTES?*

Modern computers transmit data in digital language composed of bits, the smallest unit of data. Computer language is created in digits of two numbers, a one and a zero, called a *binary system.* Computers use an infinite combination of these two numbers to form words, images and numbers. One bit is a binary digit. Bits can also be interpreted as "on" and "off" switches instead of numbers.

Bytes (pronounced "bites") are used to describe the amount of storage of bits. A byte equals a string of eight bits, the unit of data needed to store one character, such as a letter or number. For example, a byte to make the letter *A* requires the eight digits 01000001. The more bytes in a document, the larger the file or the storage of bits.

A document that contains 1 million bytes equals one megabyte of storage. A floppy disk contains about 1.4 megabytes of storage space, meaning it can store 1.4 million bytes, while a Zip disk contains 100 megabytes. Computers and some portable disks now can store as much as a billion bytes, called a *gigabyte,* or several gigabytes.

WHAT IS *BANDWIDTH?*

Bandwidth is the amount of data a cable or network can transmit. Web designers often say that when bandwidth increases, multimedia documents will become more common because they will load faster. Right now a document with many images or multimedia can take a long time to load on your computer because the bandwidth is limited, especially if you are using a modem.

WHAT IS AN *ISP?*

ISP stands for Internet service provider, which is the company or main computer that provides your connection to the Internet. Your university may be your ISP; the largest commercial provider is America Online (AOL).

WHAT IS *RAM*, AND WHY IS IT IMPORTANT?

RAM means random access memory, the amount of memory your computer has to run programs. New computers these days come with 16, 32 or more megabytes of RAM. That's not the same as the storage memory for computers, which is often 750 MBs (megabytes) or more. Newer computers contain two or more gigabytes.

WHAT IS *FTP?*

FTP stands for file transfer protocol, the rules that allow computers to transfer files back and forth to each other. When you download software, you often get it via FTP.

WHAT IS A *BBS*?

A BBS is a bulletin board system or a group discussion. The Internet contains many bulletin boards where you can send and receive messages.

WHAT DO *CLIENT* AND *SERVER* MEAN?

A *server* is a computer that contains software that allows it to deliver information to another computer. A client is the application on your computer that requests the information from the server. When you want to retrieve a Web document, for example, your machine is a client and the machine that contains the document is the server that will "serve" or deliver it to you.

WHAT DOES *DNS* MEAN?

DNS stands for Domain Name Server, a standard system of addressing sites on the Internet. The domain is the place where a Web site resides, basically the address, much like your own address, which contains a street, city, state and ZIP code. Most Internet addresses include the name of the server, the name of the organization, and the type of organization such as *edu* for educational, *com* for commercial, *gov* for governmental or *org* for organization. The parts of the address are separated by dots. Your university Internet address probably ends with *edu*. The *Chicago Tribune* domain is *http://www.chicago.tribune.com,* which stands for an address on the World Wide Web, the organization name and a commercial site. Internet addresses are converted to numerical addresses when they are accessed.

WHAT IS *BETA TESTING* OR A *BETA VERSION*?

Beta testing is probably something you should avoid unless you know how to fix your computer if it crashes. A beta version is a version of software that hasn't been released in final form because it needs to be tested (beta tested) for problems called "bugs." Software companies like to have computer users test the programs so they can find out what problems exist and fix them before releasing a program to the public.

WHAT ARE *GOPHER SITES?*

Gopher is a system of organizing and transferring files on the Internet that was developed by the University of Minnesota and named after its mascot, the gopher.

WHAT IS A *SEARCH ENGINE?*

A search engine software application that allows you to search for documents on the Internet. You'll find out more about them in Chapter 3.

http://www.mhhe.com/socscience/comm/
rich/ch1/

1–1 Web Words Safari

The Internet has spawned a new set of terms, including scores of acronyms. To decipher geek-speak, you need glossaries, and you'll find many of them on the World Wide Web, including one for this book. If you know how to use a Web browser, take this interactive quiz on our Web site. You can check your answers there, too. If you are still contributing to dead trees, take this multiple-choice quiz, and print out your answers.

1 Cyberspace is

    a. a space between documents on the Internet.

    b. a term coined by William Gibson in his science fiction novel *Neuromancer*.

    c. a place in a community of Internet users.

2 URL is

  a. an acronym for user's resources locations.

  b. an acronym for unified religious legions.

  c. an acronym for an Internet addressing system, Uniform Resource Locator.

3 HTML is

  a. an acronym for a type of Web coding software, Helvetica Talk Medium Logos.

  b. an acronym for a World Wide Web document coding system, HyperText Markup Language.

  c. an acronym for a Web coding language, HyperText Medium Logistics.

4 The Internet is

  a. a network that connects computers internally in a university.

  b. a network that connects only international computer systems.

  c. a collection of computer networks that are interconnected through cables, phone lines or satellites to share information.

5 ISP is

  a. an acronym for Internet service provisions.

  b. an acronym for Internet service provider.

  c. an acronym for Internet service protocols.

6 The World Wide Web is

  a. a network of computers that spans the globe.

  b. a system for storing and retrieving Internet documents created in a common language called HTML, characterized by links.

  c. a worldwide network available only through university computer systems.

7 HTTP is

  a. an acronym for HyperText Talking Platforms to transfer documents on the Web.

  b. an acronym for HyperText Transfer Protocol to transfer documents on the Web.

  c. an acronym for Hypermedia Transfer Protocol to code documents on the Web.

8 BBS is

 a. an acronym for best built sites on the Web.

 b. an acronym for bulletin board systems.

 c. an acronym for bits and bytes systems.

9 FAQ is

 a. an acronym for frequently asked questions.

 b. an acronym for fully authenticated questions.

 c. an acronym for frequently accessed quizzes.

10 DNS is

 a. an acronym for Digital News Service.

 b. an acronym for Digital Name Server.

 c. an acronym for Domain Name Server.

11 RAM is

 a. an acronym for random access memory.

 b. an acronym for realtime access modems.

 c. an acronym for radio audio modems.

12 A gigabyte equals

 a. one million bytes of storage.

 b. one billion bytes of storage.

 c. two binary systems of storage.

13 Hypermedia are

 a. very fast loading media at a hyper pace.

 b. text-only documents written in HTML.

 c. HTML documents featuring audio, video and graphics.

14 FTP means

 a. fast typing protocols to move documents quickly on the Web.

 b. file transfer protocols to send and retrieve documents on the Internet.

 c. file transfer points to indicate where documents should go on the Web.

15 Bandwidth means

 a. a large band of bytes to transfer Web documents.

 b. the amount of data a cable or network can transmit.

 c. the width of a computer cable.

1-2 **Discussion**

* How has the Internet changed your life?

* For what purposes do you use the Internet?

* How has e-mail changed your communication with friends and other people?

* How do you think the Internet will affect newspapers, magazines, television and other media?

Chapter 2
BROWSING BASICS

Goals

* To learn terms related to navigating the Internet.

* To learn how to use a browser, a software program that retrieves documents to your computer. The most popular browsers are Netscape Navigator and Microsoft Internet Explorer.

* To use browsing skills to explore some media sites.

Hyperleap

If you already know how to use browsers, leap to the end of the chapter and travel on some safaris to a wide world of media sites and connect to our Web site. But first, make sure you know the terms in the glossary. For newbies using Netscape Navigator, instructions start on Page 25. If you use Microsoft Internet Explorer, leap to instructions on Page 31.

Our Web site for this chapter is:

http://www.mhhe.com/socscience/comm/rich/ch2/

Web sites

The following Web sites are cited in this chapter; you can link to them on our Web page:

American Journalism Review:
http://www.ajr.org

Lynx, a text-only Web browser, version 2-7:
ftp://ftp2.cc.ukans.edu/pub/lynx/lynx2-7

Lou Montulli's home page:
http://people.netscape.com/montulli/index.html

The Amazing Fish Cam:
http://live.netscape.com/fishcam/fishcam.html

Other Web sites are included in the safaris.

Glossary at a Glance

Some of the terms here have been repeated from the previous chapter. A full glossary is in the appendix and on our Web site at:

http://www.mhhe.com/socscience/comm/rich/glossary.html

BOOKMARK A menu feature in Netscape that allows you to save addresses of Internet sites you want to revisit, like a bookmark in a printed document that saves your place. In Internet Explorer this feature is called *Favorites.*

BROWSER A software program that allows you to explore documents on the Internet. Netscape Navigator and Internet Explorer are the two most popular browsers, but many others are offered by Internet providers.

CACHE The storage place in a browser that keeps a record of the Internet sites you recently visited.

DOMAIN The part of an Internet address that identifies the name of the computer serving the information, the organization and the type of site, such as *edu* for educational, *gov* for governmental, *org* for organization, or *com* for commercial.

DNS Domain Name Server (or Domain Name System), a standard system of addressing World Wide

Web sites; also a synonym for an Internet address.

ENCRYPTION Scrambling of data so that only authorized people can see it. If you are sending your credit card to an online source, you would want an encrypted site.

HOME PAGE The entry page to a Web site.

HTML HyperText Markup Language, a coding system for all documents on the World Wide Web.

HTTP HyperText Transfer Protocol, a code for the rules by which documents are transferred from one location or computer to another. All HTML documents on the World Wide Web start with *http* in lower case.

HYPERLINK A link, usually underlined or in a different color from the text, connecting one HTML document to another; also called *links*. Images also can be links.

INTERNET A global collection of computer networks connected through cables, phone lines or satellites to share information.

INTERNET EXPLORER A browser made by Microsoft Corporation.

NETSCAPE NAVIGATOR A browser made by the Netscape Communications Corp.

SERVER A computer that connects with other computers and contains software that delivers or "serves" information through a network.

SURF, SURFING Slang for *browsing* the Internet.

URL An Internet address, called a *Uniform Resource Locator,* to locate sites on the Internet, much like your street address identifies where you live.

WORLD WIDE WEB A worldwide system of storing and retrieving Internet documents coded in a format that includes links, graphics and multimedia.

Lou Montulli

Scott Adams, creator of the Dilbert cartoon, wasn't far from the truth when he credited some college kid with inventing a browser. But Lou Montulli wasn't drunk when he created an Internet browser, Lynx, while he attended the University of Kansas. Montulli, who describes himself as a "really weird person," barely has time to eat. These days he works 110 to 120 hours a week at Netscape Communications Corp. developing software.

At age 23, just six credits away from getting his degree in computer science at KU, Montulli left school to become one of the original team of programmers at Netscape Corp., which produces a popular browser for the World Wide Web. Shortly thereafter, he became a multimillionaire.

He says he'd like to get his degree some day and chuckles as he describes the note posted on his computer at Netscape headquarters in California: "Call your adviser, call your adviser, call your adviser!" Montulli says the Dilbert cartoon in this chapter is also posted in the Netscape office, and the character bears striking resemblance to Mark Andreessen, one of the founders of Netscape.

Montulli says he and Andreessen had been corresponding by e-mail about new ideas for Web development in the early 1990s. In 1994, when Andreessen and Jim Clark, chairman of Netscape's board of directors, cofounded the company, they asked Montulli to join them along with a handful of other computer gurus.

Considered a genius by his former colleagues at KU, Montulli also developed the "blink" tag that you often see on advertisements in Web sites. This time he came closer to mirroring the Dilbert cartoon. Montulli confesses that he created the HTML code for the blink "after one night of drinking heavily."

In addition, he created the Amazing Fish Cam, a video camera connected to an Internet server. The camera, positioned in front of a fish tank, produces images on a Web site that change every minute, so you can enjoy watching the virtual fish, but you don't have to feed them.

DILBERT reprinted by permission of United Feature Syndicate, Inc.

LYNX

When he was in college, Montulli and two other KU colleagues created the Lynx browser, which is a text-only way to access and view Internet documents. Although Netscape Navigator and Microsoft's Internet Explorer now dominate the browser market, Lynx still is used by thousands of people who don't want to view graphics in documents because this browser downloads documents in text-only format very quickly. It is particularly helpful for visually impaired people because they can download documents without images and use audio-reading equipment. Montulli was inducted into the World Wide Web Hall of Fame in 1994 for his contribution to Lynx and Web development discussion groups.

These days Montulli works on the networking applications at Netscape. He was instrumental in developing Netscape Communicator, the software we will use to browse and create Web pages. Instructions also are provided in this chapter for Microsoft's Internet Explorer browser.

You can download Lynx from the University of Kansas and view documents from the World Wide Web and other Internet sites in text versions. However, Netscape and Internet Explorer make it easy and more fun to explore the World Wide Web because you can link to documents and view them with graphics, audio and video if the sites contain these elements.

Eric Meyer has made it even easier for journalists to browse through media sites. A journalism professor who also operates an Internet consulting company, Newslink, Meyer has created the Web site for *American Journalism Review* (AJR), which is an excellent starting place for journalists. The site contains about 6,000 links to newspaper, broadcast, and magazine sites throughout the world. Meyer also provides links to scores of media organizations and other resources for journalists.

Meyer spent part of one summer browsing through more than 2,000 of about 3,600 online newspaper sites to check the links on his Web site. He wasn't too pleased with what he saw. "They're all doing the same thing; there's a lot of bandwagon mentality," he says.

He claims that most online users are browsers, not readers. "Headlines become more important online than in print," he says. "People aren't reading text; they aren't reading stories. They are information seekers. The audience that makes this medium is browsing."

Once you begin browsing on the World Wide Web, you may find yourself spending hours clicking into links that provide an amazing array of information. Set a time limit for yourself.

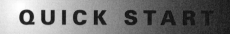

QUICK START

Here's a quick start to browsing; complete illustrated instructions follow later in the chapter.

✳   Click twice on the icon for Netscape or Explorer to open the browser.

✳   In the location bar at the top of your browser, type this Internet address (called a *URL*) for *American Journalism Review:*
     http://www.ajr.org
     Then hit return. Type this address carefully with no spaces between the slashes and dots.

Location : |http://www.ajr.org/

✳   Click once on the links, which are underlined in a different color from the text, and have fun "surfing" the World Wide Web of media sites.

To learn more about browsing for Netscape or Explorer read on. If you have never used a browser, read these instructions for Netscape's browser or skip to Page 31 if you are using Microsoft's Internet Explorer browser.

NETSCAPE FOR NEWBIES

The icons and screen images in this chapter are based on versions of Netscape Communicator's Navigator 4.0. Browsers continually improve and change their appearance, but they provide the same basic functions described here. If you are using an earlier or later version of Navigator, the icons may look different, but the functions will be similar. Netscape Navigator's appearance also differs slightly on Macintosh and PC machines. These steps will get you started browsing the Web.

Open Netscape Navigator   Locate your Navigator icon in your Netscape Communicator folder or on your desktop and double-click your mouse to open it. If you click your Communicator icon in Windows, it will also work as a navigator.

Wait to Load   While the page is downloading (starting to appear on your screen), shooting stars will move through the N on the right of your screen, and a toolbar will open at the top of your screen. The bottom of your screen will also tell you how much of the document is loading. Wait until the N stops moving.

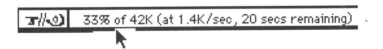

Composer may open a component bar on your screen, offering you choices of browsing, getting mail, using discussion groups or composing a Web page (which we'll use later in the book). If you don't want this bar to show, click on the

Explorer menu at the top of your screen and pull it down to "Dock Component Bar." In Windows, pull down the Communicator menu and do the same.

Type a Web Site Address In the address bar next to "Netsite" or "Location," depending on your browser version, type an address, called a *URL*, which means Uniform Resource Locator, a uniform system of addressing sites on the Web. Follow these steps:

✳ Delete the Netscape address in the bar by highlighting it and hitting Delete (or Back Space in PCs) or just use the delete key.

✳ Type the address for *American Journalism Review:*
http://www.ajr.org
The bar will change to "Location."

Put colons, slashes, dots and tildes (~ the wavy character, usually at the top left on your keyboard) in exactly the right place with no extra spaces. All URLs on the World Wide Web start with *http://* (*http,* for HyperText Transfer Protocol, followed by a colon and two forward slashes). Most browsers automatically insert the *http://* as a default, but you should know how to type a full address anyway. *American Journalism Review* is a good starting place because it contains links to print and broadcast media and hundreds of resources for journalists.

✳ Hit Return (or Enter on PCs) and wait for the site to load on your screen.

SCROLLING

Once you connect to an Internet site, you can scroll up and down by using the down arrow in the scrollbar at the right of the document or by using your up and down cursors on your keyboard.

CONNECT WITH HYPERLINKS

You can also connect to another location by clicking on a hyperlink, a word or phrase that usually is underlined and/or in a different color than the rest of the text, such as <u>Newspapers</u> in the Sites box of *American Journalism Review.* Click on the link to <u>Newspapers</u>. It will connect to newspapers in the United States and other countries or allow you to search for an online paper you want.

SITES
<u>Year's best</u>
<u>Hot site</u>
<u>Top 10</u>
<u>Newspapers</u>
<u>Magazines</u>
<u>Radio/TV</u>
<u>Resources</u>

BOOKMARKS

If you like the site you accessed and want to revisit it often, save the site address as a bookmark.

* Pull down the bookmark icon at the top of your screen next to the Explorer icon in Macintosh and click on "Add Bookmark." In Windows the Bookmarks menu is on your toolbar near the Location bar. Try this by saving the AJR site as a bookmark.

﹡ After you have saved a bookmark, you don't have to type in a URL for it again. Just pull down your Bookmark menu to the site you saved. Try it again by using your bookmark to call up the AJR site.

NETSCAPE TOOLBAR

The toolbar offers you many navigation shortcuts. The icons differ in various versions of Netscape, and they look slightly different in Macintosh and Windows, but their functions are the same. You can do many of the same functions by pulling down the menus at the top of your screen, but toolbar buttons simplify the tasks.

This is how the toolbar looks in Macintosh:

This is the how the toolbar looks in Windows 95.

Here is what the buttons do.

﹡ **Back:** Returns you to the previous document you viewed. If you keep clicking "back," you'll return to other documents you viewed. The Go menu offers you the same options and also keeps a history of the last 10 or more sites you have visited. You can click on a site in the Go menu, and Netscape will retrieve it for you. If you pull down the Communicator menu to "History Page," you'll get a list of all sites you have visited. By clicking on any site in the history page, you can access the document. This is very useful if you have forgotten a URL and don't want to search for it again.

✳ **Forward:** Returns you to the preceding document you viewed, but it works only after you've clicked on the back button. The last document you viewed will be displayed.

✳ **Reload:** If you want to reload a document that doesn't look clear, click this button. This is very helpful when you are designing Web pages so you can view your changes.

✳ **Home:** Returns you to the home page of your browser. It defaults to the Netscape home page, but you can set up your home page as you wish by pulling down the Edit menu and clicking on "Preferences." Then type a URL you prefer for your home page.

✳ **Search:** To find documents about a subject, person, or specific site, hit the Search button, and several search engines (software to search the Web) will open. Navigator usually offers a different search engine each time you access this page. We'll learn searching skills in the next chapter, but you should try this button now as well. Type a topic, such as journalism, in the address bar of whatever search engine appears, and see how many thousands of documents you can retrieve.

✳ **Guide:** The Guide button offers some interesting sites selected by Netscape in conjunction with the Yahoo! search engine for various categories.

✳ **Images:** Some people prefer to turn off images so pages can download faster. You can do that by setting preferences under the Edit menu, then clicking "Advanced." Then click the box with "Automatically load images . . ." to remove the X or check. Instead of images, a small icon will appear. Clicking the images button will reload images on documents. In Windows this button doesn't show up on the toolbar unless you have turned off the option to automatically load images.

✳ **Print:** Click this button to print any document you have downloaded.

✳ **Security:** This button tells you whether the site has encrypted data, meaning scrambled data that can be read only by authorized people. If you are sending your credit card for online shopping, you would want an encrypted site. This button also opens a menu that allows you to choose whether you want warnings if information you are sending is not secure. Click the button and then click the Navigator link to set preferences for warnings.

✳ **Stop:** If you want to stop loading a page because it takes too long or it is not what you wanted, click the Stop button.

✳ **Saving Documents:** To save a copy of a Web document, go to the File menu and pull down "Save As." Then name your document and click Save. The document will be saved as text without images.

OTHER TOOLS

❋ **Go Offline:** After you locate a site, if you want to read a document offline, go to the File menu and click on "Go Offline." This is helpful if you get charged for time online.

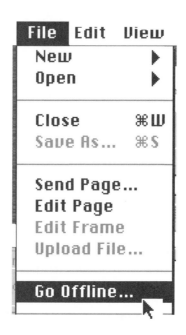

❋ **Help:** If you need help using your browser, click the Help menu on your toolbar in Windows or the question mark icon on the right of your screen in Macintosh.

❋ **Mail:** You can set your browser to send and receive e-mail by pulling down the Edit menu to "Preferences." Under "Mail and Newsgroups," click the arrow downward on Macintosh or click the plus sign to minus on PCs. Fill out information in each category, listing your server and your preferences. For more information about setting up newsgroups, see Chapter 5.

If you don't plan to use Microsoft's Internet Explorer, skip to Safaris at the end of the chapter.

MICROSOFT INTERNET EXPLORER

These instructions are for PC users on Windows 95 platform. If you are using Explorer in a Macintosh, the toolbox will look different but the functions will be the same.

Open Explorer   Click on the Internet Explorer in your computer. The Explorer icon or another Internet service provider's icon will move until the page downloads.

Type a Web Site Address   In the address bar, type an address, called a *URL,* which means Uniform Resource Locator, a uniform system of addressing sites on the Web. Follow these steps:

❋ Delete the default address for Microsoft by highlighting it and hitting Back Space or Delete on a Macintosh.

> Address http://www.msn.com/

❋ Type a new address as illustrated:
http://www.ajr.org
This is the address for *American Journalism Review,* which is a good starting place for journalists. Type carefully, with colons, slashes and dots but no spaces.

> Address http://www.ajr.org

❋ URLs for the World Wide Web start with *http://* (*http* in lower case with a colon followed by two slashes, for HyperText Transfer Protocol, which stands for the rules by which HTML documents are transferred on the Web).

❋ Hit Return or Enter and wait for the site to load on your screen.

SCROLLING

Once you connect to an Internet site, you can scroll up and down the site by clicking in the scrollbar at the right of the document or using the up and down cursors on your keyboard.

CONNECT WITH HYPERLINKS

You can connect to another location by clicking on a hyperlink, a word or phrase that is usually underlined and/or in a different color than the rest of the text such as <u>Newspapers</u> in the Sites box of *American Journalism Review.* Click on the link to <u>Newspapers</u>; it will connect to newspapers in the United States and other countries or allow you to search for an online paper you want.

SITES
Year's best
Hot site
Top 10
Newspapers
Magazines
Radio/TV
Resources

FAVORITE SITES TO SAVE

If you like the site you accessed and want to revisit it often, save it by adding it to your Favorites menu.

* Pull down the menu and click on "Add To Favorites" in Windows or "Add Page To Favorites" in Macintosh, or click on the Favorites button in the toolbar. Try this with the AJR site. After you get the site on your screen, add it to your favorites.

* The next time you want to get the site, you don't have to type in the URL. Just pull down your Favorites menu to the site you saved.

The toolbar offers you many navigation shortcuts. The appearance differs on a Macintosh and PC and in newer or older versions of Explorer, but the functions are the same. You can do many of the same tasks by pulling down your menus (File, Edit, View, Go, and Favorites), but toolbar buttons simplify the tasks.

These are the toolbar functions:

* **Back:** This button returns you to a previous document. You can also use the Go menu. If you pull down the Go menu to "Open History Folder," you'll get a list of all sites you have visited. By clicking on any site in the history page, you can access the document. This is very useful if you have forgotten a URL and don't want to search for it again.

> Open History Folder

* **Forward:** The forward button, when highlighted, returns you to the next-to-last page you visited after you have clicked the back button.

* **Stop:** If you want to stop loading a page because it takes too long or isn't what you wanted, click the X button, which is the Stop button.

* **Refresh:** If the page you loaded isn't clear, this button reloads it to get a better version.

* **Home:** This button takes you back to the browser's home page or one you have designated to serve as your starting page. You can change your home

page and many other ways you view documents in your browser by going to the View menu and clicking on "Options." Then click on "Navigation" to change your home page or other options to set your preferences.

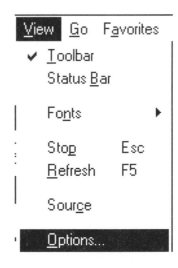

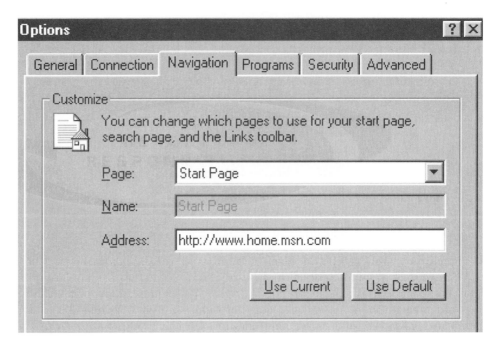

* **Preferences:** In Macintosh, you can click the Preferences button on your toolbar or use the Edit menu and click "Preferences" to change your home page or select other options if you want to customize your browser for viewing and navigation.

* **Search:** This button will open search engines.

* **Favorites:** This button will add a site to your list of favorites as an alternative to pulling down the File menu to add a favorite site.

* **Print:** Click the print button to print a document you have loaded.

* **Font:** The font button with small up and down arrows allows you to increase or decrease the size of the type you are viewing. There are five different settings, from largest to smallest; keep clicking until you get your desired font size.

* **Mail:** You can set up Explorer to read your mail and you can read newsgroups, which are discussion groups on the Internet. To set mail preferences, pull down the Options menu to "Programs." Fill out the information as directed. (This isn't advisable if you are working on a shared network at your school because your e-mail address will remain for others to use if you don't delete it.)

* **Edit:** When you begin to create Web pages, the Edit button will launch your favorite Web editor, which automatically codes Web pages. We will use the Netscape Page Composer for creating Web pages.

* **Help:** For more help, pull down your Help menu to "Help Topics."

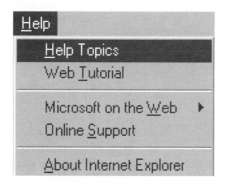

Netscape or Explorer won't open: If several other applications are open on your computer, your machine may not have enough memory to connect to your browser.

Macintosh users: Place your cursor on the computer icon at the top right of your screen and pull down a menu showing the open applications. Scroll to an application, open it, then quit it by pulling down the File menu and clicking quit or typing Command Q.

Windows users: Open each application listed on your taskbar at the bottom of your screen. Close each one by clicking the X (close) bar on the corner of the application, or pull down the File menu and click on "Exit."

Now click again on your browser application to open.

No home page or document appears on your screen: If the browser application is open but you have no document, pull down the File menu and click on "New Web Browser" in Netscape or "New Window" in Explorer.

No connection occurs: The browser may give you a message that the server could not connect or is busy. It also may say you have no DNS (a Domain Name Service), which is the address of the computer to which you are trying to connect. The Netscape connection could be busy, but you could have typed the address incorrectly. Check the address. If you have repeated problems trying to connect, quit the browser and restart your machine or the application.

The browser is cranky: Like overworked college students, browsers get tired and cranky, especially when they've been retrieving a lot of documents. If your browser isn't connecting to new documents, it may have too many sites stored in its memory or "cache." The browser stores connections to sites you have retrieved. When you call up a site, the browser retrieves it from your cache. To get the latest version of a document, hit Reload or Refresh on your browser. If you clear the cache, you will lose the sites you have accessed, so make sure you don't want to store them anymore. You also can clear the cache to remove your previous documents as follows:

* In Netscape, go to the Edit menu and pull down "Preferences." Click on "Advanced," then "Cache" and "Clear Memory Cache." The memory cache stores the documents you have visited during this Internet session; the disk cache stores your documents in your history folder. If you want to clear your history, click on "Clear Disk Cache" in Windows or "Clear History Now" in Macintosh.

* In Explorer, on Windows, pull down the View menu, click "Options," click on "Advanced," click on "Settings," and click on "Empty Folder." On Macintosh, pull down the Edit menu and click on "Preferences" or click the Preferences button. When the menu appears, click on "Advanced" under "Web Browser"; then click on "Empty Now" in the button near "Cache."

You can take this safari by reading the instructions in this book or you can find many more treasures and links for this exercise by accessing the McGraw-Hill Website for this book. You will need the password that comes with your book.

http://www.mhhe.com/socscience/comm/ rich/ch2/

Safaris

2–1 Media Resources

Type these URLs in your browser, or go to our Web site and click on the links in the 2–1 Safari. If you followed the interactive directions in this chapter for using a browser, you already will have discovered the *American Journalism Review* site, which links to hundreds of media resources. Check out starting points for journalists on the AJR resources page:

http://www.newslink.org/spec.html

Now explore some of these other media resources. (Some of these site addresses may have changed. If you can't connect, go on to the next site. In the next chapter you'll discover searching methods when you don't have a URL.)

1 You're looking for a job or internship in newspapers in the news, advertising or marketing department. Check Editor & Publisher Interactive and scroll down the page until you can click on the link to the online classified ads.
http://www.mediainfo.com/

2 A major disaster has occurred and you want to check the latest online news on CNN Interactive:
http://www.cnn.com

3 You are planning a career in advertising. Check out the American Association of Advertising Agencies and type this address carefully, noting the capital letter A's:
http://www.commercepark.com/AAAA/index.html

4 You have a test in media law and need to check the Supreme Court decision on the Communications Decency Act. Check FindLaw Internet Legal Resources page at:
http://www.findlaw.com

5 You are planning a career in public relations. Check the Public Relations Student Society of America at:
http://www.prssa.org/

6 You'd like some comic relief. After all, the Internet is supposed to be fun. Check out the Dilbert Zone by Scott Adams at the United Media site:
http://www.unitedmedia.com/comics/dilbert/

Chapter 3

SEARCHING SKILLS

Goals

* To learn about different search engines.
* To understand Push technology.
* To learn searching tips.

If you know how to search and are familiar with the glossary terms, you can proceed to other sections in this chapter.

Hyperleap

* Leap to the section on Push technology on Page 43.
* Leap to tips for organizing and saving bookmarks on Page 48 and 52.
* Leap to the Safaris to find people, career resources and map search tools.

  http://www.mhhe.com/socscience/comm/ rich/ch3/

These Web sites are mentioned in the first part of this chapter.

Yahoo! history page:
> http://www.yahoo.com/docs/pr/history.html

FishWrap:
> http://fishwrap.mit.edu

Pointcast:
> http://www.pointcast.com

A full glossary is in the appendix and on our Web site.

http://ww.mhhe.com/socscience/comm/rich/
glossary.html

COOKIES A coded piece of information that tracks where users browse in Web sites. A Web site with a cookie sends the code to your computer, and the next time you call up the site, it can identify you by your unique code number. Because of privacy concerns, browsers like Internet Explorer and Netscape issue warnings when cookies are installed in a Web site and allow users to turn off the cookie mechanism in the browser. Cookies are helpful to managers of Web sites, particularly in the media and advertising, to determine readers' preferences.

CRAWLER An indexing program that scans documents on the Internet for keywords.

HITS The number of text and graphic items downloaded when a page is accessed. The term is misleading because you can have 10 or more hits on a page. A preferable term is *page impressions* or *page views* meaning each time a page is accessed, it counts as one page view or page impression.

PROTOCOLS Rules that govern the way information is conveyed on the Internet.

PUSH Technology that delivers information the user chooses to his or her computer via headlines scrolling across the screen like a screensaver or by sending documents to the user's e-mail. It is akin to an electronic clipping service.

PULL An expression for browsing, where the user seeks information by typing Internet addresses or searching.

ROBOT A program or tool that scans documents on the Web in search of information for indexing, errors or keywords.

SEARCH ENGINE A computer program that finds documents on the Internet at the user's request.

SPIDER A program that scans documents on the Internet for keywords or indexing.

SERVER A computer that connects with other computers and delivers information through a network.

URL An acronym for an Internet addressing system, Uniform Resource Locator, whereby all addresses on the World Wide Web conform to the same rules, called *protocols,* starting with *http* for HyperText Transfer Protocol.

DILBERT reprinted by permission of United Feature Syndicate Inc.

SEARCH ENGINES

In 1994 when David Filo and Jerry Yang were doctoral candidates at Stanford University, they developed a computer program to keep track of their favorite sites on the World Wide Web. Like Lou Montulli in the previous chapter, Filo and Yang are among a group of young millionaires who have made fortunes from their computer skills. Within three years, Filo and Yang, then 28 and 30, were each worth more than $140 million from their invention, Yahoo!, the most heavily used search engine in the world.

A search engine is a software program that allows people to seek and retrieve information from the World Wide Web by typing keywords.

Filo and Yang were studying computer science in the engineering school when they invented their search engine as a nighttime hobby. One night they looked in the dictionary to name their program and latched on to *Yahoos,* a term used in *Gulliver's Travels* for uncultivated brutes. Filo and Yang claim the term fit them, but they say Yahoo! officially stands for "Yet Another Hierarchical Officious Oracle," according to their Web site. Although they dropped out of school before gaining their doctoral degrees, they endowed a $2 million chair at Stanford.

Since their invention, scores of other search engines have been created to help people find information just by typing in words to describe a topic. But these search engines have become so good at retrieving information that searching can become tedious.

You can get more than you want. When you type a request for information about student loans, you get 2,382,670 documents with the Infoseek search engine.

You can get less than you want. When the author tried to find her name and e-mail address in several people-finder search engines, she discovered that she didn't exist, but more than a dozen other people with her name were listed in other states.

You can get confused by the responses different search engines give for the same query. A request for journalism organizations retrieved 40,000 sites in Lycos, starting with Journalism Library: Journalism Organizations, whereas a search in the HotBot search engine returned more than 22,000 documents, starting with PR Place.

PUSH TECHNOLOGY

Enter Push technology. Instead of "pulling" the information from the computer via a search engine or by typing a URL, you can get news, magazines, travel sites and a wealth of other information you want delivered directly to your e-mail or in headlines scrolled across your computer screen. The information is "pushed" to you at your request.

Push was also an idea created by college students—this time by freshmen at the Massachusetts Institute of Technology as part of a class in the MIT Media Lab, where many futuristic media ideas originate.

Their Push product is called fishWrap®, an experimental personalized newspaper named for the expression, "Yesterday's news wraps today's fish." Students using the service fill out a personal profile and get news tailored to their interests and their home towns.

This personalized news service was a forerunner to Push technology, which has now been incorporated into major browsers such as Netscape Navigator and Microsoft Internet Explorer, as well as a number of independent services that update the news you select throughout the day. The concept also is called *Webcasting, channeling, niche casting, narrowcasting* and other names. It is like a personalized clipping service.

One of the earliest Push products to use the concept of scrolling headlines across the computer monitor like a screensaver was PointCast, a free Push software program supported by advertising. You can choose the news, but the advertising comes with it, a reason advertisers embrace Push technology as well.

For the media, Push technology offers the equivalent of home delivery of newspapers, magazines and online broadcast sites to your electronic door via e-mail. Customizing their products even further, some media sites allow you to choose which sections of their online products you want delivered to your computer each day such as the sports section or stock market listings.

Nor is this technology limited to the news media. If you are interested in receiving information about travel, games, technology or other subjects, Push services will deliver Web sites with those topics to your e-mail or by scrolling headlines from the sites across your computer screen.

An advantage of Push is that you don't have to search for the sites you want to visit regularly. A disadvantage is that you might be missing news and information you need but didn't request.

This technology renews the age-old journalistic argument: Should consumers of news get what they want or what they need?

PUSH AND PULL

Chances are you will need both: Push technology to give you the information you want daily and pull techniques to find other information you don't use regularly. The World Wide Web contains millions of documents, and thousands are updated or added every day. Whether you are searching for sources, background for a news story, or for something you aren't even sure exists on the Internet, you'll need an understanding of search engines and searching skills.

SECURITY

Once you start searching and browsing through Web sites, you may receive an ominous warning from your browser such as this one from Netscape Navigator that lets you know whether or not the site has encrypted data, meaning information that is scrambled to protect you:

> **Any information you submit is insecure and could be observed by a third party while in transit.**
>
> **If you are submitting passwords, credit card numbers, or other information you would like to keep private, it would be safer for you to cancel the submission.**
>
> [Don't Show Again]   [Cancel]   [OK]

This is the warning in Microsoft Explorer:

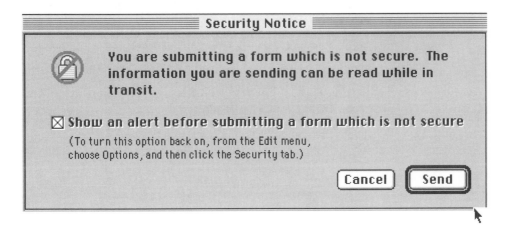

Security Notice

> **You are submitting a form which is not secure. The information you are sending can be read while in transit.**
>
> ☒ **Show an alert before submitting a form which is not secure**
>   (To turn this option back on, from the Edit menu, choose Options, and then click the Security tab.)
>
>   [Cancel]   [Send]

COOKIES

Big Brother or Big Sister, in effect, is watching where you go on a Web site with a code called a *cookie*. It's akin to the telephone service Caller ID. A cookie gives each computer an identification number, so it can track sites the user visits. Media publishers and advertisers, as well as other Web site producers, use cookies to determine user preferences. Despite some initial fears, most sites with cookies are not seeking to invade your privacy.

You can turn off the warnings by pulling down the Edit menu in Netscape Navigator to "Preferences," and clicking on "Advanced." Then click whether you want to accept cookies, disable them, or be warned before accepting them. In Internet Explorer, you can turn off the warning by pulling down the View menu, clicking on "Options," then on "Advanced." If you prefer to be informed when a site has a cookie, you will see something like this cookie from ZDNet, a Ziff Davis site that offers technology information:

However, if you disable your cookie function, which is another option, some sites such as *The New York Times* may not allow you access.

START YOUR ENGINES

Netscape Users   Open Netscape Navigator and click on the Search button in your toolbar. A page will open giving you a choice of several search engines. A different search engine will appear each time unless you customize your page by selecting your favorite search engine as directed on the search site. A list of other search engines also will appear on the page. We'll discuss the differences among search engines later in this chapter.

Choose a search engine and fill in the bar with your request. For example, select Excite, type "journalism scholarships," and click the Search button.

Excite	Infoseek	Lycos	Yahoo

journalism scholarships   Search

Internet Explorer Users   Open Explorer and click the Search button. A page of search engines will appear. Choose one by clicking on a button, typing your request, and clicking on "Search." Try it by typing "journalism scholarships."

journalism scholarships   Search   ☐ Set as Default

Search the Web:

- ◉ **NetGuide**Live
- ○ **HOTBOT**
- ○ **Microsoft**
- ○ **WEBCRAWLER**
- ○ AltaVista
- ○ MAGELLAN
- ○ **AOL NetFind**
- ○ YAHOO!
- ○ eXcite
- ○ ⓘ infoseek
- ○ LYCOS

Search Newsgroups:

- ○ DEJANEWS

47

Whether you chose Excite, Lycos, or another search engine, chances are you received thousands of documents. Don't be deceived. There aren't that many journalism scholarships, but there are that many documents containing the words, *journalism* and *scholarships*. The sites even feature advertisements for scholarship sites.

How do you know which search engines will return the best matches? Try the same request in different search engines to see what you get. After a while, you may develop a preference for a particular search engine, and you can customize your search page to default to that engine. Even though you may get thousands of matches to your request, usually the first 10 or 20 will provide the closest matches.

BOOKMARKS IN NETSCAPE

If you find a site you want to revisit often, don't forget to add it to your Bookmark menu (in Netscape Navigator) or your list of Favorites (in Internet Explorer). Your bookmarks function like an address book; you don't want to search repeatedly for a site you use frequently. To add a bookmark, pull down the Bookmark menu in Netscape or the Favorites menu in Explorer and click on "Add Bookmark" or "Add the Page." (See Chapter 2 for more details if you skipped the navigation instructions.)

You will accumulate a huge list of bookmarks very quickly. You need to save them so they are portable, especially if you create them in a classroom. To manage and save your bookmarks, take these steps, which differ slightly for Macintosh and Windows users:

Open the Bookmark File Type Command B (in Macintosh) or Control B (in Windows) to open the Bookmark file. You can also pull down the Communicator menu and scroll to "Bookmarks." Your bookmark folder will open.

File   Edit   View   Go

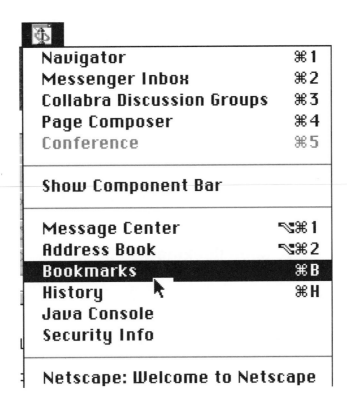

Windows users have another option: Click the Bookmark icon on the toolbar and click on "Edit Bookmarks." Your Bookmark folder will open.

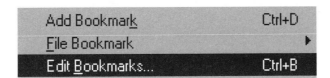

Delete Unwanted Bookmarks   Highlight the bookmark you want to delete. Then pull down the Edit menu to cut, copy, delete or select all.

❋   To delete several bookmarks in a block at the same time, highlight one bookmark, hold down your Shift key, and scroll to others you want to delete, then cut.

❋   To selectively cut several bookmarks that are not in sequential order, highlight one and hold down your shift key on Macintosh or the control key in Windows while you select others to delete. Then hit "Cut" from the Edit menu.

Organize Bookmarks Just like files in a filing cabinet, you can put your bookmarks in folders by topic. Pull down your File menu and choose "New Folder." Give it a name and then drag the bookmarks you want into it. You can also insert separators between topics.

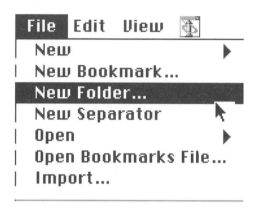

View bookmarks in folders as follows:

✳ Macintosh users: Click on the arrow next to the folders. When the arrow faces to the right, it shows just the folders. When you click the arrow again, it will face downward and reveal the bookmarks inside the folders.

✳ Windows users: To view bookmarks within folders, click on the plus sign. A minus sign will open, revealing the contents of the folders. To show only the folders, click on the minus sign and it will change to a plus.

Find Words in Bookmarks To search for words or topics within the bookmarks, make sure your Bookmark file is open. Then pull down the Edit menu and scroll to "Find in Bookmarks." A dialogue box will open allowing you to type words to search for within your bookmarks. It should look like this in Macintosh:

In Windows, the dialogue box looks like this:

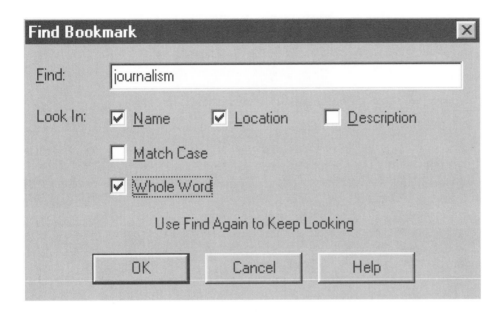

Save your bookmarks to a floppy disk, another folder or another drive! You'll be sorry if you lose them. Highlight the bookmark and drag it to your floppy. To move them all at one time, click your main Bookmark folder to the right arrow (or to the plus sign in Windows) and drag the folder to your floppy or other destination. You also can pull down your file menu to "Save As" and choose the file or floppy disk where you want to save the bookmarks; then click the Save button.

BOOKMARKS IN INTERNET EXPLORER

Pull down your Favorites menu or click on the Favorites icon. Then click on "Organize Favorites."

A dialogue box will appear offering you various choices:

Organize:	Move...	Rename	Delete		Open
	Select one or more files from the list above, then click one of the buttons to organize them.				Close
	Click the ⊡ button above to create a new folder.				

C r e a t e   F o l d e r s   b y   T o p i c s   Click on the folder button. Name the folder and drag related bookmarks to the folder.

D e l e t e   U n w a n t e d   B o o k m a r k s   Highlight them and click the Delete button in the menu on your screen (in Windows) or hit your Delete key.

S a v e   B o o k m a r k s   Save your bookmarks to a floppy disk or another folder or drive! Losing them is like losing your address book. Highlight the bookmark and drag it to your floppy. To move them all at one time in Windows, pull down the Favorites menu to "Organize Favorites." A window will open showing your bookmarks. Select the Favorites folder in the folder bar; drag it to your floppy or destination. On a Macintosh, go to File and click on "Export," select the destination and click the Save button. Or pull down your File menu to "Save As," choose the file or floppy where you want to save the bookmark, and click the Save button.

SEARCH
ENGINE GUIDE

Can you imagine a search engine that contains 50 million documents you can access with just a few keywords? Some search engines, such as HotBot and Excite, boast of such huge databases. Who scans all those documents to find the keywords? Programs called *spiders, crawlers,* and *robots* tunnel through Web documents finding and indexing keywords or other information that will match your requests. Search engines look for pages containing one or more words you typed. Then they retrieve the documents and rank them by how frequently the words you requested appear in them.

For example, one religious organization advocating sexual abstinence wanted its Web site to appear first or second when search engines retrieved documents for queries about sex, so it used the word *sex* almost 100 times in its document. Sure enough, it came up first on the list when several search engines retrieved documents about sex.

However, robots in search engines differ in the way they retrieve documents. Some robots are programmed to search only in titles and may return hundreds of choices for you, whereas other robots search for keywords within documents and return thousands or even millions of choices. To check the differences among search engines, see how they respond to the same topic you type. New search engines are created constantly because they are major uses of the Internet, and they generate advertising. Here are some characteristics of popular engines:

Yahoo!   One of the most widely used search guides, Yahoo! technically is more of a directory than a search engine. Yahoo! uses human beings to catalog Web pages by topics, such as journalism or news and media. Then you can search within that category, which narrows the topic to more relevant matches. The topics also list many subcategories to help you narrow your search.

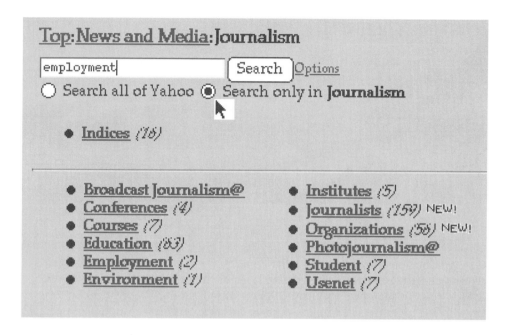

Try Yahoo! If you click the News and Media link, it will lead you to organizations, institutes, and a host of other good sites for journalists. You can click on a category link or type another request and click on "Search." If you want a more thorough search, Yahoo! directs you to another search engine, Alta Vista.

Alta Vista This search engine catalogs individual pages within Web sites, not just the home pages of the sites. With more than 35 million Web pages, this is a thorough search engine that updates its pages with a spider every few months. It indexes every word on all those pages and in newsgroups. To use this engine more effectively, use quotation marks around the words in a proper name, such as "Washington Post," otherwise you'll retrieve millions of documents containing the words, *Washington* and *Post*. Capitalize proper names in Alta Vista.

Lycos This is another thorough search engine that catalogs individual pages within Web sites, so it returns vast numbers of documents, although the first 20 usually are close matches. Lycos also lets you select whether you want to search the entire Web or search by subject, pictures or sounds.

Excite Another search engine with a mammoth database of more than 50 million documents, Excite can search documents by keywords or concepts. A request for public relations will also return documents about communications and career resources that may include public relations jobs as well as documents containing the term *public relations.* The first 20 documents usually are a close match. Excite also offers you the choice of receiving Web sites by topic or receiving individual pages within a Web site. For example, if you found a document for "journalism scholarships," Excite will offer you a chance to click on "More like this," for other sites related to this concept.

AOL Netfind   Like several other search engines, American Online's search engine offers categories of subjects such as "business" or "health." It also provides categories to search for people, newsgroups (discussion groups), and reviews of Internet sites provided by the Excite search engine. It provides a special search engine, "for kids only," to search sites of interest to young people.

Infoseek   This search engine catalogs Web sites in directories of topics as well as by individual sites, somewhat like Yahoo! Let's say you requested "public relations." Infoseek will retrieve documents containing the words *public relations,* and it will offer broader related topics such as "advertising," "Web site promotion," and "schools of journalism" that teach public relations. Make sure you capitalize proper names with this search engine as well.

HotBot   This search engine is one of the largest, boasting more than 50 million pages. Developed by Wired Ventures, which also publishes *Wired* magazine and the HotWired Web site, HotBot offers pull-down menus that give you a choice of viewing documents that match all the words, any of the words or the exact phrase of links to documents you retrieve. This site uses Boolean connectors of AND, OR, AND NOT. So a search for the *Washington Post* would be "Washington and Post" or "Washington and Post and not George."

Webcrawler   With a smaller catalog than other search engines, Webcrawler makes it easy to receive documents with close matches. You type a request and some synonyms. For example, if you wanted to find employment opportunities in journalism, you would type several choices: "journalism," "jobs," "careers," "employment," "internships," "resources."

PEOPLE FINDERS

Would you like to find an old friend or a source for your news stories? Try a people-finding search engine. Almost all browsers and search engines have directories to find people by name, address, phone number and/or e-mail addresses, but many of them contain outdated information or no information at all. It's like using a telephone book that is three or more years out of date. The best advice for journalists is to ask your sources for their phone numbers and e-mail addresses instead of relying on Internet directories. However, if you need to track down someone you can't find locally, it's worth checking the electronic phone books.

In addition to the people searchers on Netscape and Explorer, here are some other sites devoted to finding people:

❋   Bigfoot offers e-mail and residential addresses and phone numbers.
  http://www.bigfoot.com

❋   WhoWhere offers e-mail, residential and Yellow Pages directories, government pages and toll-free phone numbers.
  http://www.whowhere.com

❋   Four11 offers residential and Yellow Pages. If you aren't listed, you can click on "Add me."
  http://www.four11.com

❋   Infospace offers extensive directories of Yellow Pages, residential, business guides, government listings, and various city guides.
  http://www.infospace.com

❋   Switchboard offers residential and business listings.
  http://www.switchboard.com

You'll get your chance to test more people search engines in the safari at the end of the chapter.

NEWSGROUPS

In addition to searching for Web sites, the major search engines offer you the chance to search through Usenet newsgroups. These are electronic bulletin boards where people can post messages about various topics. Unlike listserv bulletin boards, which require users to subscribe to them, Usenet groups are available to anyone as long as the Internet service provider agrees to offer them. These newsgroups discuss hundreds of topics, ranging from literature to sex.

However, the sex-related newsgroups have become controversial and are subjects of First Amendment legal battles. Opponents of these newsgroups want them banned from college and university computer systems, but media groups want to protect the right to free speech. We'll discuss newsgroups and bulletin boards in more detail later in the book as well as legal issues.

MAPPING SEARCH PROGRAMS

Assume that you are a reporter on assignment. You need directions to a fire, an interview, or a location in a different city, state or country. The World Wide Web offers scores of mapping programs, which allow you to fill in your origination point and your destination. The program then gives you a map with your exact destination plus driving directions if you desire. Almost every search engine includes map search programs on its home page.

Whether you are searching for a map or a Web site with a search engine, here are some tips to make your search more productive.

SEARCHING TIPS

* Backtrack. If you connect with a site but you don't get the document you want, backtrack to the end of the domain name so you get the home page. Chances are you can find the site through the home page. For example, if you were looking for the jobs files on *Editor & Publisher's* site, the URL for the classifieds is:
  http://www.mediainfo.com/ephome/class/classhtm/class.htm

  If that file won't appear, delete everything back to the *com* (commercial) domain, so you have the main page at this URL:
  http://www.mediainfo.com/

* Type carefully. Upper or lower case letters don't affect searches unless you are searching for proper names of people and places. But spaces, plus and minus signs, and connecting words do make a difference.

* Capitalize names and titles.

* Use quotation marks around words in a phrase or title that must appear together in the document; for example, "American Journalism Review." That eliminates the millions of matches for "American" or "Journalism" or "Review" alone.

* Use a plus sign (+) and no spaces to join words when you want both or all words to appear in the document. Some search engines, such as Webcrawler, use Boolean connecting words—AND, OR—to indicate you want a document to contain both words; for example, online+journalism. The Boolean example would be online AND journalism.

* Use a minus sign (–) with no spaces between words to indicate the word or words that must not appear in documents; for example, pearl–jam. This will give you documents about pearls but not about the musical group, Pearl Jam.

✳ Use commas to separate names if you want the search engine to find documents containing more than one name. Without commas the search engine will treat the words as one name; for example, Walter Cronkite, Tom Brokaw, Diane Sawyer.

✳ Use wildcards. Use an asterisk (★), which is a wildcard symbol, to allow for plurals and other variations of your keywords; for example, broadcast★. The search engine will find documents containing *broadcast, broadcasting, broadcasts, broadcaster.*

Boolean Searching   The method called *Boolean logic* uses connectors called *operators,* such as AND, OR, BUT NOT. For example, if you request "Gannett or Knight-Ridder," you will get documents with one or both media companies. You can also type a plus or minus to indicate AND or NOT. The method is recognized by most browsers, but it doesn't always work. In most cases, it's preferable to use quotation marks around proper names or phrases.

http://www.mhhe.com/socscience/comm/rich/ch3/

3–1 **People Safari**		Find yourself and your friends in a white-page directory or people search engine. You can access the "people" directories on the search pages of Netscape Navigator or Internet Explorer or use some of the people-finding Web sites. Don't give up if you don't find yourself. Try a few different directories. For links to the people finders discussed in the chapter, click into the book's Web site for Safari 3–1. You might not be able to find your name and address in the people search engines, but chances are better that you can find a map showing the location of your apartment or house if you take the Travel Safari (3–3) in this chapter.
3–2 **Career Resources Safari**		Find three good resources related to your field of interest by testing at least two different search engines. When you find good sites, bookmark them. You will use them in the next safari. For suggested sites in news, broadcast, public relations, magazine and advertising, click into the book's Web site for Safari 3–2.

3–3 Travel Safari

The Internet is an amazing resource for all sorts of information related to travel, including hotels, restaurants, and maps of cities you might want to visit for business or pleasure. If you are covering any news story in or out of your town, you can use these resources to find lodging, maps, sources in that city and other valuable information. Locate some of this information as directed or check our Web site for links.

Clue: Check Yahoo! or Infoseek directories for travel. Start locating cities and information you need from that point.

a. You are covering floods in the Midwest, and your editor sends you to Des Moines, Iowa. Before you cover any disaster, you ought to check maps. In this case, you will work from the offices of the Des Moines Register, located at 715 Locust St.

   1. Find the location of the newspaper on an interactive map.

   2. Find a hotel near the newspaper where you can stay.

b. Now that you have found interactive maps, try to find a map that lists the location of your home or apartment. Clue: Check Excite's "City.Net travel" site for one interactive map source. **http://he.net/~brumley/world/cities.htm**

c. You are planning to spend a summer in France in a "Study Abroad" program. Your school is getting a tour rate on the airlines, but you want to arrange your own living accommodations, preferably at some youth hostels. You want to stay on the Left Bank as cheaply as possible.

   1. Find youth hostels in the area of the Left Bank by checking directories and maps to make sure you are in walking distance of the Sorbonne on the Left Bank.

   2. While you are in Paris, you want to visit the Louvre and the *International Herald Tribune.* Find them on the Internet.

Chapter 4
ONLINE MEDIA CRITERIA

Goals

* To learn to think interactively.
* To understand linear and nonlinear presentation.
* To develop criteria for media Web sites.

Hyperleap

If you want to connect to the Web sites mentioned in the chapter as you read it, call up our Web site.

You also could leap to the Interactive Journalist Safari on our Web site before reading the chapter to see the interactive techniques online media sites are using.

http://www.mhhe.com/socscience/comm/rich/ch4/

Web sites

The *Philadelphia Inquirer* and *Philadelphia Daily News*
> http://www.phillynews.com

Health Philadelphia
> http://health.phillynews.com/

Philadelphia Inquirer series on "America, What Went Wrong," free Web version
> http://www.phillynews.com/packages/america96/

Philadelphia Inquirer/Daily News Star Wars site
> http://www3.phillynews.com/packages/starwars/index.html

Chicago Tribune
> http://www.chicago.tribune.com

Sun Herald, Sunline
> http://www.charlotte-florida.com/

The New York Times
> http://www.nytimes.com

College Press Network
> http://www.cpnet.com

Glossary at a Glance

A full glossary is in the appendix and on our Web site.

http://www.mhhe.com/socscience/comm/rich/glossary.html

ANIMATED GIFS Images with motion.

CHAT A discussion via e-mail among people who are online at the same time in a specified location, often called a *chat room* on a Web site. Think of it as a computer conference call, but the participants speak to each other by typing messages, although audio and video chat software is available.

COMMUNITY Online communities are groups of people who share a common interest. Discussion groups, chats and other interactive forums help build online communities.

FRAMES Like picture frames that enclose paintings, Web frames are containers for Web documents. A site with frames can have two or more documents on the same screen, each within a frame that can have its own scrollbar. However, borderless frames without scrollbars also are popular. Although frames are useful for navigation, they divide screens, making the viewing area smaller.

HOME PAGE The main page of an online site, like a front door to a home.

INTERACTIVE Active participation by users in a Web site via e-mail, discussion forums, quizzes, games or other features.

LINEAR Information offered in a preordained sequential order such as a newspaper story printed in lines of text from beginning to end or a television news broadcast.

NONLINEAR Information that can be read or viewed in any order such as hyperlinks on a Web document.

PARTNER OR PARTNERING A collaborative arrangement.

REPURPOSING Reusing information online from another medium such as print. It is essentially the same information used for a different purpose—online distribution.

SHOVELWARE A pejorative term for dumping information online without changing the format or content. A newspaper story presented online exactly as it appeared in print is called *shovelware,* similar to *repurposing.*

Robin Palley's fingers dart over the keyboard as she types information for a new medical Web site she is creating for the online versions of *The Philadelphia Inquirer* and *Philadelphia Daily News.* The site includes a database of information about thousands of physicians, hospitals, support groups and prescription drugs. At the same time, Palley is keeping track of news for the next day's online newspapers.

Then the phone rings. A copy editor from another newspaper wants to know whether she should take an online media job. Palley encourages her.

"I'm having as much fun as I've ever had but in a whole different way of thinking," says Palley, a Web editor for Philadelphia Online, the World Wide Web version of the two newspapers. *The Philadelphia Inquirer* and *Philadelphia Daily News,* owned by the Knight-Ridder Corp., operate independently in the same building, but they share a common online home page.

Robin Palley

THE INTERACTIVE MINDSET

For Palley a different way of thinking is an interactive way of thinking. For a user of an online site, interactivity means actively participating in the information by sending e-mail, taking quizzes, playing games or posting messages to a chat or discussion forum. For a journalist, interactivity requires interpreting information creatively to make the audience responsive.

Palley used her creativity by adding interactive quizzes and games to the online version of an *Inquirer* investigative series about the economy. Readers can take the multiple choice quiz by clicking the buttons and then linking to the answers. Test your economic IQ with these sample questions (answers come later):

You can earn more than $200,000 a year and owe no federal income tax at all.

❋   True

❋   False

Among the richest 1 percent of the nation's households, the average income is about:

✳   (a) $109,000

✳   (b) $143,000

✳   (c) $465,000

✳   (d) $532,000

✳   (e) $729,000

An interactive game, "The Blame Game," gives readers a chance to act as government and business leaders and make decisions about the economy. Another method of interaction, a discussion question, accompanies the Pulitzer-Prize-winning *Inquirer* series, "Seeking a Good Death," about right-to-die issues. Readers can e-mail their responses to this query: "Do you think assisted suicide should be constitutionally protected?"

When she gets a spare minute, which isn't often, Palley likes to demonstrate the "Star Wars" games on the Philadelphia Online site. May the force be with you as you try to win these games.

The online newspapers aren't offering just news; they're also entertainment providers. If parents are going to spend time online with their kids, Palley wants them to play video games on her site.

"Everything people can do with their leisure time is our competition," Palley says. "It's a whole new definition of competition."

Palley says she could get hooked on playing the games at work if she weren't disciplined. But she doesn't have time for games. She's too busy building the mammoth medical site.

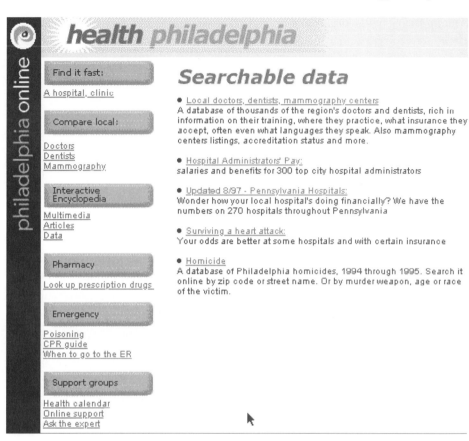

The searchable medical database includes names of about 20,000 doctors, where and what they practice, the type of health insurance they accept and other medical information for the consumer. It also includes an interactive encyclopedia about health, data on prescription drugs, news stories, salaries of health administrators and other health-related information.

But Palley isn't inputting all that data. She has contracted with a database company to provide the information in a growing arrangement called *partnering*. The newspaper gets the data, and the company gets to share the profits of any advertising the paper sells on the site. "Everyone is willing to share the risk because the Web is so new," Palley says.

The content also involves a new concept. The site includes information
Philadelphia area hospitals want to distribute such as information about new
medical procedures. Publishing such promotional material on a newspaper site is
a move that some people see as a departure from the traditional journalistic
standard to avoid conflicts of interest.

"In many ways it's fairer," Palley said. "We used to pluck two paragraphs from a
news release. Now you can provide the full text and let the reader decide what is
important."

However, the source of information produced by the hospital is clearly labeled
and topped with the hospital's logo, not the newspaper's logo, so users will know
this is not independently produced news.

The medical site is just one of many interactive databases in Philadelphia Online.
A user can call up the murder database to find out if any of the 2,100 homicides
committed in the past five years were in his or her Philadelphia neighborhood. If
you don't get murdered in Philadelphia, you don't want to have a heart attack
there either, especially if you check the database of survival rates for heart attack
victims in southeastern Pennsylvania hospitals. On a brighter note, you could find
a home at the New Jersey seashore by searching the newspaper's database of
90,000 properties or let the Restaurant Rover help you choose one of 400
restaurants for your dining pleasure.

That's what makes online products useful, Palley says. They shouldn't just be
duplicates of the print version. That's called *shovelware,* just shoveling the print
product online, a concept that makes Palley cringe.

LINEAR VS. NONLINEAR

Shovelware defeats the purpose of the World Wide Web, where hyperlinks change the way people read online. Newspapers are limited to linear presentation, which is information offered in a set order the user can't control except by turning to another story or page. For example, news stories are written in "lines" from beginning to end.

Television broadcasts also are linear: You get what you are given in the order the broadcast is presented. Viewers' control is limited to clicking the channel. But on the World Wide Web, information can be presented in nonlinear form with links that don't require the user to follow a preordained sequence. That means journalists must consider the nonlinear presentation when reporting, writing and editing information for the Web.

REPORTERS' RESPONSIBILITIES

Palley says that when reporters cover events, they should take disks with them and ask if the full text of speeches or reports is available in computer form for the online version. For example, a speech by the president or a local official might be published online several ways: audio and video clips, a digest version, and a full-text print version, plus reader reactions in online discussions via e-mail. A feature story about a science fair could link to the complete list of winners.

"Reporters need to think of photos and graphics," Palley says. "And think full text and video." Philadelphia Online has several Knight-Ridder staffers who shoot video just for the online publications.

Reporters also need to consider the next phase of a story. Online editions will publish all day, Palley predicts. "If we don't stay in the gee-whiz zone, people won't keep coming back. We have to produce even before they can get it in print or on TV. It's sort of a return to the past. Ten or 15 years ago we published all day long. All we're talking about is flipping back the clock before delivery problems."

QUALIFICATIONS

Speaking of clocks, that's how Robin Palley became a Web editor. She was an assistant city editor at the *Philadelphia Daily News* when the two newspapers decided to go online. Management decided to create an online staff by taking people from the print newspapers.

"I'm a gadget person," Palley says, admitting she knew nothing about online publications. "Someone said, 'You have a watch with 42 phone numbers.'" That was her qualification to be Web editor.

A few weeks later, armed with a book, *Teach Yourself Web Publishing with HTML in a Week,* Palley became one of four original editors producing Philadelphia Online in 1995. Two years later the staff grew to seven editors, a general manager, three programmers, a systems staffer and the video crew.

Editors still produce the home page and section fronts in HTML (HyperText Markup Language) every day, but the rest of the newspaper is automatically converted into HTML by a computer program.

COOPERATION WITH PRINT NEWSPAPERS

Every day the print editors meet with online editors at daily news meetings to discuss how the online editions can complement and enhance coverage, particularly with interactive elements such as reader polls or discussion questions. If a major news story is breaking, the online editors will suggest that the video crew shoot footage for the story.

In the past, print editors considered their online versions competitors. But increasingly, when major news stories occur, newspapers break the story first in their online versions to be competitive with television and other online news sites.

Interactivity is working at Philadelphia Online. The online site receives at least 200 to 300 e-mail messages a week for the sports section alone and a few hundred more on general topics. Despite the heavy e-mail, Palley's phone rings constantly with questions from online viewers and requests for tours of the operation. "It's like working in a train station," Palley says. "This whole Web thing is so fascinating!"

P.S. The answers to the quiz questions are

True, you can earn $200,000 and avoid paying taxes.

The answer to the second question is c: $465,000. That's the average income of people who are in the richest 1 percent of the nation's households.

TRIBUNE MEDIA SERVICES INTERACTIVITY

Chances are you aren't in that richest 1 percent. If you are like most college students, chances are that you are in debt. What should you be doing to improve your financial situation? You can get an online financial checkup tailored to you. Or do you need some neck exercises because you've been working too long at your computer.

Tribune Media Services (TMS), a division of the Tribune Company, offers answers to all these questions in several interactive ways. TMS creates online packages for several of the company's newspapers, including the Chicago Tribune. With an interactive calculator, you can input your financial information and get advice that fits your profile. If you want to find out how fit you are, you can take a fitness quiz.

But interactivity isn't limited to games and feature sections of news. You can use these techniques to personalize hard news for your readers. For example, if you are writing a story about local tax rates, plan interactive forms for your site. Readers can insert their current tax rate, property value, and the new tax rate to find out how the story affects them.

WINNING WEB SITES

The *Chicago Tribune*'s online site was named the "Best Overall Newspaper Site" in 1997 by the Newspaper Association of America in the large newspaper category. It was lauded for its interactivity, multimedia, and its Digital City community sites, which offer complete guides to entertainment and cultural life in Chicago and its suburbs.

Another consistent winner in online newspaper contests in the small newspaper category is Sunline, producers of the *Charlotte Sun Herald* in Charlotte Beach, Fla.

"One of the best in the areas of community service, interactivity and imaginative original content," the judges wrote. "Its 'In Memory' Tributes area enables users to write tributes to departed friends and relatives—and to write their own obits in advance!" The Sunline home page screams, "Named #1 online newspaper in the world!"

What makes a Web site a winner? Before you create your own Web documents, you should discover the criteria that make good Web sites so you can apply them to your pages.

* Download time: How long are you willing to wait for a site to load on your screen?

* Content: Does the site have content that makes you want to return?

In an annual Interactive Newspapers contest conducted by *Editor & Publisher, The New York Times* won top honors one year for best overall service and best editorial content. The criteria the 21 judges used were:

* Design and navigation.

* Innovation and creativity.

* Editorial content.

* Timeliness, how current the information is and how often it is updated.

* Original content, instead of shovelware.

* Online community, interactive elements such as chats, discussions, e-mail, and sites geared to special interests.

* Advertising.

College newspapers also compete annually in a contest conducted by the College Press Network. Here are the criteria the judges used:

✳ Timeliness: Is it up to date?

✳ Content: Does it provide comprehensive in-depth coverage of college and community?

✳ Navigation: Is it easy to find information?

✳ Innovation: Is it innovative, fun or thought provoking?

✳ Technology: Does the site take advantage of new technology?

✳ Creativity: Is the site daring and creative? Does it hold readers and bring them back for more?

Here are some other criteria and questions for you to consider when you evaluate sites and create your own.

✳ Design: Is it attractive and appealing without taking too long to load?

✳ Links: Are they useful? Do they take you out of the site? Is that a good or bad quality for the site you are viewing? Most online media producers want their viewers to remain in their sites. But if your purpose is to provide a comprehensive list of links from your site, then clicking to other sites may be acceptable. However, every time someone clicks to a link outside of your site, he or she may not return to your site.

✳ Useful: Does the site offer helpful content you want to know or use?

✳ Uniqueness: Does the site provide something original and different from other sites?

✳ Interactivity: Does the site have interactive elements such as e-mail, chats, discussion items, games or other features that encourage users to participate?

✳ Multimedia: Does the site offer audio, video and other multimedia components (important factors for news sites, especially broadcast)?

✳ Advertising: Is the advertising appealing?

✳ Enduring: Does the site make you want to return?

The last question may be the most important, especially for media sites. Content is always one of the most important qualities of a publication, whether in print, broadcast or online. If the newspaper, broadcast, magazine, public relations or advertising site does not offer content you want to use frequently, it doesn't achieve its purpose of being a good information provider. When you create your own sites, consider content that will make people return and become frequent users.

Now you decide the criteria for a good Web site. What pleases or annoys you when you access a site? Which sites would you want to add to your bookmarks or list of favorites? That's a real clue as to whether they are successful. So you be the judge and conduct your own site contest in Safari 4–2.

http://www.mhhe.com/socscience/comm/
rich/ch4/

4–1	**Interactive Journalist Safari**	Take a safari to sites that will give you interactive ideas and models on our Web site. Then answer the questions and see if you have gained the interactive mindset.
4–2	**Site Contest Safari**	Evaluate at least 20 online sites, preferably media sites, and choose your top five favorites. Rank your winners in order of first to fifth place. Write a brief comment after each winner, explaining why you chose that site as one of your favorites. Then write a brief critique (one or two lines) of the 15 other sites you visited, listing their strengths or weaknesses. These can be the best or worst sites you visited; you can learn just as much by viewing bad sites as good ones. Use at least five criteria to judge the sites, including content and navigation ease. Develop your own criteria of other factors you consider most important for Web sites. You may make a chart or a list of the winners.
4–3	**Quizzes and Questions**	a. Using a story in your campus or local newspaper, devise an interactive discussion question. b. Using the same story or a different one, make up a multiple choice quiz for the story.

Chapter 5

ONLINE COMMUNITIES

Goals

* To understand the Internet concept of community.

* To learn about the legal issues concerning newsgroups.

* To learn about newsgroups, chats, listservs and forums.

* To become familiar with journalism listserv resources.

To find some of the online resources as you read this chapter, click into our Web site.

http://www.mhhe.com/socscience/comm/rich/ch5/

Some other highlights include:

Hyperleap

* Instructions for setting up a Netscape newsreader on Page 80.

* Instructions for setting up a Microsoft Explorer newsreader on Page 84.

* Information about journalism listservs on Page 87.

Web sites

DejaNews, a newsgroup search group:
http://www.dejanews.com

IRC help (information about Internet Relay Chats):
http://www.irchelp.org

Journalism Newsgroups:
http://www.newslink.org/email.html

MSNBC:
http://www.msnbc.com

Yahoo! news and media chat listings:
http://events.yahoo.com/News_and_Media

Glossary at a Glance

A full glossary is in the appendix and on our Web site.

http://www.mhhe.com/socscience/comm/rich/glossary.html

BULLETIN BOARDS Discussion groups to which you subscribe, most without charge, and post or reply to messages.

CHAT A discussion via e-mail among people who are online at the same time in a specified location on a site, usually called a *chat room*. These simultaneous e-mail discussions often are called *real-time chats* and resemble a computer conference call.

COMMUNITY Online communities are groups of people who share a common interest. Discussion groups, chats and other interactive forums help build online communities.

FORUMS Another term for discussion groups on a particular issue.

FLAME Responding to another person's message with an abusive or sarcastic reply.

INTERNET RELAY CHAT (IRC) Software that sets up a chat area in a server connected to networks of servers around the world that feature the same software, like a global conference call. IRCs feature channels in which people can log in and communicate with each other simultaneously by typing messages.

LISTSERVS Discussion groups that are "served" to your e-mail. You must subscribe to this type of discussion list before you can post messages.

LURKER Someone who reads messages in discussion groups but does not respond or actively participate by posting messages; he or she "lurks" behind the scenes.

MAILING LIST Same as a listserv; a discussion group sent to your e-mail.

MAJORDOMO An automated software program that manages subscriptions to a listserv-type mailing list.

NETIQUETTE Etiquette on a network, particularly when sending messages to discussion groups.

NEWSGROUPS Electronic bulletin boards where users may read and post messages on various topics.

POSTING Sending a message to a discussion group.

REAL TIME A software program that allows computer users to simultaneously converse via typed or audio/video messages to each other while they are connected to the Internet as though they were communicating face to face or on the telephone.

SERVER The computer that contains software to retrieve your request and "serve" you information from the Internet.

SMILEYS Symbols that describe a person's mood when sending e-mail messages, such as happy, sad or jesting.

SPAM Electronic junk mail.

SYSOP System operator.

THREADS A discussion of messages on a specific topic.

USENET A worldwide group of electronic discussion lists, part of a network named for "users' network."

She claimed she was a 25-year-old blonde actress named Nancy. She posted messages to newsgroups, which are freewheeling discussion groups on the Internet. She began corresponding with a man in one of these groups. One day she boarded a train from Baltimore to North Carolina to meet her Internet acquaintance. She left her husband a note saying, "If my body is never retrieved, don't worry. Know that I am at peace."

Her nude body was found three days later in a shallow grave in the North Carolina woods.

Nancy was really Sharon Rena Lopatka, a 35-year-old Maryland housewife who had dark hair and weighed 189 pounds. And the newsgroups to which she had posted messages were sex-related forums about bondage, torture and erotica. A 45-year-old North Carolina computer analyst was charged with her murder. Based on e-mail messages found on Lopatka's computer, police said she expected to be sexually tortured and killed by a man she met on the Internet.

Lopatka was one of millions of people who post messages to Usenet newsgroups, discussion groups on thousands of topics. Unlike discussion groups to which people must subscribe, Usenet groups are accessible to anyone if an Internet service provider agrees to offer them. The Internet contains more than 25,000 Usenet newsgroups, which predate the World Wide Web. These discussion forums are not named for news. They are interest groups, organized in hierarchies, such as *bio* for biology, *rec* for recreation, *sci* for science, and so on.

Newsgroups that don't fall into the hierarchies of the Usenet system named for "users' newtork," are grouped in *alt* categories, meaning alternative categories. Journalism is grouped under *alt.journalism,* not because it's alternative journalism but because it didn't have its own hierarchy. Included within this journalism category are newsgroups for journalism students, photojournalists, gay journalists and others.

Whether it is a discussion about journalism, sex, music, or forums and chats provided in online media, these opportunities for expression are among the most popular uses of the Internet. They are ways to build "community," a buzzword for creating Internet neighborhoods where people congregate to share common interests even if they are separated by continents. While Usenet newsgroups are available to anyone, many other discussion groups are limited to members who subscribe to them.

Although Usenet newsgroups and other discussion groups offer valuable information, they should also be viewed with caution. Like "Nancy," people who post messages to discussion groups don't always reveal their real names. And the information they post may not be reliable enough to use in a news story. However, they can be helpful to journalists for finding sources and sharing ideas.

In Lopatka's case, a news researcher at the *News & Observer* in Raleigh, N.C., searched Usenet newsgroups to discover some insightful background about the woman. Using DejaNews, a Usenet search engine that allows you to type in a keyword and search messages in newsgroups, the researcher did a search for the woman's e-mail address, which she had obtained from police. She found dozens of messages the woman had posted in a newsgroup about sexual bondage. Clearly, that information was useful in the newspaper story about this woman's murder.

USENET
COURT CASES

Usenet newsgroups are the subject of controversy, particularly the groups that contain explicit sexual material. While some organizations want to restrict access to these newsgroups, media and civil liberties advocates claim any restrictions would violate First Amendment rights of free expression.

That was the situation at the University of Oklahoma. A group called Oklahomans for Children and Families, which opposes the distribution, sale, and access of material that it considers pornographic, cited a state law that makes it a crime to allow obscene material to appear on state computers. The group threatened to go to the media with examples of pornographic materials that could be accessed through the university computer system.

The university's president, David Boren, decided to restrict access to a number of newsgroups that appeared under the *alt.sex* heading and a dozen others under *alt.binaries,* which carried graphic or pictorial material. The student congress condemned the action and created links to the blocked newsgroups on its Web page.

Bill Loving, an associate professor of journalism who teaches media law, filed a suit in federal court claiming that the blockage constituted prior restraint in violation of his First Amendment rights. The university responded by creating a new computer policy that went into effect shortly before the trial. Under the new policy, the university established two newsgroups servers. One server would contain noncontroversial newsgroups available to everyone. For access to the second server, which would offer all newsgroups, users would have to agree that they were using the newsgroups for academic purposes.

At the trial, Loving claimed the university had created a public forum in its computing system by allowing any and all speakers access to the newsgroups server prior to the blockage. He claimed that a restriction of a public forum constituted a violation of his First Amendment rights. But the university argued that its newsgroup server was not a public forum and that Loving could have access to the newsgroups in question through alternate means. The trial judge ruled in favor of the university, saying that Loving had failed to show his First Amendment rights had been harmed. Loving appealed the decision.

CARNEGIE MELLON CASE

That wasn't the first time, nor is it likely to be the last, that restrictions to newsgroups have created a furor on college campuses. In 1994 the vice president for computing services at Carnegie Mellon University in Pittsburgh issued a memo stating that the university would withdraw some of its newsgroups with sexual content from its computer system because state law prohibited distribution of sexually explicit material to people under age 18 and obscene material to anyone regardless of age.

As a result, the university removed all newsgroups in the *alt.sex* category and others believed to contain sexually explicit images and text. After protests from the American Civil Liberties Union and other groups defending First Amendment rights, the university kept the ban on newsgroups with sexually explicit images but restored access to those with text-only materials.

The legal issues involving newsgroups are of particular concern to the media because the First Amendment to the U.S. Constitution protects freedom of speech. For that reason, although some messages posted to newsgroups may be offensive, media advocates have defended the right of users to express them.

CONCERNS ABOUT LIBEL

Legal issues involving newsgroups and other discussion forums on a network are not limited to topics of sex. The issue of liability is of equal or even greater concern to media organizations and other Internet service providers that offer discussion groups.

Consider this situation: In an online newspaper's discussion forum about sports, one of the participants posts a derogatory message about a team coach. The coach claims the message is libelous because it defamed his or her reputation. To be libelous, an accusation must be published, must be false and must damage the person's reputation. Whether the message really was libelous would have to be decided in court. But these other issues also need to be resolved:

❋ Is the media organization or Internet service provider that offers the discussion group on its server responsible for libel if one of the participants in the forum writes a libelous message about someone else?

❋ Should these discussion areas be monitored and censored by the online media provider?

In 1998, a U.S. District Court judge ruled that America Online was not responsible for the comments published on its service by cybercolumnist Matt Drudge. White House aide Sydney Blumenthal sued AOL and Drudge for libel, slander and invasion of privacy for publishing rumors that Blumenthal had tried to cover up a "spousal-abuse past." Although Drudge retracted the unsubstantiated rumors, Blumenthal sued anyway and sought $30 million in damages. Judge Paul Friedman ruled that the Communications Decency Act of 1996 protects Internet service providers from liability for content transmitted by their users. The judge dismissed the case against AOL but not against Drudge.

It was the third decision of its kind absolving AOL from responsibility for content transmitted on its service, and it signaled increased protection for Internet service providers. In the past the responsibility for content was not as clear as evidenced by the following two cases that were often cited in questions of liability of Internet service providers.

CUBBY V. COMPUSERVE

CompuServe, an Internet service provider, carried many discussion groups, including one called the *Journalism Forum,* which posted a daily newsletter, *Rumorville USA,* about the television and radio industry. In 1990, Cubby Inc., a company that planned to publish a competing electronic newsletter, claimed that it was defamed by statements carried in *Rumorville* on the CompuServe forum. Cubby sued CompuServe for libel.

CompuServe claimed it only distributed the information and had no editorial control over the statements carried on the forums. In 1991 the U.S. District Court in the Southern District of New York granted CompuServe's motion for summary dismissal. The court decided that CompuServe had no liability for the content because it had exercised no control over it.

Although it was only case law, that ruling sent a message to sysops (system operators) that if they don't edit the material in discussion groups, they aren't liable for any comments that users make. Many online media sites take this position in dealing with their chats and forums.

STRATTON OAKMONT V. PRODIGY

Four years later, another New York case concerning bulletin board operators resulted in a different decision. A securities investment banking firm, Stratton Oakmont Inc. sued the Internet service provider, Prodigy, for statements posted by an unidentified user in the ISP's Money Talk bulletin board. Stratton Oakmont claimed that the defamatory statements made about a stock offering it had planned to issue ruined the value of the stock.

On May 24, 1995, a New York state trial court issued a summary judgment that Prodigy was responsible for the potentially libelous statements because the service provider had exercised enough editorial control over the messages in its forum to be considered a publisher. This was based on the fact that Prodigy had marketed its service as a "family-oriented" computer network that used a software screening program to block offensive bulletin board messages. Prodigy also required its users to adhere to content guidelines that prohibited posting messages that were insulting, harassing or harmful to maintaining a harmonious online community.

Stratton Oakmont agreed to drop its $200 million defamation suit if Prodigy offered an apology. The parties settled out of court, but Prodigy filed a motion to rehear the court's ruling. Although Prodigy had changed its policies and no longer monitored bulletin boards, the court refused to reverse its decision.

NEWSREADERS

Before you can read or post messages to a newsgroup, you need a newsreader. When you got your e-mail account, it probably came with a newsreader such as *news* or *tin* or others for reading Usenet. Commercial services such as America Online also provide readers for Usenet newsgroups. And several shareware software programs are specifically designed to be newsreaders. But you also can use Microsoft's Internet Explorer or Netscape's Navigator to read your newsgroups if you set them up properly. You just need to fill out the name of your server and newsreader—information available from your Internet service provider.

With more than 25,000 newsgroups and new ones added all the time, you don't want to sift through all of them every time you want to read a particular one. Your newsreader will ask you to "subscribe" to the newsgroups you want, meaning you select the newsgroups you want from a list. They are free and you can cancel them at any time. We will discuss the journalism newsgroups, but the process for subscribing, retrieving and sending messages is the same for all the groups.

Before you subscribe, however, be forewarned that these discussion groups generate a lot of "spam," which is unwanted solicitation, and some include messages that you might consider offensive. While it is useful for you to know about newsgroups, you may not want to read them regularly.

JOURNALISM NEWSGROUPS

Journalism-related Usenet newsgroups include about 10 subgroups, and more are added periodically. For example, if you want to communicate with other journalism students, you might subscribe to the *alt.journalism.students* newsgroup. Some other groups include *alt.music, alt.journalism.criticism,* and *alt.journalism.newspapers.*

If you have set up your Internet browser to read newsgroups, you can access them easily via the *American Journalism Review* site, created by Eric Meyer, a journalism professor and Internet consultant who owns NewsLink Associates.

✳ Call up the Usenet groups on the AJR site:
http://www.newslink.org/eunet.html

✳ Click on the links to journalism groups in which you are interested. In Netscape you will receive a dialogue box telling you how many messages were posted and asking you how many you wish to download. Microsoft's Internet Explorer will tell you the number of messages in a group after you subscribe and go to it. Here are directions for reading newsgroups in Netscape; if you use Microsoft's Internet Explorer, skip to Page 84.

NETSCAPE MAIL
AND
NEWSREADER

When you set up your discussion groups, you can also set up your server to read e-mail in Netscape. The directions are similar, but instead of clicking on the newsgroups server, choose the mail server.

* Pull down the Edit menu to "Preferences."

* Click on "Mail and Groups." Click the arrow to face down on Macintosh or the plus sign to a minus on Windows.

* Fill out information under identity, the types of information you want, and the name of your Internet service provider's e-mail server. You can create a signature to be included in your messages as well. In the mail server dialogue, you can opt to leave messages on your server, but if you are going to subscribe to newsgroups and discussion lists, you may receive hundreds of messages—more than the allowed space you have on your server.

The newsreader in Netscape's Communicator is Collabra, but if you are using an earlier version of Netscape, the instructions for setting up a newsreader are similar. You may not be able to do this on a network if you share your computer with other students because you need to use your own e-mail address. However, you can follow these directions if you want to download newsgroups on your own computer.

* Pull down the Edit menu to "Preferences." When the dialogue box opens, click on "Mail & Groups." In Macintosh, click on the arrow to face downward; in Windows, click on the plus sign to change to a minus so the subcategories will be revealed.

* Click on "Groups Server." Another dialogue box will open. Fill out the name of your news server that you received from your network administrator. Netscape comes with a default newsreaders set as "News." This may default

to your news server, or you may need a more specific name. It might be *news* plus your Internet provider's domain such as *news.your university Internet abbreviation.edu.*

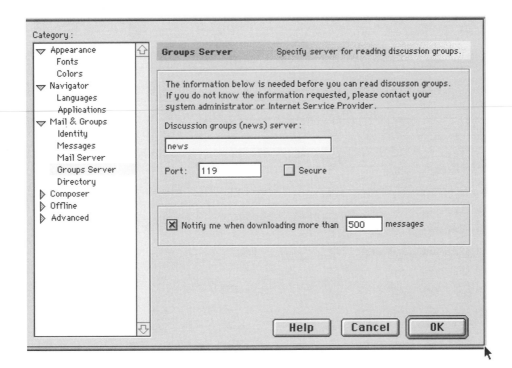

* Fill out how many messages you want to download before being notified. In Windows you also may want to specify the file where you want your discussion group folder.

* To access your discussion groups, pull down the Communicator menu to "Collabra Discussion Groups" or "Message Center." Either one opens e-mail and newsgroups.

* To subscribe to discussion groups, click on the Subscribe menu button, called "Join Group" in Macintosh, or use your File menu. Wait until the newsreader loads the major newsgroups categories. This may take a while.

✳ If you know the name of the group you want, type it in the discussion Group bar. If not, scroll through the groups and click "Subscribe" or just click on the button next to the groups you want to read and an arrow will appear. When you want to stop subscribing, click the checkmark again or click on "Unsubscribe."

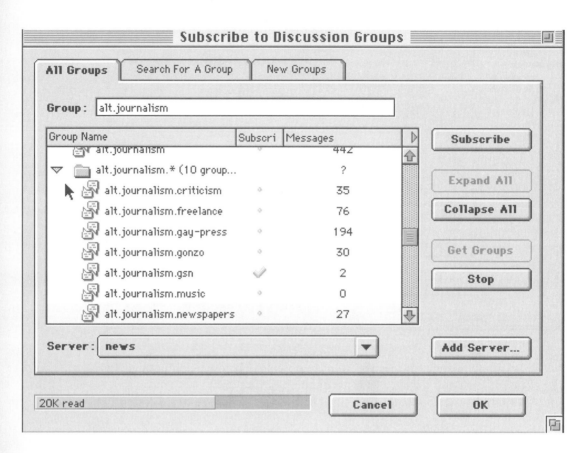

✳ After you have selected your groups, return to your "Message Center" to read and reply. When you call up your "Message Center," your groups will be listed and you don't have to scroll through a huge list.

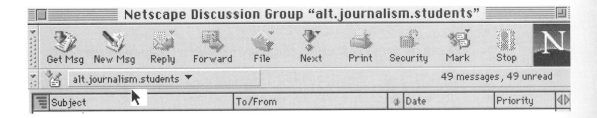

Folder Name	Unrea	Total
▽ 🖳 Local Mail		
📧 Inbox	0	5
📨 Unsent Messages		
📑 Drafts		
📰 Sent Mail	0	120
🗑 Trash	1	12
▽ 💬 news		
📰 alt.journalism.gsn	2	2
📰 alt.journalism	442	442
📰 alt.journalism.students	49	49

✳ To get messages, click twice on the newsgroup. As they are loading, Netscape will tell you how many messages there are. You can stop loading at any time. Some newsgroups contain hundreds and even thousands of messages.

✳ To post messages, after the messages have loaded, click the appropriate Reply buttons on your toolbar. To reply to an individual, click Reply. To post a new message to the group, click New Msg.

			Netscape Discussion Group "alt.journalism.students"							
Get Msg	New Msg	Reply	Forward	File	Next	Print	Security	Mark	Stop	N

📰 alt.journalism.students ▼   49 messages, 49 unread

Subject	To/From	Date	Priority

✳ Windows users have more options of replying to individuals or the group after they click the toolbar Reply button.

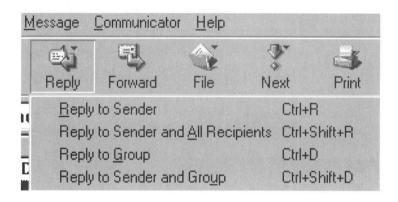

Message	Communicator	Help		
Reply	Forward	File	Next	Print

Reply to Sender	Ctrl+R
Reply to Sender and All Recipients	Ctrl+Shift+R
Reply to Group	Ctrl+D
Reply to Sender and Group	Ctrl+Shift+D

✳ Other newsreading buttons: Next reads the next message, Print does what it says, the Mark button marks it as read, File saves it in your designated folder on your computer, and so on.

MICROSOFT'S EXPLORER NEWSREADER

Find out the name of the news server your Internet Service Provider uses. When you set up Explorer to read newsgroups, you can also set it up to receive your e-mail.

✳ Click on the mail icon and pull down the Mail icon menu to "Read News." The Internet News box will open. Pull down the News menu to "Options" and click once to open the dialogue box.

❋ Click on "Server" in the dialogue box:

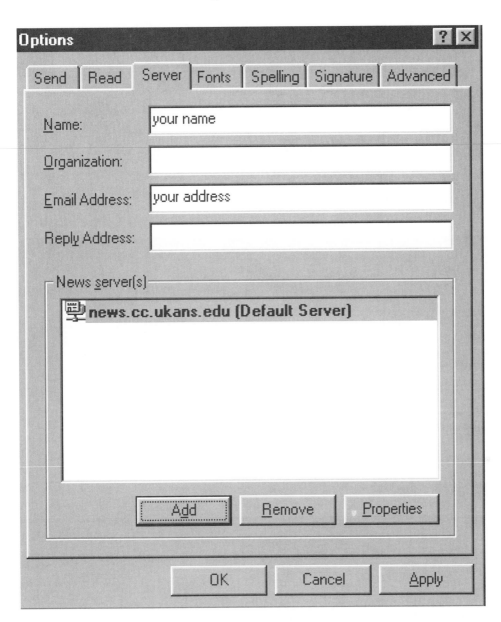

❋ Fill out your name and e-mail address.

❋ Click on "Add" to insert your news server if the one listed is not your provider. Your news server might be *news* plus the domain name of your university or your provider.

✱ If your news server requires you to log on (many don't), fill in your account name. Click "Set Default" if you want to use this server all the time.

✱ Set other options such as fonts, your signature, and so on, by returning to the Options box if you wish to read your messages in any form other than the default style. If you want to include a signature in your messages, click on "Signature" and fill out your preferences. Click "OK" after each entry when you are finished.

✱ If you prefer to see your messages vertically instead of horizontally, pull down the View menu and set it accordingly.

✱ Click on the Newsgroups button, and the main hierarchy of newsgroups will download. This may take several minutes.

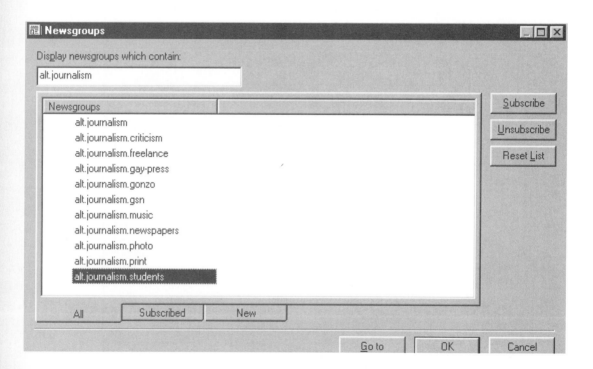

✱ Subscribe to the newsgroups you want. If you know the name of the group, fill out the top bar. If not, browse through the groups. Click on "Subscribe" when you want to join a newsgroup, and click on "Unsubscribe" when you don't want it anymore. To see the newsgroups you have subscribed to, open the Newsgroups icon and click on "Subscribed" at the bottom of the box.

✱ Read messages. Click on the newsgroup you want to read and click "Go to."

❋ Post messages. To reply to a message, click it open and then choose your
   options at the top of your menu bar to post a new message or reply to the
   group or just the author of the message.

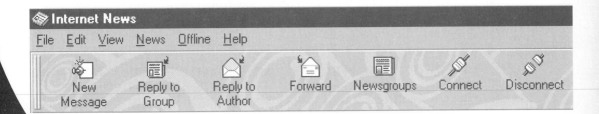

LISTSERVS

In addition to Usenet newsgroups, many other types of discussion groups exist,
and many of these are geared to specific areas of journalism. These are called
listservs because they are discussion lists that are served to your e-mail after you
subscribe to them. Most of them are free. Several journalism listservs are excellent
resources for networking, jobs and information you can share about your media
careers.

You can acquire an amazing amount of knowledge about your field from
journalism listservs because many of the people who contribute to them are
outstanding professionals in their fields. The questions and answers posted to these
lists can serve as a supplemental course of study in the media. However, because
many of the participants are professionals, questions from students are not always
tolerated well, and you should not use these lists for doing basic research that you
might gather elsewhere.

You don't have to post or reply to any messages to gain a wealth of knowledge
from the lists. If you just want to read the posts, you can be a "lurker," a person
who doesn't actively participate in the discussions. When a question is posted that
generates replies, the related discussion that ensues is called a *thread*.

For example, if you belong to the Online-News discussion group, some threads
concern legal issues, online design, copyright and other emerging problems of
online journalism discussed by some leading Web editors, designers and professors
in the field.

If you want to become a photojournalist, you can join the National Press Photographers Association discussion group. Learn about investigative reporting through the discussion group of Investigative Reporters and Editors. Copy editors have their own discussion group, as do broadcast and magazine journalists. And if you are interested in putting your college newspaper online, you might want to discuss issues with other student journalists in the Student Electronic Paper Mailing List.

You can join all of these journalism listserv discussion groups easily by accessing them through *American Journalism Review,* where Eric Meyer has compiled an excellent list of them.
http://www.newslink.org/e-mail.html
You also can find links to these and others in journalism on our Web site for this chapter under the Listserv Safari.

Some of these discussion groups generate up to 100 or more messages a day, so if you don't have daily access to your e-mail, you might not want to subscribe. However, you should join a list at least for a while so you can get a sense of the type of information exchange that might be of value to you.

HOW TO SUBSCRIBE

When you access the sites to subscribe to listservs, carefully follow the directions for signing up. In most cases you will address your sign-up request to the listserv or a "majordomo," which isn't a major or even a human being. It's a software program that manages subscriptions to a listserv mailing list. Keep your sign-up request short, and insert exactly what the directions specify. Don't add "please" or other unnecessary words that the robot isn't programmed to understand or care about anyway.

For example, to sign up for the "Student Electronic Papers" discussion list, you would address your message to *listserv@vm.temple.edu,* and in the body of your message you would write, "Subscribe STUEPAP" and your name.

One of the most active lists, which generates scores of messages a day, is the Computer-Assisted Reporting list. You can learn tips about how to find and use statistics and other electronic data by addressing your subscription request to *listserv@ulkyvm.louisville.edu,* and in the body of your message just write "Subscribe CARR-L" and your name. Directions for other groups are listed in the AJR site linked to our Web page for this chapter.

Soon after you sign up, you will receive a message confirming your membership and telling you how to unsubscribe. Print out these directions and save them because many times people can't get off the list. The instructions for unsubscribing usually are simple—just your name and the word "unsubscribe" plus the name of the list—but, for some reason, innumerable people send messages to the list because they can't remember how to get off it.

ETHICAL USE OF MESSAGES

Messages posted to the list are intended for discussion, not for publication. So if you plan to quote anyone or use a message from the list in a news story, it's ethical to notify the person who wrote the message.

The legality of whether a person's message is copyrighted property of the sender is not clear. Some experts maintain that anything you post to the Web is copyrighted automatically as your own, while others claim that messages don't qualify and are in public domain because they are posted to a public forum. Whatever the legal case, take the ethical approach and inform someone before you use his or her comments in a publication.

CHATS

A chat is a software program that allows two or more people to chat online by typing their comments back and forth in real time, meaning at the same time, in a specified location called a *chat room* or *cafe* or something similar. It is just as though they were conversing on the telephone but they are conversing in print messages. America Online made this type of communication popular. Many major media sites now feature chat rooms with celebrities at specific times so users can ask questions or just discuss an issue with other participants.

A popular use of a chat room on local news sites is for sports. The chat can feature a coach, player, or just an online discussion issue that is moderated by the media site. For example, MSNBC offers news chats as a regular feature, and Yahoo! offers lists of chats that are conducted daily on news and media subjects.

Newer software programs will allow users to meet in chat rooms and see and hear each other with audio and video as well as print messages. But that defeats some of the freedom people enjoy in chat rooms because they are so anonymous. In many cases, they use a nickname or pseudonym.

Internet Relay Chats are a form of real-time discussion that has been likened to CB radio because the chat area is called a *channel,* where many people can connect simultaneously. IRC is a chat area in a server connected to servers around the world that feature the same software, like a global conference call. This type of chat is extremely useful in time of disaster. When the Oklahoma City federal building was bombed, people all over the world instantly began communicating on an IRC. As with any information in discussion groups, journalists should use the messages only as tips that must be checked for accuracy.

NETIQUETTE

When you post or reply to a message in a discussion group, some rules of etiquette should be followed. When people communicate via e-mail, in personal messages or in discussion groups, the tone of their messages often can be misunderstood. Intonation and gestures that give clues to meaning when you communicate in person or on the telephone are missing. Unlike letter writing, e-mail messages are more spontaneous and often lack good grammar and good manners.

When people give a sarcastic or abusive response to messages in a forum, it is called *flaming*. And there is a lot of it, especially when the person posting the messages is using a pseudonym. The behavior of many people on these forums is akin to the way some people behave when driving on a crowded freeway.

To prevent misunderstanding, a code of symbols, known as *smileys,* developed in the early days of e-mail and bulletin board forums. For example, a happy face, meaning this message is sent with good wishes, is written (:-); parenthesis, colon, dash and end parenthesis. Look at it sideways. A frown just reverses the end parenthesis, (:-(. And just kidding is a wink made with a semicolon, (;-).

Although these codes are still used, they aren't popular anymore, nor do they take the place of old-fashioned courtesy. Here are some tips for good netiquette:

* Sign your message with your name and some identifying information, such as a title or affiliation. Although your messages will include your e-mail address, they don't always include your full name or pseudonym, so anyone wanting to reply to your message may not know how to address you.

* Don't write messages in all capital letters. That's considered shouting or screaming. It's also hard to read all caps.

* Try to keep your messages short. Long e-mail messages are hard to read, and your browser even gives you an option to reject messages that are over a certain number of words.

* Take a few seconds to proofread. If you can't spell or use proper grammar, you are making a bad impression, especially if you are a journalist!

* Don't say anything in a message that you wouldn't want other people to read, whether it is a personal message or posted to a discussion group. E-mail is not private. Remember that messages can be forwarded to anyone.

⁕ Don't quote any message from a discussion group in a news story or other publication without notifying the author of the message. That's common courtesy and that's ethical behavior.

⁕ Don't spread rumors on discussion groups. If you wouldn't use the information in a news story, don't post it to a group.

⁕ Read the FAQs (frequently asked questions) if the group posts such a page. You don't want to post common questions or ones that have been asked prior to your subscription or questions.

⁕ Before you post a message to a discussion group, lurk for a few days. Read the messages that are sent so you understand the nature of the group and type of discussions that are warranted. Keep the focus of the group.

⁕ Save the information about signing off from a listserv discussion group. It is annoying to a group when you send messages asking how to sign on or off.

Safaris

http://www.mhhe.com/socscience/comm/ rich/ch5/

5—1	**Usenet Newsgroup Safari**	Choose one of the journalism Usenet groups and lurk for a day or two. Before you download all the messages, you might request that your browser download just five or 10, so you can get an idea of the types of messages. Use the DejaNews search engine to search Usenet groups for a particular topic, such as something related to your career. **http://www.dejanews.com**

5—2	**Listserv Safari**	Join a listserv in your field. Check the American Journalism Review site: **http://www. newslink.org/email.html** You can click directly to it from our Web site. ⁕ Write three story ideas based on the discussion in one of your groups. ⁕ After lurking for a week, identify three sources you consider knowledgeable in your field and useful for networking or news stories.

5-3 **Chat or Forum Safari**

Using your local or campus newspaper, devise three ideas for chats or discussion groups that would be of interest to your audience. For ideas, check MSNBC, or the Yahoo! list of chats. You can link to them on our Web site for this chapter or use the Web site locations at the beginning of this chapter.

Chapter 6

BASIC HTML

* To learn the basics of HTML coding.
* To code online resume with HTML.

If you know how to code HTML, read the beginning of the chapter but leap over the instructions on Page 100 and create your own resume.

Check our Web site for HTML tutorials, graphics and job resources.

http://www.mhhe.com/socscience/comm/rich/ch6/

Glossary at a Glance

A full glossary is in the appendix and on our Web site.

http://www.mhhe.com/socscience/comm/rich/ glossary.html

SNAIL MAIL: Mail sent the old–fashioned way—by the U.S. Postal Service or other countries' postal services.

TAGS: HTML codes enclosed in brackets. While other languages require an alphabet, HTML requires tags with codes that make the document readable in a browser.

ASCII: Officially stands for American Standard Code for Information Interchange, a worldwide standard system for code numbers that computers use to represent letters and numbers. For writing purposes, when you save or write a document in ASCII format, it is plain text that can be read by any word processing program or Internet browser. It does not retain any formatting, such as boldface type, sizes or special fonts.

FREEWARE: Software that you can download or receive without charge.

GIFS: Images for Web documents in a format called Graphic Interchange Format, which compresses image files. Images in this format can be read by all browsers.

HTML: HyperText Markup Language, the coding system for documents on the World Wide Web.

HTTP: HyperText Transfer Protocol, the rules that govern how computers transfer World Wide Web documents from one computer to another.

JPEGS: Images for Web documents in a format developed by the Joint Photographic Experts Group; this format is better for photographs. It also compresses images.

SHAREWARE: Software you can download from the Internet without charge initially, but you are expected to pay a fee to the developer after a trial period.

DILBERT reprinted by permission of United Feature Syndicate Inc.

Wanted: journalists with online media skills, preferably HTML coding. Such advertisements appear weekly in *Editor & Publisher* Interactive and numerous other journalism resources. Consider some of these job postings:

* "Online editor for electronic media at a major metropolitan newspaper. Responsible for creating cohesive online packages for breaking news and sports, including writing headlines and editing copy. Sound news judgment and editing skills required. Excellent interpersonal, communication and organizational skills. Attention to details both in word editing and coding for electronic publication. Bachelor's degree along with 4–6 years news experience required. HTML coding experience preferred. Excellent benefits and 401k package. Beginning salary: $715 to $1,072 a week."

* Online news editor for **Washingtonpost.com,** the online version of *The Washington Post.* Although this job no longer is available, note the requirements: "The successful applicant will have excellent headline writing skills and experience editing on deadline. Either Internet experience or a willingness to learn HTML is mandatory."

* This ad is from an online real estate news service. "Seeking an aggressive, versatile writer. A thorough knowledge of the Internet is required. The position will focus on coverage of the massive changes facing the real estate and related industries brought about in large part by the emergence of the Internet. We syndicate news and columns to more than 100 print and online news organizations and other technology, industry and media sources. Salary is $45,000 per year plus benefits."

* Web content manager: "I'm looking for a specific, superior person to help me manage Web content on the [name of company] site. As a former journalist, I know the skills in newspapering/reporting will go far toward what I need—especially if you've taken the care to learn HTML and Photoshop and have a strong work ethic. The job pays in the $40–$60K range, depending on experience. Since the person I need will have strong writing and online skills, I'll be asking you to apply by e-mail and will send you back instructions on how to complete a demonstration of your Web authoring/content creation skills on a subject of my choosing."

Don't expect to earn $60,000 just because you have some skills in online journalism. But you can expect to earn more than journalists who lack knowledge of the Internet, as much as 30 percent more.

Nor do you need to limit your job search to traditional media fields in newspapers, magazines, public relations or broadcast. Journalists are becoming more in demand in many areas because so many businesses are adding communication components online and offline. Almost all major media sites, such as CNN, Mercury Center, Wired and those of nonmedia companies, feature listings of jobs at their organizations on their Web pages.

Mary Kay Blake, recruitment director for the Gannett Co., said the best and the brightest journalism students have many more options now. "The recruiting of journalism students is not only being done only by newspapers, but also by many other companies that are interested in people with strong communications skills," she said in an interview with *Editor & Publisher* Interactive. "There is a whole realm of opportunity that was not out there before, and the competition for the best is growing more intense."

Bob Sullivan discovered that fact shortly after he graduated from the University of Missouri in 1994. He started his career as a print reporter for a New Jersey newspaper. But he says he was impatient to succeed and make more money, so he taught himself HTML, HyperText Markup Language, the coding for all documents on the World Wide Web.

"I got involved in Web publishing because the money was rolling in," says Sullivan, a reporter/producer for Microsoft's MSNBC operation in Redmond, Wash. "Suddenly I was getting calls from *The New York Times.* It was one big shortcut to success for me."

Meredith Artley, night editor for the online edition of *The New York Times,* had a similar experience. She, too, graduated from the University of Missouri but with a broadcast degree and taught herself HTML. Before graduating, she began interviewing with Web sites and was hired at the online *New York Times.*

They discussed their experiences at a conference of journalism educators.

REASONS TO LEARN HTML

Although many online media editors and producers say you don't need coding skills in HTML to work on Web sites, Artley and Sullivan think some knowledge of HTML is important.

"If you are going to get involved in the Web, it helps a lot if you understand how that works," Sullivan says. "It's fundamental."

Artley agrees. "We kind of hound them [applicants to the online *New York Times*]. If you are coming here, you're going to be doing some HTML."

Mitch Lazar, a producer for new business development at CNN Interactive, downplays the importance of HTML and stresses good writing skills. "I think you should learn the fundamentals of HTML and then use a Web editor," he says.

That is exactly what we are going to do. We'll begin creating an online resume in this chapter using the basics of HTML. In the next chapter, you can learn to design and enhance your resume with a Web editor, a tool that helps you create Web pages without coding.

Even though Web editors eliminate the need for knowledge of HTML, even the best Web authoring tools create errors. Sometimes images don't appear in your documents when you use a Web editor. Other times strange characters appear in place of the letters you typed. Understanding HTML allows you to fix your documents if something is wrong and to use Web authoring tools more effectively.

As you learn how to code with HTML in this chapter, you can start creating your online resume. You can find many resume forms on the Internet. Word processing programs such as Microsoft Word and WordPerfect also contain resume forms for Web documents. You just fill in the blanks. But that type of formatted resume shows little originality or creativity, qualities that journalism students should possess. Do it yourself. Here is how to get started.

HTML PREREQUISITES

You can use any word processing program to code your HTML document. You just need to save the document in ASCII ("text only," nonformatted text that can be read by any computer program or browser). Some versions of WordPerfect, Microsoft Word and other word processors offer options to save your document in HTML format. Text editors such as SimpleText or TeachText for Macintosh and Notepad for PCs already are in ASCII format, so you don't need to save your text in any special way. After you learn how to code with HTML, you may want to convert an existing document in your computer to a Web page by inserting codes in it. You can save any existing document in ASCII format as follows:

✻ Open the document you want to save.

✻ Go to the File menu, pull down "Save As."

File	Edit	Insert
New		⌘N
Open...		⌘O
Open Latest		▶
Templates		▶
Close		⌘W
Save		⌘S
Save As...		

✻ Pull down the menu that offers you ways to save. It will say "Save File as Type" or "Format." Pull down the menu to "Text Only" in Word or "Text Export" in WordPerfect or the equivalent in other word processing programs.

Save Current Document as:

resume

Save File as Type

Text Only ▼

✳ Save your document on your desktop (unless your network prevents it) if you plan to create a Web page with it. It's easier to go back and forth between your browser and the desktop when you want to view it. After you have clicked on "Save As," and saved as "Text Only," click "Desktop" on the right part of the dialog box on Macintosh. On Windows, use the scrollbar until Desktop appears in the "Save In:" menu bar.

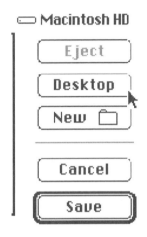

HTML RULES AND TIPS

Here are some general HTML rules and tips.

✳ HTML codes are instructions for browsers to read the document.

✳ Every HTML code must be enclosed in angle brackets, <codes inside these brackets>.

✳ Bracketed codes are called *tags*.

✳ Almost all codes need a pair of tags, one to open and one to close the commands. Tags to start a command go before the text or image; tags to end a command are placed after the text or image.

* Opening tags are codes inside brackets, like this: <html>

* Closing tags have a slash before the code, like this: </html>

* Type codes carefully, and leave no spaces in your codes except in specific cases as instructed.

* Use lower case in most instances; case generally doesn't matter. It's just easier to type everything in lower case.

* Note brackets, quote marks, slashes and equal signs; they are part of the codes.

* Spaces or extra lines are not recognized by HTML browsers. It is easier for you to check your coding errors if you put codes on separate lines.

* Save your document after almost every line so you don't have to retype codes if your computer or your network encounters a problem.

* Windows users: When you save your document for the first time, name it with a dot and *html* or *htm* extension such as resume.html, and save it as All Files (*.*). If you don't use this extension, you won't be able to view it in a browser in Windows. Macintosh users also use an *.html* extension even though you can view it in a browser. When you upload it later on the Internet, you will need an *.html* or *.htm* extension anyway.

* Save shortcut: Instead of pulling down your File menu to save, use Command S (that's the apple plus the letter *s* on a Macintosh) or Ctrl-S on Windows.

HTML BASICS

Let's start creating your resume. Open a word processing program, preferably SimpleText or TeachText in Macintosh or Notepad in Windows, by clicking twice on the application icon. Type the codes and brackets as they appear here and follow the instructions, but don't type the explanations that appear within parentheses. Remember to save your document repeatedly.

<html> (All HTML documents start with this code.)

<head> (This identifies the file but does not show up when viewed on the Web.)

<title> (This is the title that appears in the browser bar. After the bracket, leaving no space, write a short title): My Home Page or [Your Name] Home Page.

</title> (This is the end tag for the title; note the slash for ending codes.)

</head> (This is the end tag for the head, meaning the header instructions end here.)

<body> (This tag starts the information that will show up when you view your document in a browser. It is the beginning of the document that people see.)

<h1> (Headline that identifies your document. This headline may be the same as your title, but this does show up in the browser. This is the largest headline size. Headlines go from sizes 1 to 6, with **<h1>** the largest and **<h6>** the smallest.)

(Write a headline after the code): Your Name Resume. (Save your document.)

</h1> (End headline tag. If you don't close the tag like this, your whole page will be in headline-size type.)

<p> (This is a paragraph code. You need this code every time you start a new paragraph.) Start typing a few lines of text. For example, write your e-mail address. You don't need an ending </p> tag.

<p> Career Objective: To get an internship or a job as a [reporter, copy editor, producer or whatever is appropriate for you].

</body> (This code ends the body of your document; note the slash.)

</html> (End tag for the document.)

Save your document. Make sure you save it as "Text Only" if you are not using a text-only program, such as SimpleText or Notepad.

That's the bare minimum of HTML coding. You should have the beginnings of your first Web document. Your coded page should look like this:

<html>

<head>

<title>Your Name Resume

</title>

</head>

<body>

<h1>Your Name Resume

</h1>

<p>Your e-mail address

<p>Career Objective: To get an internship or a job as a. . . . (Type another line or two if you wish.)

</body>

</html>

VIEWING THE DOCUMENT

Let's see how your document looks on the Web. Remember to save it with an *.htm* or *.html* extension. In Windows, add *.html* or *.htm* after File Name, and also pull down the arrow in the "Save as type" bar to All Files (*.*). Even though you will be able to see this in Netscape Navigator or Internet Explorer, this document is not on the Internet yet, so no one else can see what you are doing. Transferring documents to the Web is another process that comes later.

These instructions are for Netscape Navigator in the Communicator browser; Internet Explorer instructions follow.

✳   Open Netscape Navigator.

✳   Pull down the File menu at the top of your screen and click on "Open." Then move your cursor to "Page in Navigator."

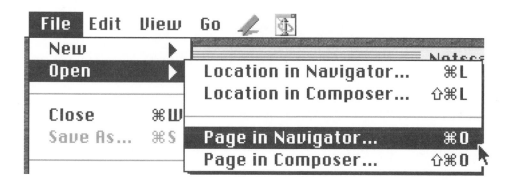

✳   A directory of folders in your computer should open. Click open folders and files until you find the document you are coding. If you have saved your document on your desktop, your file should look something like this:

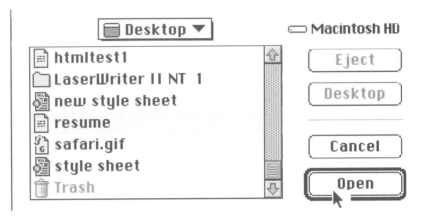

✳   In Explorer, go to the File menu and click on "Open." (In Windows, if you can't find the name of your file, use "Browse" until you locate your file. Then click "OK.") Explorer will show it as a Web page even if you don't give it an .html extension.

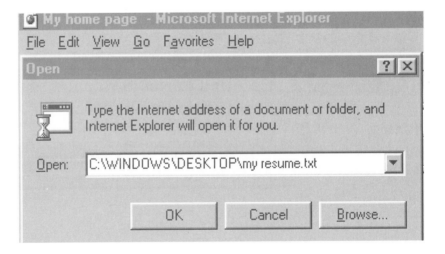

✳   View your file. Your document should look like this in either browser:

Your Name Resume

Your e-mail address

Career Objective: To get an internship or job as a reporter (or whatever you typed).

✳ Keep this browser file open while you make changes in your document! You will be clicking back and forth from your browser to your document as you create it.

✳ Go back to the document. Add a new paragraph before the end body tag:

<p>I am learning online journalism skills.

✳ Save again.

✳ View the changes. Click back to the browser. Click the Reload button on Netscape or the Refresh button on Explorer. You don't have to keep opening the file unless you closed it. Your changes should show up. Make sure you inserted the new paragraph before the end body tag. **</body>**

Always save after every change or the changes won't show up when you browse again. If you don't click Reload or Refresh, you will get the old version of your document.

HTML LISTS

Now let's expand your resume with some lists. HTML has four kinds of lists.

✳ **Unordered** lists use bullets, the most common kinds of lists.

✳ **Ordered** lists number items as 1, 2, 3, and so on.

✳ **Descriptive/definition** lists offer descriptions of list items. This is very helpful for resumes. For example, if you listed your experience and wanted to briefly describe your duties in each job, you would use this type of list.

✳ Nested lists

　　✳ These are bulleted lists within lists.

　　✳ They would look like this, and the bullets differ in each nest.

Let's add to your resume with each kind of list. We'll start with an unordered list, characterized by bullets. The <ul> code means unordered list. The <li> code means a list item.

✳ Call up your HTML resume document.

✳ After the last paragraph you wrote but before the ending </body> tag, write a size 3 heading and some list items. Don't type the explanations that appear here in parentheses. Your codes should look like this:

<h3>Experience

</h3> (This ends the headline code.)

<ul> (This starts the unordered list.)

   <li>Campus newspaper reporter, dates

   <li>Student Senate representative, dates

   <li>Server at Starving Student Pub, dates

</ul> (This ends the unordered list. You don't need an ending code for the <li> items.)

✳ Save the document.

✳ Go to your open browser, click Reload or Refresh (or reopen the file if you closed it by accident) and view your document in your browser. The headline and list should look like this:

> **Experience**
> - Campus newspaper reporter, dates
> - Student Senate representative, dates
> - Server at Starving Student Pub, dates

✳ Now create a numbered list right after the previous items using the code <ol> for ordered list and a smaller headline <h2> so you can see what a size 2 head looks like:

<h2>Preferred Media Jobs

</h2>

<ol>

    <li>Copyediting

    <li>Design

    <li>Reporting

</ol>

Don't forget to save your document. Now view it in your browser by clicking Reload or Refresh. It should look like this:

Preferred Media Jobs

1. Copyediting
2. Design
3. Reporting

✳ Now create a descriptive list, which is very useful in a resume. Add this right after the numbered list. Use a size 4 **<h4>** headline this time. The code for a descriptive/definition list is **<dl>.** The **<dt>** code stands for descriptive term and **<dd>** means definition or description of the term. No closing tags are needed for **<dt>** or **<dd>** but one is needed for **</dl>.**

<h4>Job Duties

</h4>

   <dl>

   <dt>Intern at CNN, Summer 1998

      <dd>Monitored the wires, fetched coffee

   <dt>Server at Starving Students Pub, 1997–98

      <dd>Waited on tables, took cash, begged for tips

   </dl>

It should look like this:

Job Duties

Intern at CNN, Summer 1998
        Monitored the wires, fetched coffee
Server at Starving Students Pub, 1997-98
        Waited on tables, took cash, begged for tips

✳ Suppose you want to add a descriptive definition to a bulleted list item. Just add the <dd> code after your bulleted item. Go back to the earlier bulleted list. After the item, <li>Server at Starving Student Pub, dates, add a descriptive term as follows:

<li>Server at Starving Student Pub, dates

<dd>Waited on tables, took cash, begged for tips

It should look like this in your browser:

Experience

- Campus newspaper reporter, dates
- Student Senate representative, dates
- Server at Starving Student Pub, dates
  Waited on tables, took cash, begged for tips

✳ Let's do a nested list, which is also useful for resumes or proposals. The code is the same as for a bulleted list with secondary items.

<ul>

<li>University Activities (This is the first list item with a bullet.)

  <ul>(Starts a secondary list.)

    <li>1998: Student Council representative (First item in list within a list.)

    <li> 1997 Campus newspaper editor (Another sublist item.)

    <li> 1996: Freelance reporter for campus newspaper (Another sublist item.)

  </ul> (This ends the secondary list.)

<li>Hometown Community College (Second main list item.)

  <ul> (Secondary list code.)

    <li> 1995: Campus newspaper editor (Another sublist item.)

    <li> 1994: Slept in classes (Another sublist item.)

  </ul>(This ends the sublist.)

</ul>(This code ends the entire nested list.)

This is how a nested list looks in Netscape; note how the secondary list bullets differ from the main ones. Different browsers use other bullet forms, but the concept is the same.

- University Activities
    - 1998: Student Council representative
    - 1997: Campus newspaper editor
    - 1996: Freelance reporter for campus newspaper
- Hometown Community College
    - 1995: Campus newspaper editor
    - 1994: Slept in classes

HYPERLINKS

Now you are ready to add links to your document. Before you begin, you might want to check the URLs for some favorite sites or check the URL of your college or university so you can create a link to it in your resume. There are two basic types of links: external and targeted internal links.

* **External links** connect your document to other documents on the World Wide Web.

* **Targeted internal links** create links within your own document such as "Back to top" or others you might want to use for navigation or other purposes.

All links are created with anchor tags <a href="URL enclosed in quotes">. Think of it as an abbreviation: The letter *a* equals anchor, *href* stands for hyperlink reference, and the URL in quotes is the proper name of a URL. Note the space between the letter *a* and *href*. You also need text after the end bracket to describe the link. This is the clickable text that characterizes hyperlinks, which usually are underlined and in a different color to distinguish them from other text. (Their appearance can be set in browser preferences.)

E x t e r n a l   L i n k s   Go back to your HTML resume and create a link at the end of your last list. The following URL will link to CNN Interactive, but you can substitute any URL you prefer.

<p> (for new paragraph)

<a href="http://www.cnn.com">CNN Interactive

</a>end anchor tag

Save your changes. Open the document in your browser and click on the link. It should connect you to CNN Interactive or the URL for the site you chose. Don't forget the ending anchor tag </a>.

T a r g e t e d   I n t e r n a l   L i n k s   These links target a specific area within your document and link to it. Most often you will use internal links for navigation such as "Back to the top" or to a specific heading within your document. We'll create them for that purpose. Here are the two codes involved:

* First, target the words you want to link to, and put the anchor plus name of target code before those words and an end-anchor code after the words or image.
  <a name= "the words or image you want to link to">words or image that were previously there**</a>**

* Then, create the link with an anchor code, quotation marks and a pound sign plus the name of the link.
  <a href="#the word or image to link to">clickable link name</a>
  Try it.

* Locate the heading or words you want to link to within the document. In this case, link to the first word in your first headline, "Your Name Resume," or whatever you called it. Make sure you type lower or upper case letters exactly as they appear in the word you want to link to. Note the spaces between *a* and *href* within these codes.

* In front of the headline or word that you are targeting such as "My Resume," type this target code, which identifies the words you will link to, and put an end anchor tag after the existing words.
  <a name="My Resume">existing words**</a>**

* Now go to the bottom of your document where you want to create a link called "Back to top," but make sure you create the code before the end body tag </body> or your link won't appear. Write the following code with a pound sign, indicating you will link to the word after the pound sign. Then write the words, *Back to top,* for your clickable link. Add an end anchor tag.
  <a href="#My Resume">Back to top</a>

* Save and test it in your browser.

❋ Now create a reverse targeted internal link from the top to the bottom of your document.

❋ Go to the bottom of the page and type the word *bottom*. Next, create this target code before the word *bottom* that you just typed.
<a name="bottom">bottom</a>

Then go to the top of the page and create a clickable link with this next code:
<a href="#bottom">bottom</a>

You can link to a specific place in another document, but it isn't a good idea because you have no control over other people's documents. However, if it is another document you created, you can create the links as follows:

❋ Locate the place you want to link to in the document and define it:
<a name="name of heading or first words where you will connect">target text</a>

❋ Now create the link in your document with the full URL and a pound sign.
<a href="URL#name of heading or first words where you will connect">clickable descriptive text</a>

E-MAIL LINKS

You can create a link to your e-mail address or anyone else's address with a link anchor tag and the word *mailto:* before the address. If you typed your e-mail address earlier, you can go back to it and add the address link or create a new e-mail link now.
<a href="mailto:your e-mail address">e-mail address</a>

❋ Don't put any spaces between the mailto: and your address.

IMAGES

Images in World Wide Web documents can only be displayed in two forms:

❋ **GIF: Graphic Interchange Format.** This type of image can be viewed on all types of computers and browsers.

❋ **JPEG: Joint Photographic Experts Group.** This format is preferable for photographs.

When you insert an icon, picture or other image, it must have a *.gif* or *.jpg* tag at the end of the image to tell the browser what type of image it is. You can't just type those labels after the name when you save the image. You have to save the images in those formats in such programs as Adobe Photoshop, Graphic Converter (available as shareware), Paint Shop Pro for Windows, or other software programs that offer those options.

Both formats compress images for the Web, meaning they reduce the amount of bytes or Web space that pictures and images require. Without compression, images would consume more computer memory and take longer to load.

Many icons, graphics and photographs are available free on the Internet from hundreds of sites. However, check the copyright requirements before you use images in your documents.

You might want to link to your university or college home page and select an image. We'll use these images to code into your resume. Here is how to get an image from a document on the Web.

On Macintosh: Put your pointer on the image, and hold down your mouse button until you get the menu asking you to "Save this Image as." After you click this option, it will ask you to name the image and will tell you whether it is a jpg or gif file. Save it to your desktop or folder in your computer.

```
Back
Forward

Open this Image
Save this Image as...
Copy this Image
Copy this Image Location
Load this Image
```

On Windows: Hold down the right button on your mouse and click on "Save Image As" in Netscape or "Save Picture as" in Explorer. Then click on your left mouse button, and a menu will appear asking you to name your image and tell what type of file it is, a gif file or a jpg file.

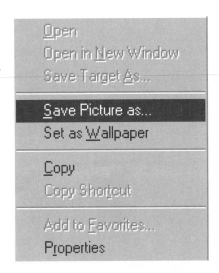

Give your image a brief name ending with *.gif* or *.jpg* (that's dot *gif* or dot *jpg*). The image should be saved automatically in .gif or .jpg form, but make sure it also is labeled with one of those tags. Save it to your desktop or folder in your computer.

Image Tags   To insert an image in your document, you need an image code <img> before the image, but you don't need a closing tag. It is preferable to save an image in your own computer instead of linking to one on someone else's site. Make sure you type the name of the image exactly as you have saved it, including lower or uppercase letters. Here are the codes for inserting images; note the space between *img* and *src* and the quotation marks around the name of the image or URL:

* If the image is saved in your desktop, use this code for a .gif or a .jpg:
  <img src="name of image.gif"> or **<img src="name of image.jpg">**

* If the image is saved in a folder in your computer, use this code with name of folder, followed by a slash, then the name of the image:
  <img src="folder name/name of image.gif or name of image.jpg">

* If you are linking to an image on another site, use this code:
  <img src="URL of the image with end tag .jpg or .gif">

Aligning Images   To align the image in your document, use these codes:

Middle alignment: <img src="name of image" align=middle>

Left alignment: <img src="name of image" align=left>

Right alignment: <img src="name of image" align=right>

However, don't spend much time on alignment now because it is much easier to use a Web editor, which we'll do in the next chapter.

FORMATTING CODES

Formatting also is much easier with a Web editor, so you don't have to do this now, but if you want to understand the concepts, here are the basics of style codes. Formatting codes are expressed in two types:

* **Logical style** directions are expressed with words such as *strong* for "bold." They use information more than codes to tell the browser what to do.

* **Physical style** directions are codes such as *b* for boldface, *i* for italics, and so on.

Here are some formatting tips you might want to use in your resume:

Headlines Sizes   Headlines come in sizes 1, the largest, to 6, the smallest. You've already used some of these headline sizes in your document. Try different sizes to see what you want for your subheads:

<h1> Largest headline, usually reserved for your title.

<h3> Medium-size headline, good for subheads.

<h6> Very small head.

Typeface Codes The most common are boldface and italics. Don't underline for emphasis because that usually indicates a hyperlink.

boldface (Don't forget the end code or the rest of your document will be in boldface.) You also can write this code in logical style.

****synonymous with boldface****

<i> Italics**</i>**

**
** Line break. Use this code after a line if you want the equivalent of carriage return without a new paragraph, which always adds a line space. This will give you single spacing. You don't need an ending code.

<p> Paragraph tag. This tag will insert a space between paragraphs. If you just want to add an extra line anywhere, you can use the <p> tag. No ending tag is necessary.

<hr> Horizontal rule. This will create a line across your page, like a break between your name and the body of your document. No ending tag is necessary.

<pre> Preformatted text **</pre>** This command tells your browser to display the text exactly as you typed it. It is useful for columns or unusual spacing. The disadvantage is that preformatted text will be displayed in 10 point Courier font, which is hard to read. It is the font used in e-mail.
```
Courier font looks like this.
```

For more advanced layout and formatting, we'll use a Web editor in the next chapter. This information should give you a basic knowledge of HTML so you can create your resume or another Web document. After you have created your document in basic HTML and beautified it with a Web editor, we will transfer it to the Internet in Chapter 8. In the meantime, store all the images and your document in a folder on your computer and also save them on a floppy disk.

VIEWING CODES IN DOCUMENTS

If you want to know how any Web document is coded, you can find out easily. It's a good way to learn how to format documents or use a code for an item or style you like in a Web site. Copying the code is not plagiarism, but copying the content is.

❊   Go to the View menu in either browser—Netscape or Explorer.

❊   Click on "Page Source" in Netscape Navigator ("Document Source" in older versions of Navigator) or "Source" in Microsoft Explorer. The source codes will open in SimpleText or Notepad so you can view them. You can do this with your own Web documents, too, so you can check your coding.

Safaris

http://www.mhhe.com/socscience/comm/
rich/ch6/

6–1	**HTML Tutorials**	To find links to online HTML tutorials, click into our Web site.
6–2	**Job Safari**	Check our Web site for links to job sources so you can see what type of media jobs are available.
6–3	**Graphics Safari**	Check our Web site for links to sites that offer free graphics. Observe copyright restrictions. Many images are available for use on personal home pages and resumes.
6–4	**Your Resume Safari**	Create a basic resume using HTML. Code the information you need. You'll learn design tips and use a Web authoring tool to beautify your resume in the next chapter.

Chapter 7

BEYOND BASICS

Goals

* To learn how to use a Web editor.

* To design and create a resume.

* To explore online resumes of media Web designers.

* To explore online media job sites.

If you know how to use Page Composer, the Web authoring tool from Netscape Communicator, or another Web editor that you prefer, read the design tips in the beginning of the chapter and leap to the online Safaris to view leading media Web designers' home pages and explore media job sites. If you want to leap to different parts of the instructions, here are some highlights:

http://www.mhhe.com/socscience/comm/rich/ch7/

Hyperleap

Rich Beckman's home page
http://sunsite.unc.edu/rbeckman/Remembrance

Public Domain Graphics at Sunsite
http://sunsite.unc.edu

Netscape home page
http://www.netscape.com

Web designers' home pages and graphics sites are in the online Safaris.

A full glossary is in the appendix and on our Web site.

http://www.mhhe.com/socscience/comm/rich/glossary.html

WYSIWYG An acronym for "what you see is what you get," used to describe Web authoring tools that allow you to create a Web document that will look the same way when you view it in a browser.

ANCHOR The word, phrase or image you connect to with an internal link, one within the same Web page you are viewing or creating.

EXTERNAL LINKS Links to other Web pages.

HOME PAGE The entry page to your Web site.

INTERNAL TARGETED LINKS Links that connect to words or images within the same Web document you are viewing or creating, not to another document.

PIXELS A derivative of "picture element," pixels are the dots that make up images or characters on computer screens.

RGB Red, green and blue, the values used to create different colors in computers. The combinations and strengths of the colors determine the hues.

TARGET Same as an anchor; the word, phrase or image you connect to with an internal link.

The first page of Rich Beckman's online resume features a photograph of the family he loves. Susie and her offspring aren't his wife and children; they're bears. But the photos of bears, an elk and some wood storks reveal more about Beckman than his own photo or words.

Beckman is an award-winning photojournalist who specializes in environmental issues, particularly endangered species, and he wants your first impression of him to be the work he loves. The photo of the grizzly Susie and her cubs is from a documentary he produced in Alaska.

Beckman is also a journalism professor at the University of North Carolina, where he coordinates the visual communication sequence. But you have to click to another page on his resume to get that information.

"Design a single screen first," Beckman says. "Make an impression on the front page."

In print the first impression you make on an employer is through a cover letter. When you create an online resume, the first screen of your Web site takes the place of a cover letter. But that first impression doesn't have to be a verbal one.

HOME PAGE

Your entry page is a home page, and it doesn't need to reveal everything about you. That would be like hanging all your most important possessions on the front door of your home or apartment. You can create a link on the front page to another page on your site that offers more written information about you.

Beckman suggests that you design the entry page to your resume to reflect something special about you. "It could be teasers of what you have done," Beckman says. "Perhaps you've had a good internship that sells you."

For example, if you are a photojournalist and you have an award-winning picture, put it on your first screen, Beckman says. If you are going to be a graphic designer, your first screen should reflect good design skills. And if you plan to be a reporter, copy editor or magazine writer, you might display an abstract of a story you wrote or an introductory paragraph that compels readers to find out more about you, he says.

Designing a single screen that entices people to continue learning more about you isn't easy. What you leave out of the page is as important as what you put in it. "Give it your best shot," Beckman says.

HOME PAGE LINKS

The home page of your Web site should contain links to your resume and other Web pages within your site. You'll find examples of online resumes for some leading media Web designers in the Resume Safaris Web site for this chapter.

Beckman's home page features a simple design, containing one large graphic with photographs and links to his resume and work examples. The only other elements on his Web page are four navigation buttons providing links to his syllabi, his school, his department and an online software site associated with the University of North Carolina.

Although Beckman describes his credentials in his resume, the links to excerpts of his work reveal more about his talents. Here is a passage from a documentary he created about grizzly bears in Alaska:

> Three years ago, I stood on the trail to Brooks Falls at the base of the Aleutian Peninsula staring at two grizzlies. Our paths crossed at the crest of a knoll. I knew to get off the trail, to drop down in respect, to not look into their eyes—instead I stood calmly and quietly and fell forever in love.
>
> What I learned that day and since changed who and what I am. I count my time with the grizzlies among the happiest and most enlightening days of my life. My pictures and words are a mere shadow of experience, but I hope they will promote understanding and plant the seed that will allow you to fall forever in love.

NAVIGATION

Regardless of the information you include in your home page or entry resume page, you should provide good navigation links at the top, bottom or on the side of your entry page to other documents within your site. Your resume might be one link on a home page. Other pages within your site should have navigation links back to your home page. Make it easy for a reader to use your site.

Your resume also may have internal navigation links such as "back to top" or links from the top of the page to various subheadings on your page, particularly if your page requires a viewer to scroll for two or more screens to read the entire document. Apply the criteria you developed for good Web sites in Chapter 4.

E-MAIL ADDRESS

When Peggy Kuhr wants to hire a college student for an internship or job at *The Spokesman Review,* she looks for his or her e-mail address on a resume. It's hard to reach college students by telephone because they are in and out of their residences so much, says Kuhr, managing editor of the newspaper in Spokane, Wash. She says it's much easier to contact a student by e-mail.

Whether your resume is in print or online form, your e-mail address should be as much a part of it as your telephone number. Your e-mail address should also be part of any Web site you create.

In one case Kuhr even interviewed a candidate through e-mail. An American reporter working in Eastern Europe had responded to an advertisement Kuhr put into the online version of *Editor & Publisher*. "He directed me to a Web site where I could read some of his award-winning stories," Kuhr said. "We communicated only by e-mail because the cost of phone calls and the time differential were problems."

Although that candidate didn't get the job at *The Spokesman Review* because he couldn't start work when Kuhr needed to fill the position, his online resume and clips earned him an interview he otherwise would not have received. That's another reason you might consider converting some of your stories or other work to Web pages that can be linked to your resume.

ETHICAL CONCERNS

How much should you reveal about yourself on your Web site? Unfortunately, crime exists in the virtual world as it does in the real one. Stories of stalkers seeking victims via online documents or discussion groups are common.

One journalism student scanned her picture into her resume. She was about to list her address and phone number just as she would in her print resume when she became concerned about potential stalkers. She knew that mapping programs on the Internet can provide directions to any street address. (Check the Travel Safari in Chapter 3 to find map searches.) As a result, she decided not to put her own phone number and address in her resume. Then she wondered whether to list telephone numbers and addresses of her references. She settled for e-mail addresses for herself and her references.

Other students in an online journalism class decided to use the phrase, "References available on request," in their online resumes, which isn't advisable in a print resume. You should make it as easy as possible for a prospective employer to get information about you, especially if you are just starting your media careers. That is why it is preferable to list names and telephone numbers of your references on print resumes, but online resumes call for different measures.

Because of the privacy concerns created by online media, you should ask your references if they have any objections to listing their business phone numbers on your online resume. A safer bet is to just use e-mail addresses if your references have them. If not, "References available on request" may have to suffice. If someone is interested enough to contact you by e-mail for an internship or job, you can follow up with your print resume listing references in full.

WEB AUTHORING TOOLS

Everyone can create a document on the World Wide Web these days without knowing HTML. However, as explained in the last chapter, it helps to master the basics of HTML so you can correct errors a Web editor may insert. Several software programs are designed specifically for creating Web documents. Two popular ones are Adobe PageMill and Microsoft FrontPage. We'll use Netscape Communicator's Page Composer because it is available for both platforms without charge to academic users.

Almost all Web editors contain the same tools and functions, so if you learn how to create a document with Netscape's Page Composer, you can easily master another Web editor. If you are using an older version of Netscape's Web editor, Netscape Gold, the instructions are similar. You can download the software from the Netscape home page at *http://www.netscape.com,* and then follow the directions to retrieve the program for your type of computer.

NETSCAPE PAGE COMPOSER

Let's start by creating a new document. You can design your first screen later. For now, we'll work with the text and appearance of your resume so you can interact with the directions. Most of the illustrations here were created on a Macintosh; if you are using Windows, the directions are the same but the images will look slightly different.

✽   Open Netscape Communicator by clicking on your Netscape icon.

✳ Pull down the Communicator menu to "Page Composer." This will open a blank Web document for you to create.

✳ You also can open a new Web page by pulling down your File menu and choosing "New." Then move your cursor to "Blank Page." You will be offered other options of a template or the Netscape Wizard, which creates a paint-by-the-numbers type of document. Choose "Blank Page" so you can use your own creativity.

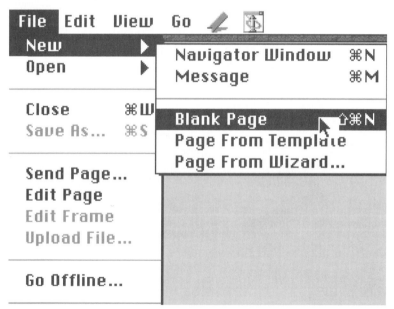

✳ The "New Page" icon also will open a blank page after you are in Page Composer.

✳ To edit an existing Web page in Composer, open the Web page. Then pull down your File menu to "Edit Page."

✳ You should get a toolbar that looks like this in Macintosh. You can use your menus at the top of your screen to perform tasks, but the toolbar makes it easier.

✳ The toolbar looks like this in Windows. Although the icons are labeled in Windows and not on the Macintosh version, when you put your cursor on any of them, the labels appear anyway.

✳ If you don't get all these buttons, pull down the View menu to "Show Composition Toolbar" and "Show Formatting Toolbar." If they are already shown, the menu will say "Hide these toolbars."

✳ Type a few words in the document such as "Your Name" or "My Resume."

SAVING STEPS

S a v e   Y o u r   D o c u m e n t   Click the Save button on your
toolbar and give your document a name. In Macintosh, add *.html* to the
end of the file name. In Windows, save your document as "HTML Files"
and an *.htm* extension will be added automatically.

✳ If this is the first Web page you have ever created and it will be your home
   page, save it as index.html. In Windows, the document will be saved
   automatically as index.htm. Change that to index.html when you save it.
   Your first home page must be labeled with an *.html* extension if this is the
   document you want to open when you call up your Web site.

✳ Save any other pages you create with a brief one-word name plus an *.html* or
   .htm extension such as resume.html. Subsequent pages may have either
   extension. Use one-word labels or labels that are linked with an underscore
   plus your *html* or *htm* extension.

✳ Save images (we'll discuss them later) with one-word names plus a *.gif* or
   .jpeg extension.

Remember to save repeatedly as you create your document. It is easier to work
with a document if you save it to your desktop as you are creating it. If your
network prohibits adding to the desktop, save it in a folder in your directory. You
can also format your document to save every few minutes. Pull down your Edit
menu, scroll to "Preferences," and set the preferences to save every five minutes,
more or less, as you choose. You should also save to a floppy disk, especially if you
are working in a classroom on a network.

Composer	Set general preferences for authoring Web pages.

Author name :   carole rich

☐ Automatically save page every   5   minutes.

VIEWING YOUR DOCUMENT

WYSIWYG Pronounced wis'-ee-wig, this acronym means "What you see is what you get." The words you typed on the page you are creating will appear exactly that way when you view them on the Web because Netscape's Page Composer is a WYSIWYG Web editor. As you make changes to your document, you can switch back and forth from the Web editor to the browser to see how it looks. This is the fun part. To view your document, take these steps:

✳ Save the document in Composer. Click the Save button or use keyboard shortcuts Command S on Macintosh, Ctrl-S on PCs. You must save every change before you view it.

✳ Click the Preview button on your toolbar. This will open the Navigator browser. Your Composer document will remain open behind the page that opens in Navigator. Keep both pages open.

✳ Return to your Composer document by clicking on it. Don't close the browser page.

✳ Save new changes in Composer. Browse again by clicking once on the open page.

✳ Reload. The browser will not recognize your changes unless you reload the page. You can do all of this offline. Now you can keep viewing your document as you create it.

Do not try to save your page under "Save" or "Save As" in your browser in Macintosh because it will save it only as text. Make sure you are in Page Composer when you save so you save it as an HTML document. In Windows, you can save from the browser or Page Composer but make sure you save it as an HTML document.

PAGE IDENTITY
AND META TAGS

You should identify the title and authorship of your page. Codes called *meta tags* also help search engines find your page, which may be useful if you want people to find your resume or Web site. These labels don't appear when you view the page.

✳ Pull down the Format menu to "Page Properties" in Macintosh or "Page Colors and Properties" in Windows. Click on "General." Fill in the title, your name, a very brief description, and some keywords that a search engine might use to find your pages. Click OK.

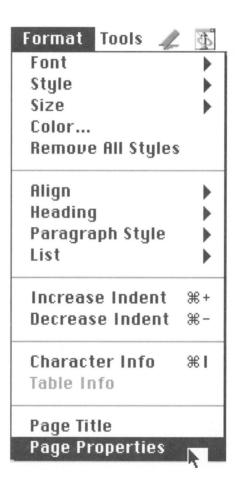

Don't use the Meta Tags panel. It doesn't provide tags you need. Now you are ready to format the appearance.

FORMATTING
APPEARANCE

Your document will open with default colors for background, text and links. The default background colors are usually gray or white unless you have set your browser preferences for a specific background color. To choose your own colors for your document, use your Format menu. Follow these steps to choose your page colors.

❋ Again pull down the Format menu and click on "Page Properties" in Macintosh (or "Page Colors and Properties" in Windows) at the bottom of the menu (see the preceding figure).

❋ A dialogue box will open, offering you several options. Select "Colors and Background" at the top of the box. After you have selected the colors you want, as explained next, click OK.

Page Properties

| General | **Colors and Background** | META Tags |

Page Colors

◯ Use Navigator's Color Settings

◉ Use Custom Colors   [Netscape Default Colors ▾]

▮ Normal Text   Normal text
▮ Link Text   Link text
▮ Active Link Text   Active [selected] link
▮ Followed Link Text   Followed [visited] link
▮ Background

Page Background

☐ Image [   ]   [**Choose File...**]

☐ Leave image at the original location

A background image will override the background color.

☐ Apply these settings to all new blank pages

[**Help**] [**Cancel**] [**Apply**] [**OK**]

❋ If you don't want to use the browser's default colors, click on the button for "Use Custom Colors."

❋ Pull down the arrow of the menu that shows Netscape Default Colors. In Windows, this menu is Color Schemes. Several choices for color combinations of text and background are offered. Choose your preference. Black text on a white background is standard and good for reading. The text color should contrast strongly with the background.

❋ If you want to choose your own colors for text and links without using the menu choices, click on the box next to each item, "Normal Text," "Link Text," and so on. A color palette will open.

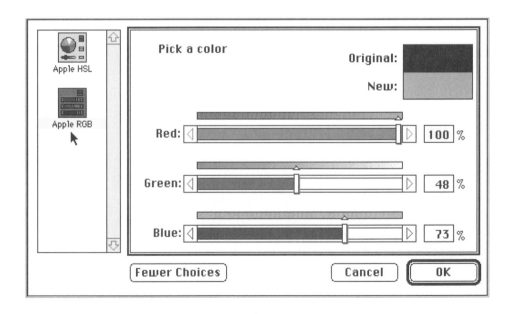

✳ In Macintosh the palette offers bars or a wheel to manipulate the choices. Adjust the bar or the wheels to select the colors you want. If you prefer a color wheel, select Apple HSL. After you select the colors you want, click OK.

✳ In Windows a color box will open. These are standard colors that all browsers can view. Select a color from the box for your text or links. To create your own colors, click on "Other." A color bar will open, and you can adjust the colors by moving the arrow on the right of the box. Then click OK.

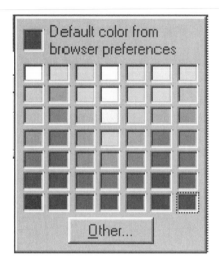
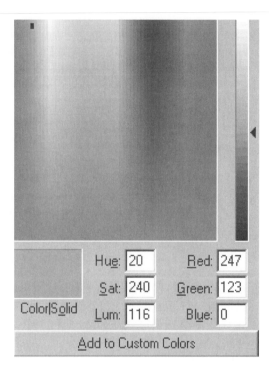

Other color format options are available. Any time you want to change the color of your text or a link, you can highlight it and click on a color button in your toolbar, or go to the Format menu and click on "Color" and the color bars will open.

On a Macintosh the toolbar color button is a palette:

In Windows it is a pull-down menu:

You should now have the color format for your document. Here are some other functions of the toolbar that you can use as you create your document.

FORMATTING TOOLBAR

If you place your cursor at the base of each button, a dialogue box will tell you the button's function in Macintosh. The functions are labeled in Windows if you set your preferences under "Appearance" to show toolbar as "Pictures and Text." Your menus, Format and Edit, perform all the same functions as your toolbar, but the buttons make it easier and faster for you to change styles as you create your document.

Start typing some more information in your document. It will automatically be coded, so don't worry about inserting any HTML codes. Then experiment with these formatting tool buttons:

Headlines and Other Styles   Pull down the first menu bar on the left side of the toolbar. It is set on the default "Normal" type. You can choose headlines from Heading 1, the largest, or Heading 6, the smallest. You can also choose the address style, which is italics, for your e-mail address. Other items include lists, which have their own buttons on the toolbar, and description text. Formatted text keeps the text spaced as you typed it, but it will default to 10-point Courier font, the font used in e-mail.

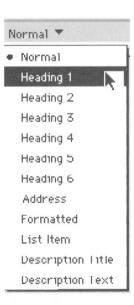

✳ Type the heading for your resume and select "Heading 1," which will be 24-point type. If you already typed it, just highlight it and click on "Heading 1." It should

look like this: # My Resume.

✳ Now type your e-mail address and select address. It will look like this: *e-mail address.* (We'll create the address link later.)

✳ Return to normal type by selecting "Normal" in the menu.

Type Size   You can adjust the size of your type by using the font size menu on the toolbar. On Macintosh operating systems, Composer shows the type size in points from 7 to 36. Windows offers more options—from 8 points to 72 points or in HTML sizes from minus 2 to plus 4.

If you want other sizes, choose your Edit menu and select "Preferences." Then choose "Appearance and Fonts." Make sure the arrow next to "Appearance" is facing downward in Macintosh or on a minus sign in Windows.

Font Style   To select boldface or italics as you are typing, use your toolbar buttons. **The first A is boldface;** *the second A is italics.* Even though the toolbar

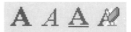

contains an underline button, don't use this because underlining is reserved for links in Web documents. The last letter A with an eraser will clear all styles if you change your mind about the formatting you chose. You can highlight text and click on the buttons to change your style anywhere in your document.

✳ Type a heading such as "Education." Now highlight it and click the boldface A. Change the size of it in your size menu.

✳ Font type: You also can format the type of font by using your Format menu and selecting "Font." Use caution because not all browsers will read unusual fonts.

C o l o r   As discussed earlier, the next button on the bottom row will open a color bar. Highlight your heading and change the color.

L i s t s   List your educational background. Click the list button if you want a bulleted list or a numbered list.

✳ To format the style of the bullets or numbers in your lists, pull down the Format menu and select "Character Info" in Macintosh or "Character Properties" in Windows.

✳ A dialogue box will open. Select "Paragraph." Then select "List Item" under the paragraph style. Pull down the other menus to choose your style of lists, style of bullets or style of numbers. If you get a pound sign instead of a number in a list, pull down the style menu to "Numbered List" and select numbers, letters or the style you want.

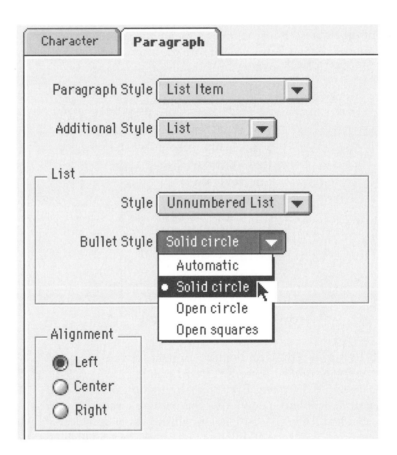

Block Quotes   Highlight the paragraph you want to justify on both sides as a block quote. Pull down the Format menu, to "Paragraph" to the "Additional Style" menu to block quote.

Alignment   You can align text with your alignment buttons.

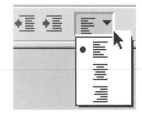

❋ To move a line, paragraph or image to the left, highlight the text or image and click the left-arrow button, which increases the indent.

❋ To move text or an image to the right, highlight the item and click the right-arrow button, which decreases the indent.

❋ To center, justify or align to the right or left, highlight the text or image and then pull down the menu under the third alignment button and click on the alignment you wish.

Cut, Copy and Paste   These buttons work the same way as word processing editing tools. Highlight the text you want to cut or copy, and click the Cut or Copy button. If you want to move the material, place your cursor where you want to paste it, and click the Paste button. These buttons are labeled in Windows but not in Macintosh. However, they look the same:

Print   To print any document on your screen, click the Print button.

CREATING LINKS

The Link button makes it easy to create links. External links connect to another document; internal links connect from one place to another within the same document and are used for navigation.

E x t e r n a l   L i n k s   First get the URL of the site you want to link to, and then follow these steps:

✳ Type or choose the word or phrase you want to be the clickable link. Highlight the word or phrase.

✳ Click the Link button. A box will open:

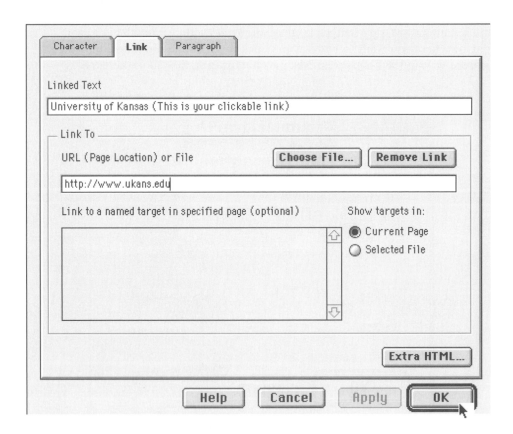

✳ Write the text for your clickable link in the top bar where it says "Linked Text." In Windows versions it says "Link Source." As an alternative, if you highlight a word or phrase on your page and then click your Link button, the word or phrase automatically will be inserted in the "Linked Text" or "Link Source" bar.

✳ Write the URL in the bar labeled "Link To."

✳ Click OK. You don't need to click on "Apply" unless you want to see how it looks.

✳ Remove link. If you don't like the link, click on "Remove Link" or highlight it on your page and use your Cut button.

✳ Dragging or copying links. If you have another Web document open that contains links you want on your page, you can just drag the links into your Composer page. You can also highlight the link on the other Web page, click Copy, and then paste it into your page.

Links to Other Pages in Your Web Site   If you are creating a Web site with several different pages that do not have URLs yet, your links should be the same names as your pages. For example, if you create a separate resume.html page that you want to link back to your home page, in the link box write *index.html*. As long as all your pages are in the same folder, your links will work.

Conversely, if on your home page (named *index.html*), you want to link to a separate resume page, write *resume.html* in your Link box.

Linking Images   Create links to images the same way you create them to text.

✳ Highlight the image.

✳ Click the Link button.

✳ Type the URL in the bar labeled "Link To." When you click on the image (after viewing it in your browser), it should link to that external site.

After you have created a link, the next words you type may appear in hyperlink style (underlined in your link color) even if you haven't created a link. To return to normal type, highlight the unwanted link-style words, then pull down your Edit menu to "Remove Link" on the new words you are typing.

Internal Targeted Links These links will take you from one place to another within the document.

❋ The word, image or phrase you want to link to is the "target" or "anchor." This is where the link takes you. Create this target first.

❋ Highlight the word, image or phrase that will serve as the target. Let's assume you want to create a link at the bottom of the page that takes you back to the top, where you have a headline, "My Resume."

❋ Click the Target button. A target properties box will open. The words you clicked will be inserted automatically. Macintosh calls it "Target Name" and Windows calls it "Enter a Name for This Target," but you don't need to do that if you have highlighted your target words. Click OK.

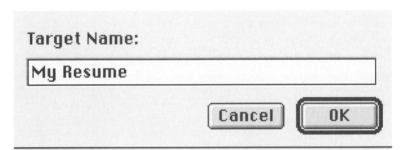

✳ Now click the Link button. The link dialogue box will open:

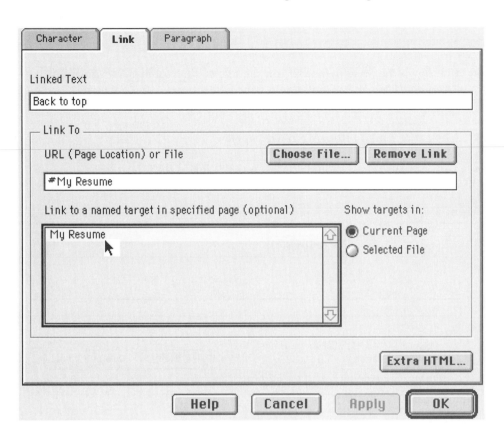

✳ Create the clickable link. In this case, assume it is at the bottom of your page and you want it to say "Back to top." Type those words and highlight them.

✳ Click the Link button. This time you will use the bottom half of the link box.

✳ The linked text should be inserted in the top bar, and your target, "My Resume," should appear in the named target bar. Make sure the Current Page button is clicked where the box says "Show targets in."

✳ Click once on the named target. It should appear preceded by a pound sign in the "URL (Page Location)" bar. If it doesn't, you can type it in. Just remember to include the pound sign, which is part of the code for targeted links. Click OK.

✳ Now check your links in your browser. Make sure you save the page and reload in the browser.

✳ If you want to link to a target in another document, which is not recommended unless you created the other document, click the button for "Selected File" in the link dialogue box. In the "Link To" bar, type the URL of the other document followed by a pound sign and the name of the target in that external Web page.

E - M a i l   A d d r e s s   L i n k   You can create a link to your e-mail
address or anyone else's address easily.

✳   Write the e-mail address in your document. Highlight it.

✳   Pull down the Style menu bar (on the left of your toolbar) and scroll to
     "Address." Or, you can pull down your Format menu, to "Paragraph," to
     "Address."

✳   Click your Link button. A box will open.

✳   Your e-mail address should appear in the "Linked Text" box:

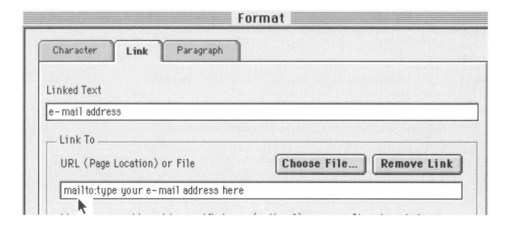

✳   Now make the link by typing *mailto:your e-mail address.* (That's *mailto* with no
     space between *mail* and *to* followed by a colon with no space and your e-mail
     address.) If you are typing someone else's e-mail address, do the same but
     substitute the other person's address.

✳   Click OK. Save the page. Go back to your browser. Reload. Test your link. If
     you are on a network and the Netscape mail program is not set up in the
     computer you are working on, the link may not connect you via Netscape.
     However, it will work on any computer in which your browser is set up to
     send or receive mail.

(The preferences in Edit under "Mail & Groups" have to be filled out for the mail
server to work.)

HORIZONTAL LINES

If you have created your title and listed your e-mail address and any other pertinent information you want at the top of your page, you might want to insert a horizontal line under the address as a divider. Use horizontal lines sparingly, however.

❋ To insert a line, put your cursor where you want the line and click your horizontal line button (labeled H.Line in Windows.)

❋ To make the horizontal line three-dimensional, click on the line in your document. If it opens in 3-D, click on it and it will return to a black line and vice versa.

❋ To change the appearance of the line, double-click on it and a box will open. You can make it wider by increasing the number of pixels in the "Height" box, and you can change the width and alignment but not the color. For fancy lines and bars, you'll have to access a Web site that offers free graphics (Link to the Graphics Safari in our Web site for this chapter.)

Horizontal Line Info

Dimensions

Height: `2` Pixels

Width: `100` `% of window` ▼

Alignment

○ Left
◉ Center
○ Right

☒ 3-D Shading

`Extra HTML...`

`Help` `Cancel` `Apply` `OK`

IMAGES

Here are some reminders from Chapter 6 in case you skipped it or forgot these steps. Web images come in two formats: Gif images are created in Graphic Interchange Format, which is good for icons and most images, and JPEG images are in a format created by the Joint Photographic Experts Group. This format is best for photographs.

You must save your Web images in either format with a program such as Adobe Photoshop or Graphic Converter. All Web images must be labeled with *.gif* or *.jpg* (with a dot before the tag). You should give your image a brief name such as *mail.gif,* and don't write anything after the gif or jpg tag, or the browser won't recognize the image. Any images that you take from the Web will be in either format, so you don't have to use a special program to convert them. Note that *jpg* as a tag is spelled without the *e* in the acronym JPEG, but a *.jpeg* tag will work as well.

Remember to abide by copyrights. Many images are free from the Internet. Don't use any images that require copyright permission unless you have obtained the rights.

Suppose, for example, you want to add an e-mail icon next to your e-mail address. The e-mail images shown here and many others are available without charge from a public domain file on the Sunsite Web site at the University of North Carolina. They are copyright free and links to the site also are available on our Web site. Take these steps to retrieve images from the Web:

GETTING IMAGES

Your instructions for retrieving Web images are the same as they were in Chapter 6 on HTML.

❋ Place your cursor on the image and hold down your mouse button. On a PC, hold down the right mouse button. A dialogue box will open.

❋ Scroll to "Save this Image as" on Macintosh or "Save Picture as" in Windows. Save the images in a folder, perhaps one named images so you can find them. Or save them on your desktop while you create your Web page.

INSERTING IMAGES

To insert an image you have saved in your folder, click the image icon on your toolbar. A box will open.

❋ Click on "Choose File" until you find the image you want from your files.

❋ Click on "Open" when you find the image in your file. The image box will reappear. Composer automatically will insert codes for the image.

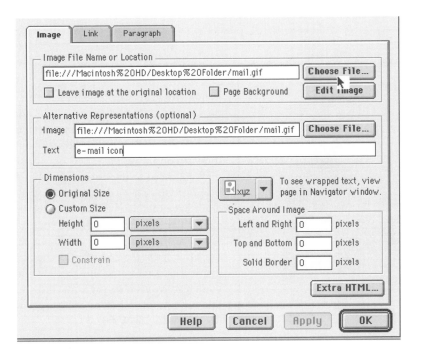

✳ Write text for your images in the "Alternative Representations" bars, if you wish. This is an option for people who choose to view Web pages without images. Instead of getting an image, these users get a description of the image. It is especially helpful for sight-impaired people and others who view Web pages in text-only format.

D i m e n s i o n s   If you want to change the size of the image or the space around it, fill in those boxes.

A l i g n m e n t   You can align your image and text next to it several ways: top, middle, bottom or wrap around. In Windows, the alignment options appear in the dialogue box; in Macintosh, the alignment options appear in a pull-down menu labeled *xyz*.

D r a g   I m a g e s   If you have a Web document open that contains an image you want to use in your page, you can drag it from the open document into your own without opening the image dialogue box.

C o p y   a n d   P a s t e   You can click once on the image you want to highlight on the external Web page, then use the Copy button on your toolbar. Place the cursor where you want the image on your page, and click the Paste button on your toolbar. This also bypasses the image box.

When you load your page into a Web directory, the image file name or location will change, but the coding may keep the original file path, and your images may not show up on the Web. This is one reason why you need to understand HTML: You may have to correct the coding so you don't have the file path as part of the image name. You also can change the coding by rewriting the image name, as shown next. For now, leave the coding with the file name or you won't be able to view it as you create your Web page. We'll discuss this again in Chapter 8 on moving your document to the Web.

Image	Link	Paragraph

Image File Name or Location

mail.gif   **Choose File...**

☐ Leave image at the original location   ☐ Page Background   **Edit Image**

Alternative Representations (optional)

Image   mail.gif   **Choose File...**

Text   e-mail icon

TABLES

To lay out items and text on your pages as you might in a design program such as Quark Xpress or Pagemaker, you need to use tables. Although browsers continue to improve their layout features, they remain very limited. However, tables give you some control over placement of information. Newer forms of HTML, some Web editors, and design programs like Quark Xpress offer more control for page design, but the basic Web editors still depend on tables for placement of text and images.

✳ Click the Table button on your toolbar; a box will open. In Macintosh it is called "Insert Table," and in Windows it is "New Table Properties." You can change your decisions later if you don't like the way your table looks. Set the properties first.

Table

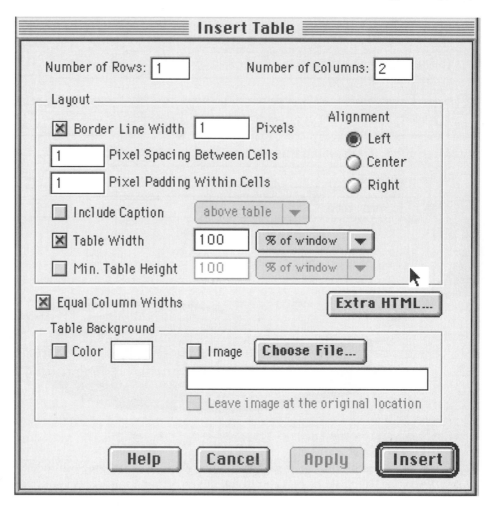

* Set the number of rows and columns. The default is 1 row, 2 columns. Rows are the number of boxes going across the page and columns are vertical. One row with two columns will give you two columns going vertically down the page. Cells are the boxes that contain information within rows or columns.

* Click the Alignment button: left, center or right.

* Border line width is the space around your table, like a picture frame. If you don't want a border, put 0 in this box. While you are designing, it helps to have a border line so you can see your tables. You can cut the borders later if you want your table to be invisible.

* Cell spacing is the amount of space between cells. If you want a column on the left and about a half-inch of space, increase the number of pixels to as much as 50.

* Cell padding is like margins, the space from the edges of the cell to the text or image. If you have a border, you may want to increase the padding so the text doesn't bump against the border.

✳ Table width: You can set table width in percentages or pixels, but no matter how wide or high you set your table columns and rows, they will expand as you insert text or images. Windows users can adjust the width of the table after it is created by placing the cursor on the outer edge of the table. When it changes from a vertical arrow to a horizontal arrow-bar, adjust the table width. Pixels provide more control.

✳ Table minimum height: If you want the column to run the length of your page, leave the height blank. Otherwise, experiment with the size you want. The length still will increase if you keep inserting information within the table.

✳ Caption: If you want a caption above or below the table, click the Include Caption button.

✳ Color: You can put color in one column and not in another or in a specific cell. To use color in the whole table, check the "Color" box and then click on the bar next to it. The color bar or wheel will open in Macintosh; in Windows the color palette box will open. Select your color.

✳ Patterned table backgrounds: To insert a patterned background to the table by using a gif or jpeg image, click on "Use image." Choose the image from your file, click "Open" and then OK.

You now should have a basic table. Here is how you can change it.

D e l e t i n g   To delete all or part of your table, pull down the Edit menu to "Delete Table." You will get another menu asking you if you want to delete the whole table, a row, a column or a cell:

Edit	View	Insert	Format	Tools
Undo			⌘Z	
Cut			⌘X	Netsc
Copy			⌘C	
Paste			⌘V	
Clear				
Delete Table ▶				Cell
Remove Link				Row
				Column
Select All			⌘A	Table
Select Table				

Inserting   To add a cell or a column, put your cursor where you want to add the item, and pull down the Insert menu to "Table." Again you will get a choice of inserting another table within your table (called a *nested table*), a row, column or cell.

Formatting Changes   To change the colors of columns or cells, alignment and other properties of your table, do the following:

✳ Put your cursor in the table or within a row or cell you want to change.

✳ Pull down the Format menu to "Table Info" in Macintosh or "Table Properties" in Windows.

✳ Select a table, row or cell, whichever you want to change. In the row and cell properties, you can change height, width or color. If your text or image is in the middle of your cell, which is the default position, click the Top button to raise it. If you want to change the color, click the Color button and then click the bar next to it to adjust color. You can do the same for rows.

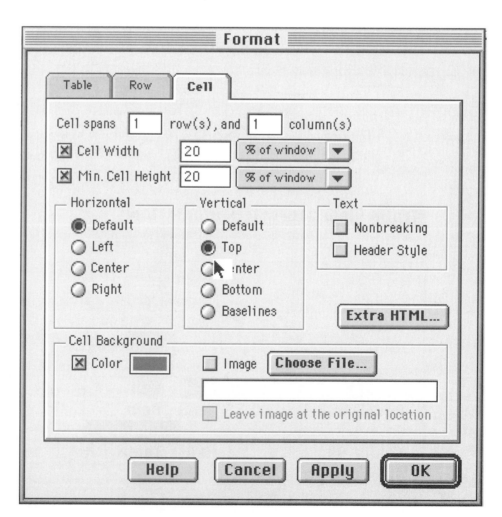

Let's experiment by creating a rather common newspaper style layout with tables. This style uses a table for the masthead, a column on the left (or right) side of the page (listing an index) and text in the center of the page. You can also use this for a resume if you had several items you wanted to link to in an index.

✳   Start with a new blank page.

✳   Click the Table button on your toolbar.

✳   Set the number of rows at 1 and the number of columns at 1. Leave everything else at its default setting and click Insert in Macintosh and OK in Windows.

✳   Put your name or the name of a company in Heading 1 style. Highlight it and center it (using the alignment button at the end of your toolbar). Move your cursor below the table.

✳   Click the Table button again. This time create a table with 1 row and 2 columns. Click Insert or OK. Type the word *Index* or something similar in the first cell.

✳   Change the size and color of the first column. Put your cursor in the first column. Pull down the Format menu to "Table Info" in Macintosh or "Table Properties" in Windows. Click on "Cell." Set the width at 15 percent (more or less if you prefer), and set the default at the top. Change the color of this cell to a color you want.

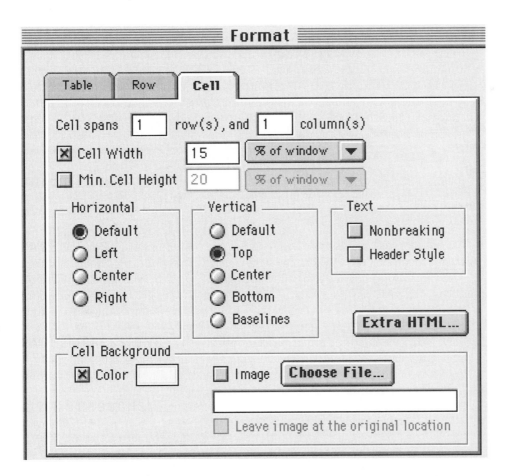

❋ Move your cursor to the second cell, and type text or insert images in it. This will be for the main part of your page.

❋ Eliminate the borders around the tables to make them invisible. Pull down the Format menu to "Table Info" or "Properties," but this time click on "Table." Change the "Border Line Width" to zero pixels and increase the pixel spacing between cells and pixel padding within cells to 10 each.

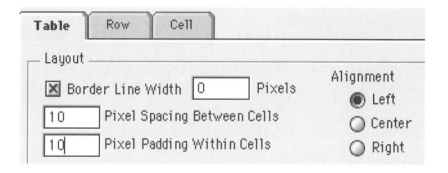

❋ If you want your tables to be completely invisible, make the colors the same as the background.

Your page should look something like this:

Your name goes here

Index with links

This cell will go the length of your page if you keep typing or hitting your return or enter key.

This cell will contain your main text and images. Set the alignment at the top.

INSERTING HTML CODE

If you wish to check or insert HTML coding in your document, first you must set your Preferences under Composer for External Editors. Choose Simple Text in Macintosh or Notepad in Windows. While your document is in the Composer mode, pull down your Edit menu to HTML Source, and change or add the coding you wish. You can also highlight text or an image and insert an HTML tag by pulling down your Insert menu to Insert to HTML Tag. You must save the document before the HTML source will work.

SPELLER

After you create your document, don't forget to spell-check it with the Spelling button on your toolbar.

VIEWING CODES IN OTHER DOCUMENTS

Netscape Composer does not support frames. If you want to create frames the easy way, use a Web authoring tool like Microsoft FrontPage, which creates them instantly. You also can add the HTML coding. Another easy way of copying the coding for the style you want is to pull down your View menu to "Page Source." Copy the coding from the document you are viewing. You aren't plagiarizing if you just take the codes, not the information or copyrighted images. You will be learning the way many other people have mastered Web page design.

CREATING AND LINKING TO A HOME PAGE

When you create your home page, the front door to your Web site, you will want to create links to other pages within your site, such as your resume. At this point, you have not uploaded these documents to the Web, so you don't have URLs for these other pages. You can still link to other documents if they are in the same folder on your computer or on your desktop. Here are some reminders mentioned earlier in the chapter:

* Create your home page. Label your home page *index.html*. This is what it eventually will be called when you load it onto the Web.

* Create other pages to which you want to link from the home page or from other pages that will be in your Web site. Label each succeeding page with its own name, such as *resume.html, clips.html, hobbies.html,* or whatever you plan to put on these other pages.

* To link back to the home page, label your link *index.html*.

* Keep all the pages and images in a folder or on your desktop so the browser can find them.

✳ Create the links from one page to another just as you linked to images: Type the words or link to an image and highlight them. Then click your Link button and label the link *resume.html* or whatever you have named the page.

✳ Use lower case; many computer systems are case sensitive.

✳ When you load your pages to the Web, if all these other pages are in your own folder on your Internet server, you may be able to keep the links as they are. If not, you will have to change the links to the full URLs when you are ready to upload them to your Web directory.

✳ If you are creating several pages with the same format, you can pull down the File menu in Composer (not in your Navigator browser) to "Save As" to duplicate the page. Then save the formatting and change the text as you wish.

TIPS FOR DESIGNING A HOME PAGE

Now that you have learned how to create documents in HTML and with a Web editor, consider designing a home page that is only one screen, as Beckman suggests. You'll learn more about design in Chapter 11, but here are some tips to help you with your home page.

✳ Consider your home page as a newspaper in a street sales kiosk, where readers only see the part of the paper above the fold. Keep it simple.

✳ Put your e-mail address on your home page. Make your address a link, but write the e-mail address as well in case users can't link to it from their browsers.

✳ Provide good navigation links to other pages in your Web site, including your resume. Link your resume to your home page so users have only one click to it.

✳ Contrast your type with your background. If you use a colored or patterned background, make sure the type over it is readable. Larger type is recommended in these cases.

✳ Consider how you would entice users into your site. Use a graphic, a quote or a simple set of links. What kind of image do you want your front door to convey about you?

TIPS FOR DESIGNING YOUR RESUME

Remember that readability is at least 30 percent poorer online than in print so keep your Web pages simple. Don't use very small type or poorly contrasting colors. If an employer wants to print your online resume, consider whether it will be readable in print as well. White type on a dark background will not print.

* Put your e-mail address on your resume and create a link to it.

* Use a career goal or objective, especially if you are a college student. State whether you are seeking a job or internship.

* Put your most important skills near the top of the page. Online readers do not like to scroll, according to most Web design experts.

* Photographs of you are optional.

* Use key words for your skills. Consider how a search engine would pick out your resume if you posted it to a career site.

* Boldface important categories: Career goal, Skills, Education, Experience, Clips.

* Link to excerpts of examples of your work.

* Keep it simple. Use lists if you have several items. Do not list all your college activities in detail as you might with a print resume.

* Use good navigation tools—internal links at the top or on the side if you have a resume that spans more than two screens.

* Check your spelling and grammar. A mistake online is as damaging as one in print. Media employers are especially critical of poor spelling, style and writing skills.

* Test your site. Ask friends or current employers to give you feedback.

* Print a copy of your resume so you can see how it would look to a prospective employer who might print a copy of it.

REVISING WEB PAGES

Here are a couple of reminders:

❋ If you want to edit your Web pages to change them, access the page and then pull down your File menu to "Edit Page." Keep the edited page open in Composer and the browser version behind it. You can do the same with any Web page you are creating before you load it to the Web.

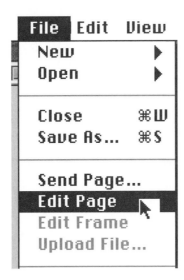

❋ To view your pages as they will look in the browser, click on the navigator wheel on your toolbar.

Checklist

✳ Have you labeled your home page *index.html* if this is going to be your first Web page?

✳ Have you checked your links?

✳ Have you named your pages and images with one word and an extension (*.html* or *.htm*)?

✳ Have you converted all your images to a .gif or .jpeg format and labeled them with those extensions?

✳ Have you put your name or logo on every page with an e-mail link?

✳ Have you created an e-mail link with the *mailto:* tag?

✳ Have you used strongly contrasting type and larger type if you used color or patterns in backgrounds?

✳ Have you printed your documents to see how they look if someone wants to print them?

✳ Have you saved your documents to a floppy disk?

Safaris

http://www.mhhe.com/socscience/comm/rich/ch7/

7-1	**Resume Safari**	Explore the resumes of some leading media Web designers in our Web site for this chapter.
7-2	**Graphics Safari**	You can link to graphics in our Web site for this chapter or for Chapter 6.

7-3 Home Page and Resume

Create a home page that will link to your resume and other documents you want to create for your Web site. A currently popular style for a home page is to limit it to one screen. That's a good mental exercise for you because it is more difficult to create one screen of information than a longer document. Then create or improve your online resume using a Web editor. Plan your design before you begin creating it. If you want to post your resume on a job site, check the job sites in the previous chapter.

Chapter 8

Goals

* To learn how to move documents onto the Web.

* To learn how to download Web documents for revision.

* To learn how to use file transfer protocols.

* To learn how telnet works.

As a prerequisite you need your login, password, and directions from your Internet service provider to upload your documents.

Hyperleap

* Instructions for Macintosh users to upload Web pages start on Page 164.

* Windows users should leap over the Macintosh instructions and start on Page 175 for directions to load upload Web pages.

* If you want to use Netscape's Publish button, leap to Page 182. It is preferable, however, for you to learn the other file transfer tools first.

* Instructions for changing and reloading Web pages in both platforms begin on Page 184.

Web sites

For FTP and telnet software, check our Web site for this chapter. Or access these sites:

Macintosh users can get Fetch, a Macintosh tool for transferring files on and off the Web
> http://www.dartmouth.edu/pages/softdev/fetch.html

For telnet software for Macintosh, get NCSA Telnet
> ftp://ftp.ncsa.uiuc.edu/Mac/Telnet

Windows users can get WS_FTP, a Windows program for transferring files on and off the Web
> http://www.ipswitch.com/downloads/ws_ftp_LE.html

Windows users can use the telnet program that comes with Windows 95 or many others available for Windows such as a shareware program QVT/Term
> http://www.frontiernet.net/~qpcsoft

Glossary at a Glance

A full glossary is in the appendix and on our Web site.

http://www.mhhe.com/socscience/comm/rich/glossary.html

DOWNLOADING Getting a document from the Web.

FTP File transfer protocol, a system that allows you to transfer files from one Internet site to your own computer. Many computer servers at universities and Internet software providers have repositories that allow you to log in with the password *anonymous* or *guest* so you can transfer files that you want without requiring an account and personal password for that site. Software programs such as Fetch for Macintosh and WS_FTP for Windows make the process of transferring files easy.

HOST The computer that provides the service that connects you to other computers.

SERVER Like a host, the server is the computer that "serves" your requests on the Internet by connecting you to other computers.

TELNET Stands for "terminal emulation protocol," which means the rules or programming that allow one computer to connect to another one at a remote location. The telnet protocol allows you to log into the remote computer system.

UNIX One of the most common operating systems for computers on the Internet. Many university e-mail accounts reside on UNIX operating systems.

UPLOADING Putting a document onto the Web.

DILBERT reprinted by permission of United Feature Syndicate, Inc.

You are on winter or summer break away from your college or university, and you want to check your e-mail, but you don't want to pay for a long-distance call to your school account. How can you do this? If you have access to a computer connected to the Internet at a library or a friend's house, you can use telnet, a program that allows you to connect to a remote computer, in this case the one at your school.

You are a reporter working on a story about AIDS, and you want a recent White House press release about the subject. Or perhaps you want a list of all the federal job openings in your area. You can call up FedWorld and transfer any of 15,000 federal documents to your computer via FTP, file transfer protocol, an Internet code that allows computers to transfer files to each other. FedWorld is at *http://www.fedworld.gov.*

You are a student who wants to get his or her home page and resume on the Web. You'll need to use FTP and telnet to do that.

Before the World Wide Web became so popular, FTP was the most common way to transfer documents from one computer to another. Now you can get most of the information you want directly from the Web when you call up a site. FTP still is used frequently to download software such as new browsers or programs you will need to make file transfers in this chapter. You also need to use FTP to load your documents onto the Web or take them off to change them.

If you are a Macintosh user, you should get an FTP program called *Fetch,* free to academic users. If you are a Windows user, a common FTP program often loaded on Windows is WS_FTP, also free to academic users. Make sure you download the limited edition, not the professional one. You also might be able to get these FTP programs free from your college or university's computer center. Check the Web sites at the beginning of the chapter for URLs or link to our Web site for this chapter.

Before you can transfer documents to the Web, regardless of the program you use, you must find out the name of the server you use at your college or university. You also should check directions at your school or Internet service provider for loading Web pages. If you use a commercial service such as America Online, follow its directions for loading Web pages. The directions that follow should work at most academic institutions.

TIPS FOR UPLOADING

Before you upload any of your documents and images to the Web, check to see if you have followed these steps:

* If you have never created a Web document, name your home page or the main page people will see when they call up your site *index.html.*

* Give your documents a one-word name with an *.html* or *.htm* extension (the latter is automatically inserted in Windows if you've saved it as an HTML document). Do not use long names or the computer will insert strange codes when you upload them on PCs.

* Use lower case for your file names, especially if your university or Internet service provider uses a UNIX computer programming system, which is case sensitive.

* Make sure your images have been created or saved as gifs or jpegs in a program such as Photoshop or Graphic Converter. If you have retrieved them from a copyright-free graphics Web site, they should be gifs or jpegs. You must label them, preferably with one word plus the dot *gif* or dot *jpg* extension such as *image.gif.* If you must use two or more words, connect them with an underscore mark, as in *my_resume.jpg.*

* Make sure your links back to your home page from other documents in your site are linked to index.html.

* Make sure your links match the names of the documents and images you plan to upload.

Here is how you can transfer your home page or resume to the Web using Fetch. Windows users should skip to the instructions on Page 175.

OPENING FETCH

✳ Double click on the Fetch icon to open the application. You will get a New Connection box. If you don't get one, click on the File menu to "New Connection":

File	Edit	Remote	Director
New Connection...			⌘N
New Bookmark List			
Open Bookmark File...			⌘O
Open Shortcut			▶
Close			⌘W

✳ Delete the Host, dartvax.dartmouth.edu, if that appears in your new connection box and fill out the rest as follows:

Host: Type the name of your computer account, probably the same name as the account from which you get e-mail.

New Connection...

Enter host name, userid, and password (or choose from the shortcut menu):

Host: your computer account

User ID: your login

Password: ••••••

Directory: /pub (delete this)

Shortcuts: ▼   [Cancel]   [OK]

User ID: Type your login.

Password: Type your password.

Directory: Delete */pub* and leave this blank. Click OK.

SHORTCUT CONNECTIONS

When you pull down the arrow after Shortcuts, you will see a number of FTP directories listed. If you plan to load and unload files from your directory frequently, you can create a shortcut for it. Fill in the information as directed previously; then pull down the Customize menu. Click on "New Shortcut." The server name you filled out in "Host" should be listed. In the future you can just pull down the shortcut menu, and it will fill in the connections box automatically.

```
┌─────────────────────────────┐
│ Customize  Windows          │
├─────────────────────────────┤
│   Preferences...            │
│   Internet Config...        │
│   Suffix Mapping...         │
│   Post-Processing...        │
│ ─────────────────────────── │
│   New Shortcut...           │
│   Edit Bookmark...          │
│   Remove Bookmark           │
└─────────────────────────────┘
```

Create a public directory for your Web documents. This is common but not universal, so you should check to see if your server requires a public directory for Web pages. If you already have a home page, you probably have a public directory, so skip these steps.

❋   Pull down the Directories menu at the top of your screen.

File   Edit   Remote   Directories   Customize   Windows

❋   Click on "Create New Directory."

❋   You will be asked to name it. Write *public_html* (that's *public* underscore, not hyphen, *html*). Click OK. Once you have created this directory, you never have to do it again. You will keep all your Web-related pages and graphics (gifs and jpegs) in your public folder.

Enter a name for the new directory:

    public_html

                                    [Cancel]   [OK]

❋ Now scroll to your public directory. Double-click to open it. Don't forget this step. If you put your files and images in your directory but not in your public folder, they won't show up on the Web!

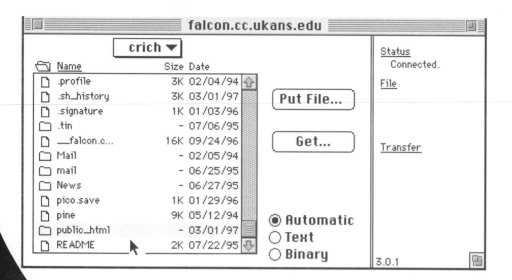

HOW FETCH WORKS

❋ "Put File" takes the file from your desktop or other folder in your computer and puts it into your public_html directory. You need to open the folder where your resume, home page or other Web documents are stored to get the files you want.

❋ "Get File" gets it from the public directory after you have put something on there. (It also gets a file from any other directory you are accessing.) You need to get your files from the public directory every time you make a change. In other words, when you want to alter your documents, you "get" them, make the changes, and then "put" them back on the Web. If you are using Netscape Composer, you can edit your documents without using FTP. Directions follow later in the chapter.

LOADING FILES AND IMAGES

* Open the folder that contains the documents you want to load to the Web.

* Click on "Put File" in Fetch.

* Highlight the file in your folder that you want such as "resume," shown here in a folder named *Web documents*.

* Click Open.

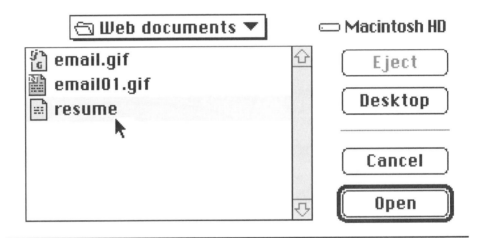

* A dialogue box will open asking you to name your document. Do not click OK yet. If this document is your home page or if it is the first and only page you are putting on the Web, you have to name it *index.html* so it will have a URL. This is not universal, but it is common. Check if your server does not require the *index.html* name for the home page.

Subsequent pages and images that you load can have other names such as *resume.html*.

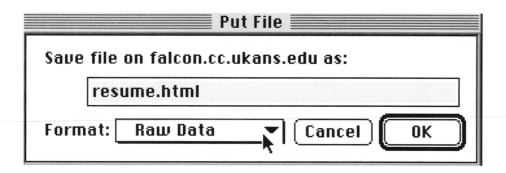

✳ Pull down the arrow in the Format menu, where it says "Text." Pull it to "Raw Data." If you don't save your files as "Raw Data," your images will show up as text. Save everything as "Raw Data" even if you are loading just text pages. That's easier than switching back and forth from text to images, and "Raw Data" will save your text pages as well.

✳ Click on OK, and a little dog will "fetch" it into your public folder.

✳ Repeat the process for every image that will appear in your document. You need to fetch each image and name it with a .gif or .jpg extension, to indicate what type of image it is so it can be read by your browser on the Internet. You can't just label images with these extensions; they have to be created in a program like Photoshop or Graphic Converter to be gifs or jpegs. Images you retrieve from free software on the Web will be in one of these forms, so you don't have to convert them. Don't forget to save each image as "Raw Data." If you forget to load every image and file connected with your pages, your images won't show up.

✳ Close the connection by clicking "Quit" under the File menu. Now you need to set the permissions to determine who can read or write this Web site.

SETTING PERMISSIONS IN FETCH

You can set permissions in Fetch, but if you are using the Publish button on Netscape or another program, you must use telnet as instructed later in the chapter. Follow these steps to set permissions in Fetch.

❋ Click on the files to highlight the ones for which you want to set permissions. If you have more than one file, hold down your Shift key to highlight several at one time.

❋ Pull down the Remote menu at the top of your screen to "Set Permissions." A dialogue box will open.

❋ Click all the boxes under "Read," giving everyone permission to read your Web site.

❋ Click only "Owner" under "Write," which means only you with your password can change this site.

❋ Click all the boxes under "Search/Execute." Click OK.

Permissions			
Set file/folder permissions to:			
	Read	**Write**	**Search/ Execute**
Owner:	☒	☒	☒
Group:	☒	☐	☒
Everyone:	☒	☐	☒
		Cancel	OK

❋ Your documents should now be on the Web.

❋ Your URL should be *http://your computer server name/~your login* (that's a tilde plus your login). Open a browser and type your URL. For example, if your computer account is on a server named *eagle* (with cc for computer center) such as one at the University of Kansas, your URL would be *http://eagle.cc.ukans.edu/~your login*. This method works on most servers; check if your server uses another one.

❋ You also can set permissions in telnet with directions that follow later in the chapter.

RENAMING OR DELETING FILES

Web editors often insert unwanted codes to match files from your computer. These may mess up your links. If you have renamed your files when you uploaded them to match the names you gave them in your document, you should have no problems. If you forgot to save your document as "Raw Data" or didn't upload it into your public directory, you can fix your mistakes.

❋ Pull down "Remote" in your Fetch menu.

Remote Directories Custom	
View File...	⌘L
View File List	
Get Directories and Files...	
Put Folders and Files...	
Rename Directory or File...	
Delete Directory or File...	
Search...	
Set Permissions...	
Set Upload Permissions...	
Send FTP Command(s)...	

✳ Click on "Rename Directory or File" or "Delete Directory or File," as you wish. Fill out the box with the names you wish to change. Then click OK.

Rename

Enter the name of the file or directory to rename and its new name:

Current name:

New name:

[Cancel] [OK]

OTHER FILE TRANSFERS

To retrieve other documents from remote servers via Fetch, follow the same directions but change the name of the host. If the other remote server allows you to sign in as an anonymous guest, your user name usually is *anonymous* and your password is your e-mail address.

To retrieve most documents from the Web these days, even if they are labeled *FTP,* you just have to click on a hyperlink. It is easier than going through remote servers on Fetch.

TELNET FOR MACINTOSH

Telnet is a computer protocol that allows you to log into a remote computer. In many cases you might be using telnet to get your e-mail at your own school. However, if you are anywhere in the world with a computer that connects to the Internet, you can access your computer account via telnet. The most common telnet tool for Macintosh users is NSCA Telnet.

You also need to use telnet after you load your Web pages if you have not set your permissions in Fetch. This is how you can use telnet to access a remote computer and then set permissions or to get your e-mail.

OPEN NCSA TELNET

✳ Double-click on NCSA Telnet to open it.

✳ Pull down the File menu to "Open Connection."

NCSA Telnet

❋ A dialogue box will open with *nowhere.loopback.edu* as the Host Session. Delete this and insert the name of your host computer, most likely the computer account you have for your e-mail unless you use a separate account for Web pages. Click Connect.

```
Host/Session      nowhere.loopback.edu      ▼
Name

Window Name       [                              ]

Terminal          <Default>

                  ☐ Authenticate (⌘A)
                  ☐ Encrypt (⌘E)

                           Cancel   Connect
```

❋ A box will open naming your account after "Digital UNIX" or the type of computer program your school uses. UNIX is a common system in universities.

❋ Type your login and password. Hit Return. You are now connected to your remote terminal at your school or wherever you have an account.

```
|Digital UNIX (falcon.cc.ukans.edu) (ttyr5)

|login: crich
|Password:█
```

❋ If you want your e-mail via Pine or another account that your school offers, type Pine or the name of your mail program and access your mail.

SETTING WEB PAGE PERMISSIONS VIA TELNET

After you have uploaded your Web documents and images, you must set the permissions in telnet after you have logged in.

❋ At the prompt ($) or (#) sign, type **cd_public.html.** That means change directory to public (underscore) html. Hit Return and another prompt ($) sign will appear.

✳ Type **chmod 755 *.*** (which means change the mode to the code, space, 755 space, star, dot, star) and hit Return. That code means only you can write this Web document, but everyone else gets permission to read and search through it.

✳ Type **exit** after the prompt. Your Web pages are now secure. Your computer screen should look like this, but instead of falcon (the name of the author's host computer), it will list the name of your computer host and your login:

```
falcon:/homeb/crich $ cd public_html
falcon:public_html $ chmod 755 *.*
falcon:public_html $ exit█
```

✳ You must set the permissions in telnet (if you haven't used the Fetch permissions box) every time you change your Web documents and reload them.

To learn how to change and reload pages in Netscape, leap to Page 184, if you are not a Windows user.

FTP FOR WINDOWS USERS

Although WS_FTP is recommended here to transfer your files, several other FTP programs are available, as well. CuteFTP is very popular and available at **http://cuteftp.com,** but it is not free. It works in a fashion similar to WS_FTP.

WS_FTP95

✳ Click on the WS_FTP icon to open. A box, "Session Profile," will open.

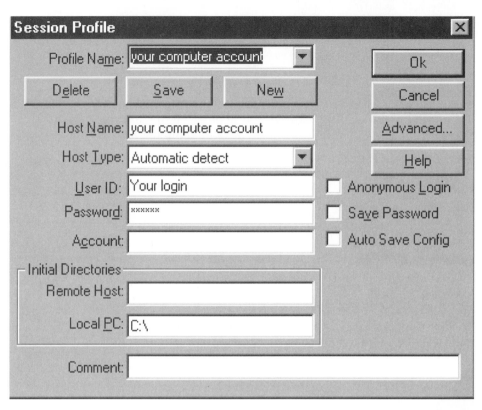

* Fill out the name of your computer server after "Profile Name." This usually is the computer account you log into for your e-mail. Don't use your name, just the name of the server. For example, if you had an account on a server named *eagle* located in the computer center at the University of Kansas, you would type *eagle.cc.ukans.edu.* If you have an account on a server named *isis* at the University of North Carolina, you would type *isis.unc.edu* for the profile and host names.

* "Host Name" is the same computer account name as your profile name.

* "Host Type" can be left on "Automatic detect," and the program will determine what kind of computer program to use.

* "User ID" is your login. Many FTP sites will allow you to log in without an ID as an "anonymous login" to get software or other documents. But to put your Web site in your computer system, you need to use your own login and password.

✳ "Password" requires typing your password for this account. Don't click on "Save Password" if you are working in a computer lab. That would give someone else access to your account. Use this feature only from your home computer.

✳ Leave everything else blank. Click OK to connect.

MAKING A PUBLIC FOLDER

✳ A box will open listing the "Local System" (this is your computer) on the left and the "Remote System" (your computer account that you typed in "Host") on the right:

✳ Create a public folder where your Web pages will be located. If you already have a home page, you probably have a public folder.

✳ Click on MkDir on the right side of the box. An Input box will open. Type *public_html* (that's an underscore). Click OK.

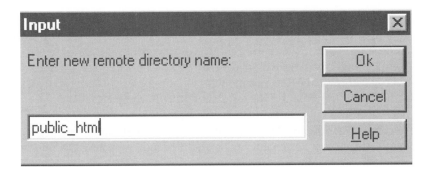

TRANSFERRING
FILES

❋ Double-click on your new public folder to open it. If you don't put the files in your public directory, they won't show up on the Web.

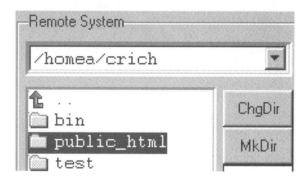

❋ Double-click to open the folder in your Local System that contains the documents and images you want to load onto the Web. If they aren't on your desktop, they might be in "My Files" in your C directory. If you need to change directories to access the folder with your files, pull down the arrow in the upper-left corner of the box until you get the directory you want:

❋ If the document you are going to load will be your home page, you need to name it *index.html*. It is a common but not universal practice to name the home page *index.html*. Check if your server does not require the *index.html* name for a home page. Do not name your home page *index.htm*. If you do, your files will show up as a list instead of your home page.

To rename your page if you loaded it with a different name, just highlight the document you want to rename, click on "Rename" on the right side of the box and type in the new name. Make sure your links back to your home page are labeled *index.html* on other documents in your Web site.

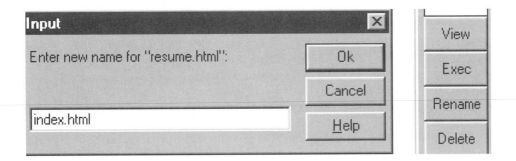

* Keep the names of your documents short, or Windows will insert strange codes.

* Use lower case for your file names if you are in a UNIX system, which is common at many universities.

* Make sure your Web pages (other than the index page) are named with an *.html* or *.htm* extension. If you saved it in Windows as an HTML document, it will automatically add an *.htm* extension. You can change the name to an HTML extension if you prefer because it is more common.

* Click once to highlight the file you want to load to your public folder such as e-mail.gif as illustrated here. Note the arrows in the middle of the box.

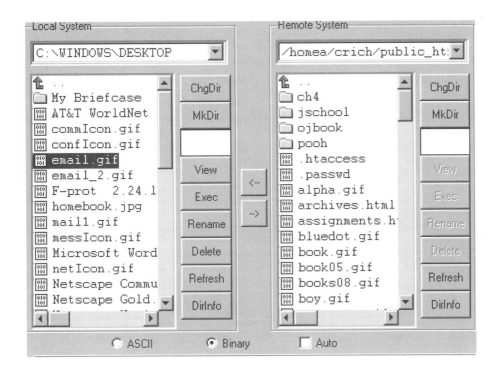

* Make sure the Binary button at the bottom of the box is clicked or your images won't show up.

* Click on the right arrow to put the file or files in your public directory. Make sure you have put them in your public folder.

* To get files from a remote system, click once to highlight the file you want; then click on the left arrow to put it in your own computer. You'll do this to change your Web documents, as explained later.

* If you want to load several files at once, click on a file and hold down the Shift key to click on the other files you want if they are all in a row or hold down your Ctrl key to highlight selected files. Then click the right arrow to load to your public directory.

* When you upload images, make sure they are labeled with a *.gif* or *.jpeg* (or *.jpg*) extension, depending on which type of image they are. Remember that you must create them in that format in a graphic program or retrieve them from a copyright-free graphics site on the Web. You can't just label them as gifs or jpegs and expect them to show up. For example, your e-mail image would be e-mail.gif.

* Don't forget to load every image and file associated with your pages or the images won't show up and the links won't work.

* If Netscape inserts codes into your directory that don't match the names of your files—and it often does, especially if your file name is long—click on the file you want to change to highlight it. Then click on rename and name it to match your files and links.

* Your document is now on the Web, but you need to set permissions in telnet to determine who can read or write the Web documents. You can use this procedure to access other remote servers as well. If they accept anonymous logins, just click that box instead of typing your name and password.

SETTING PERMISSIONS IN TELNET

Shortcut to Telnet

* Open the telnet application in Windows 95 (or use another one if you prefer). It should be in the Windows folder. If you are going to create and change your Web pages often, you should create a Shortcut to telnet on your desktop. Double-click to open.

* Pull down the telnet menu to "Remote System":

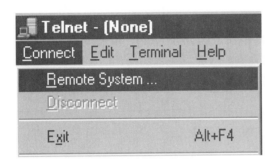

* A Connect box will open. Type in the name of your host computer, which is the computer that serves your e-mail account. Leave the Port and Terminal Type as is unless you know you have a different terminal system than the one listed. Click on "Connect":

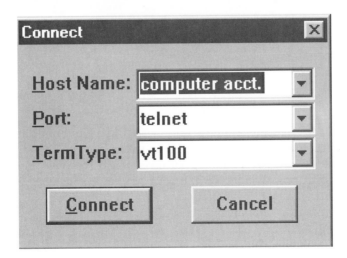

❋ After the prompt ($ or #) sign, type your login, hit Enter, and then type in your password and hit Enter again.

❋ After the new prompt sign, type the following code: *cd* (leave a space) *public* (underscore) *html,* meaning change directory to *public_html* (cd public_html). Hit Enter.

❋ After this new prompt sign, type *chmod* (space) *755* (space) ✶.✶ (that stands for change mode to 755 [space], star dot star with no spaces between the stars and dot). This code sets the permissions so that only you can write on the Web document, but everyone can read it and search through your site. Hit Enter.

❋ Type *exit* after the prompt sign to leave telnet. You have now secured your Web page. You must type these codes in telnet every time you change your Web pages. In this illustration, *falcon* is the name of the author's host computer, but your computer account would be listed instead:

```
falcon:/homeb/crich $ cd public_html
falcon:public_html $ chmod 755 *.*
falcon:public_html $ exit
```

❋ After you type *exit,* telnet may say "Connection to Host Lost." Click OK.

NETSCAPE'S PUBLISH TOOL

Once you have created a public folder, via Fetch, WS_FTP or other program, you can easily upload your Web documents using Netscape Communicator's Publish button. But you must know the name of your server, usually the same as your e-mail account. One way to find out your full server name is to go to telnet and see what it is called after you log on and get a prompt sign. Even if you know your server name, it may have an additional name in a university UNIX system, and you need that full name for the Netscape publish FTP site.

❋ Click on the Publish button.

✳ A box will open. Fill out the location to publish as follows: *ftp://your server name/your login/public_html* (for your public directory) */name of your Web document* (in Macintosh). Windows doesn't need the file name.

✳ Fill in your login and password.

✳ If you have images with this document, click on the button for "Files associated with this page," and Netscape will load all of them as well.

✳ Click Publish.

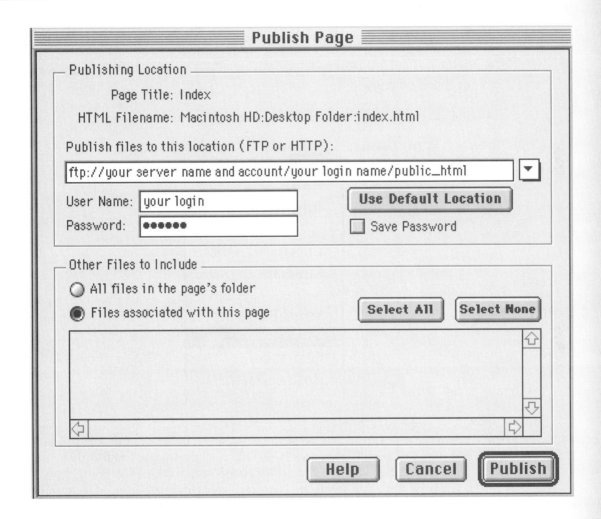

✳ Set permissions via telnet as directed previously.

✳ When the Publish button works, it uploads all the files with the page and is very easy to use. However, sometimes it doesn't work well. You must save your document for it to work. Try it one more time, and if it still won't work, use an FTP program.

CHANGING WEB PAGES

You will want to revise your Web documents to update them. Whether you are using Fetch or WS_FTP, the process is the same, except instead of loading documents, you download them. Netscape makes it easy to edit your documents.

✳ Type the URL for your Web document, and wait for it to load in Navigator or Page Composer.

✳ Pull down the File menu and click on "Edit Page" in Composer:

File	Edit	View
New		▶
Open		▶
Close		⌘W
Save As...		⌘S
Send Page...		
Edit Page		
Edit Frame		
Upload File...		

✳ When the page downloads, Netscape will ask you if you want to save it. When you click OK, it will automatically download all the images and files that accompany it. You can save it to your desktop or to a folder. Caution: Do not save a page when you are in the Netscape Navigator browser on Macintosh because it will save only as text. Make sure you are saving it in Composer, so it saves as an HTML document. In Windows you can save it in a browser or Composer but make sure you are saving it as an HTML document.

✳ Make the changes you want.

✳ Save your document.

✳ Reload it via Fetch, WS_FTP or Netscape's Publish button. If you reload the page using the same name as the document that was already on the Web, the new document will automatically override it.

Safety Tip If you want to make sure your new version of the Web document is loaded without losing the old one, rename the old document before you load the new version.

In Fetch, pull down the Remote menu and click on "Rename." Then rename your original document *old resume.html* or something different.

In WS_FTP, use your Rename button on the Remote side of your directory. Then load the new version of your Web document with the name you want to use.

✳ Secure your permissions in Fetch or telnet.

✳ Check your changes by opening them in your browser. Don't forget to click Reload or Refresh when you reload the document in your browser, or your changes won't show up.

✳ After you have browsed the new version, delete the old version using the Remote menu in Fetch or the Delete button in the WS_FTP directory.

Up to now you have transferred files and images for your Web document directly into to your public directory. If you have a complicated site with many files, you should set up folders for each part of the site. For example, a newspaper would have a separate folder for everything in the sports section and another folder to contain all the documents in the business section, and so on. Here's how:

✳ In Macintosh with Fetch, open your public folder. (Make sure your public folder is open before your create a new folder!) Then pull down the "Directories" file and create a new directory within your public folder, which will create a new folder.

✳ In WS_FTP, open your public folder by double-clicking on it. Then click the MkDir button and name a new folder. That will create a folder within your public directory.

This will add a folder name to your URL, such as *www. your server/~your login/new folder name/file name.html.* For example, here's how a URL would look if you had your resume in a separate folder named *resume* with a clips page attached to it.
http://www.ukans.edu/~crich/resume/clips.html

If you are using Netscape's Publish button, you must add this folder name to your FTP instructions. For example, if you created a folder named *resume,* your FTP location would be:

ftp://your server name/your login/public_html/resume/

Folders are very useful ways of managing documents when you create a major Web site that contains several pages. If you are working on a class project and other people are creating different parts of the site, folders are helpful so your documents and image names don't conflict. Each part of the site can have its own folder containing all the images and text for that site section.

Checklist

* Have you created a public_html directory for your Web documents?

* Have you named your home page *index.html* if this is the first page you want people to see when they connect to your Web site?

* Have you used lower case names, especially for your index page?

* Have you used one-word brief names for your files and *gif* or *jpg* extensions for your images or two-word names connected with an underscore?

* Have you uploaded your documents and images into your public_html directory?

* Have you uploaded all your files and images as "Raw Data" in Macintosh Fetch and as "Binary" in Windows WS_FTP?

* Have you set your permissions in Fetch or telnet after you loaded them onto the Web?

* Have you checked all your documents and links after you loaded them on the Web? Don't forget to hit your Reload button on your browser so your changes will show up.

* If you created a separate folder for your Web site, have you created it inside your public folder? Have you clicked open the public folder and then the new folder before you loaded your documents?

http://www.mhhe.com/socscience/comm/
rich/ch8/

8–1 **Uploading**		Load your resume or home page to the Web if you haven't already done so. If you need software for FTP and telnet, you can link to them at our Web site for this chapter.
8–2 **FTP Safari**		As mentioned in the chapter, FTP is giving way to hypertext links via the World Wide Web as a method of receiving files from the Internet. However, some sites still offer files and software via FTP. Check out some of these or link to them on our Web site.

a. Find a recent press release about a topic of your choice via FTP from the U.S. federal government site, Fedworld:

http://www.fedworld.gov

b. FTP sites with software archives on our Web site or at these locations:

* Macintosh FTP sites:

  http://www.apple.com/documents/shareware.html

* Monster FTP sites list with a good explanation of anonymous FTP:

  http://hoohoo.ncsa.uiuc.edu/ftp

* Washington University in St. Louis FTP archive:

  http://wuarchive.wustl.edu/

* PC Software related sites:

  http://www.airmail.net/pcsoft.html

Part

Creating a Media Web Site

2

Chapter 9

MEDIA SITE PLANNING

* To learn the process for planning a Web site.

* To create a Web site.

Here are some highlights of the chapter you can leap to:

* Steps to site planning on Page 197.

* Design on Page 204.

* Site planning checklist on Page 207.

Web sites

HotWired
> http://www.hotwired.com

StarNews/**Online:**
> http://www.starnews.com

Glossary at a Glance

A full glossary is in the appendix and on our Web site.

http://www.mhhe.com/socscience/comm/rich/glossary.html

DYNAMIC HTML A form of HTML that enhances design possibilities by allowing text or images on a Web page to change colors or move. For example, with dynamic HTML a headline could move across the screen or text could change color when you move your mouse over it. This allows design in layers.

GIFS Images for Web documents in Graphic Interchange Format, which compresses image files. Images in this format can be read by all browsers.

INTERFACE The designs or tools that allow a person to use or communicate with a computer. File folders on your desktop, for example, are graphical user interfaces, meaning interfaces that provide you with visual cues.

JPEGS Images for Web documents in a format developed by the Joint Photographic Experts Group. This format is better for photographs. It also compresses images so they can load faster.

PAGE VIEW A Web page accessed by a viewer with all graphics and text elements on the page count as one page view. The term is synonymous with page impression.

PIXELS Images on a computer are measured in pixels, which are dots. The equivalent for measuring space in newspapers is points; 12 points equal one pica. On a Web site, 10 pixels equal one pica. The most common design for the screen size of a Web page is 640 pixels wide by 480 pixels long.

STORYBOARD A layout of pages in order that they will appear. In Web site design, a storyboard is an outline of your site. A storyboard of the individual pages would show the content and page layout. In a cartoon, a storyboard is a layout showing each frame that will follow in story sequence.

ED STEIN reprinted by permission of Newspaper Enterprise Association Inc.

Barbara Kuhr

Barbara Kuhr sits before a white laminated chalkboard covered with sketches of redesigns for the HotWired Web site. Mrs. Peale saunters in, oblivious to the fact that she's interrupting a conversation.

"She's deaf," says Kuhr, bending to pat the Jack Russell terrier's head.

On another floor Maria, dubbed *head of security* by the HotWired staff, falls asleep on the job. The golden Labrador retriever and the terrier roam freely through this four-story, white brick South San Francisco loft that is home to Wired Ventures. The company includes HotWired, HotBot search engine, Wired News, and a handful of other Internet products. An office a few doors away houses its original print product, *Wired* magazine.

The informal working environment is in sharp contrast to the high-pressured business of producing products to compete in the ever-growing world of media Web sites that are struggling to be profitable. With an initial startup investment of $20 million for HotWired, the need to market this site concerns Kuhr as much as the creative endeavors. Kuhr and her husband, John Plunkett, are the creative directors of Wired Ventures.

"We're the 27th most visited site on the Web," Plunkett says proudly of HotWired. But because access to the site is free, popularity doesn't pay the bills for the Web magazine, launched in 1994, a year after the print magazine. Two years after Wired Ventures was created, the company suffered millions of dollars of losses on its online products. *Wired* magazine was sold in 1998.

Despite the company's economic problems, the print and online magazines made a significant impact in online media because of their innovative design and content. And the steps HotWired's staff took to redesign its online site offer insight to the process you can use when you begin to create your own Web sites. The first step in creating any Web site or other product is to decide your mission, the goal of your product. The print magazine's goal was to be a leader in the field of technology.

"We wanted to make a magazine that we wanted to read," Plunkett says. "*Wired* was the product of our personal tastes. We started by thinking of ourselves as chroniclers of the future. Now we see ourselves as agents of change."

NEW FOCUS

Change is not easy, especially revamping a massive Web site like HotWired. The 1997 redesign of HotWired reflects the company's commitment to becoming a leader in the experimental Web culture. Although the new Web site still sports the company's trademark psychedelic neon colors of its print and online magazines, the HotWired content is focused more on innovative and high-tech culture than in the past, when the site covered a broader range of subjects. However, redesigning the existing product proved more difficult than originally creating it.

"It's like trying to fix an engine of a car while it's barreling down the freeway," Kuhr says. "HotWired was always our lead project. We asked ourselves, 'What do we want to be about?' We had to rethink conceptually."

Kuhr says *Wired* was the first magazine to be devoted to reporting about the Internet culture. "We thought we needed to grow very quickly," Kuhr says of the company's original goals. "That was a mistake. What we need to be is experimental."

That's a risky decision because the technically savvy audience for such innovation could be limited, but then Kuhr and Plunkett are accustomed to taking risks in thinking, designing and living. The couple, who live in Park City, Utah, close to a ski slope, commute to the San Francisco *Wired* offices a few times a week. The rest of the time they work from their home, which, like their namesake products, is heavily wired with a direct connection to the Internet.

UNCONVENTIONAL APPROACH

From the beginning the two have been unconventional in their approach to design of the print and Web products. Friends of Louis Rossetto, founder of the company, Kuhr and Plunkett joined the organization's startup team with design experience but no journalism training.

"We didn't know the rules to break," Plunkett says. "Our editorial mission was delivery of news from the future. Louis Rossetto saw that technology would have the single biggest effect. Big media was ignoring those areas and was afraid of them. They still write that way: '50 reasons to be afraid of the Internet' or 'Watch out for pornography.' Their job is to protect the status quo. Our job is to question it."

In turn, their designs, especially in HotWired, have been questioned and criticized. Such is the price of innovative thinking. The redesigned HotWired Web site, the fourth reincarnation, was unveiled three days before a July Fourth holiday with a new form that rivaled a fireworks display. The home page featured constantly moving headlines in a coding form called *dynamic HTML* and colors like a psychedelic disco show. But the real change in the site that took six months to plan and develop was the content. It was a thorough exercise in site planning for Cate Corcoran, executive editor of HotWired, plus three editors, a designer and an engineer.

Corcoran, who majored in journalism, started her career as a reporter with *MacWeek,* so the transition to HotWired was easy. Redesigning the site was not.

SITE PLANNING PROCESS

"We spent a month just brainstorming," Corcoran says. "We gave ourselves a blank site. "Hotwired was a network of independent sites that weren't united in theme and design. What we came back to was a Wired Ventures vision. We've been in love with the Web since we first got involved with it. It's our territory. We realized we could make the Web our whole theme. We want to be active participants to help the media move forward."

Corcoran says the group decided to do a Web exercise to help them stay focused on their goals for the site. It started with a sentence: *HotWired should be . . ."* Then they listed words to describe their goals: *global, changing, surprising.* Corcoran said that while they were weighing ideas, they asked themselves if their descriptions met the overall theme of making HotWired an innovative leader in Web culture. She says they then used the same sentence to describe the design: "Hotwired design should be . . . bold, simple, primitive, innovative."

Originally the group began designing the front door, also known as the home page, to the revised site. But they soon discovered that they needed to devise all the sections of the online magazine first. They created a storyboard—an outline of the sections and pages in the order they would come.

"We wanted to break up the pages that were long pages," Corcoran says. "You get more ad impressions if you have more pages. Now we have six pages for what used to be three." They also designed the pages in print and posted them on a bulletin board so they could see how they looked before they created them on the Web.

After they were satisfied with the structure of the sections, they designed the front door to the site last. "It took a long time of building and going back and forth between editors and production and design," Corcoran says.

But they weren't finished yet. They tested the site on users. Six of the testers found a link on the home page confusing. The designers then fixed the parts of the site to make it easier for users to understand. Jeffrey Veen, interface designer for HotWired, says user testing is crucial. Get a group of people in a room and watch them as they use your site, he says. The reactions you get may surprise you.

Although this redesign was a major overhaul, like any Web site, this design won't be the last. A Web site always is a work in progress.

EVOLUTION OF AN ONLINE NEWSPAPER

Jay Small understands continual evolution of an online site. As general manager of the Star/News Online, a Web site for *The Indianapolis Star* and *The Indianapolis News,* he says the site and his job are in perpetual change. Unlike HotWired and other media Web sites that went online with many sections, Small created his company's site in stages.

Starting with only two interns, Small launched the first part of Star/News Online with a sports site in July 1995. "We decided to do the sports niche sites before approaching local news," he says. Auto racing is big business in Indianapolis and it has great national appeal, he says. So the first Web site he created was SpeedNet, a site devoted to auto racing. Four months later, a basketball site, Indiana's Game went online. From only 10,000 page views initially, the sports site audience increased to 22,000 page views within a few weeks.

In the next few months other sites were added, including daily news digests, a real estate site in partnership with the local Board of Realtors, and a Final Four site that garnered a peak audience of 475,000 page views. By 1997, Small's staff increased to eight people, and his site added classified advertisements and a city guide/business directory with maps.

Small says the home-buying guide, IndySearch, is so successful that it has the potential to fund most of the online operations in the near future. "Profitability is in sight if not in hand," he says.

STEPS TO SITE PLANNING

When you develop a media Web site for this class or in the future, you may not be thinking of profitability, but you should. If it doesn't pay, it won't stay. Most online media operations are not profitable, and Web developers are beginning to think of business plans as part of their site development. You'll learn more about the marketing and design in future chapters. For now, consider these steps to planning a Web site.

DEFINE YOUR MISSION

❋ Define your major objective: What you are trying to accomplish on your site?

❋ Write a focus statement, a single sentence defining your primary goal, just as though you were writing a headline, broadcast teaser or direct lead for a news story. To help you identify a vision for your site, try HotWired editor Cate Corcoran's exercise: This site will be . . .

❋ List the main uses for your site such as:

To inform.

To entertain.

To help consumers.

To sell products.

To provide databases, research or references to other sites.

To promote a company or cause or yourself (as in a resume).

To deliver news.

To create or serve an interest group.

IDENTIFY YOUR AUDIENCE

Who are the users you want to attract to your site? For example, do you want a target age group, a niche group, a specific type of consumer or a general audience? Your audience will influence all other factors, particularly content and design.

DEVELOP A BUSINESS PLAN

This step may not apply to your school-related sites, but it is a step you should consider early in site planning. Here are some factors to consider:

* Who will your advertisers be?

* How will your content convince advertisers to put their ads on your site?

* How will you market your site?

* What kind of pricing structure will you use? (See Chapter 10 for more details.)

* Where will you place ads on your site? (Consider this during your design stage.)

* What costs are involved in creating and maintaining your site?

PLAN THE CONTENT

What content will you provide that will make people use and return to your site?

Brainstorm   Apply journalistic principles to your brainstorming. Using some of the qualities of news, consider what content elements you want in your site.

* Proximity: Will your content be of local, national or global interest?

* Timeliness: Will you provide news or other information of a timely nature that will need to be updated? (See site maintenance if this applies.)

* Informative: What news or information will you provide that will serve your users' needs?

* Unusual: What different or unique information will your site provide that will attract users and make them return to your site?

* Helpfulness: Will your site offer information consumers find helpful?

* Entertainment: Will you provide games or other fun elements?

* Community: What features will you include that help people interact with your site such as discussion groups or questions, chat rooms, focus groups or special niche sections.

* Originality: Are you planning original content or the same content as an existing print media site such as your newspaper or magazine?

* Multimedia: Will you have audio and video components. If so, will you provide links to download plug-ins your users might need to view or hear your multimedia content?

* Brand identity: If you are planning a media or commercial Web site, does it have a brand identity with a print product, a university symbol or a company logo?

List Criteria   Refer to the list of criteria you developed in your site contest in Chapter 4. Decide which criteria are compatible with your mission.

* Strong content.

* Useful links.

* Ease of navigation.

* Interactivity.

* Currency.

* Usefulness.

* Rapid downloading.

* Highly graphic or simple design.

* A text-only alternative.

* Fun elements.

* Others.

Outline Content   List the content you want and need to get. Then decide how many pages you will need on your site and what type of content each page will contain. This should be a rough outline of content. You can plan features of specific pages after you create your storyboard, a flow chart of pages for your site.

Plan Links   Decide what, why and where you want links.

❋   What sites do you want to link to your pages? List the URLs.

❋   What purpose will your links serve?

❋   Will your links be limited or extensive?

❋   Why do you want these links? Don't link just to show that you have searched a lot of sites or that you can provide extensive links. Every external link takes a user away from your site. Make the trip worthwhile.

❋   Where do you want to place your links on your pages? Every link interrupts a thought! Don't put hyperlinks in the middle of a sentence or paragraph or even in the middle of a text story if you want readers to continue reading the story. That's like putting a jump line asking the reader to turn to another page in the middle of a sentence or thought. If you are layering information in the form of headlines or briefs, your links can be placed on the headline or inside the brief. Experiment with hyperlink placement: Try them on the sides, at the bottom, or where they might not be intrusive.

Plan Interactive Elements   What interactive elements will your site contain?

❋   E-mail contacts.

❋   Feedback links or form boxes.

❋   Search capabilities.

❋   Interactive entertainment: puzzles, games, quizzes.

❋   Archival material—will your site need to maintain archives and if so, will they be searchable?

Consider Maintenance

❋   List content that needs to be updated.

❋   Decide if someone (and who) will maintain your site?

✳ Eliminate information that is so timely it will be outdated before you can maintain or update it.

✳ List content that will be archived.

CREATE A STORYBOARD

A Web site storyboard is a flow chart for the architecture of your site. This is the structural plan that shows the relationships of different pages within a site to each other and to the home page. It is like an organizational chart that shows who reports to whom in a company. Your Web site flow chart should show how many layers your site will have. Use the three-click principle (limit layers to three clicks back to the home page). One click is even better! The storyboard will help you create navigation for your site.

Sample Storyboard

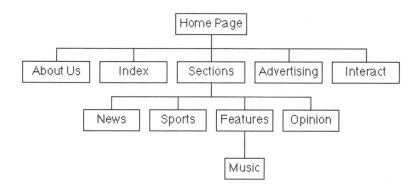

Create your storyboard three ways:

1 Create a storyboard showing the overall hierarchy of the site, outlining the relationship of each section to the home page.

2 Create a storyboard showing the relationship of each page within the section if you have a complicated site.

3 When you have developed your content, create a storyboard for individual pages. This is like laying out a page, showing the relationship of items within the page.

Work Flow Chart Once you have decided the hierarchy of your site, create a similar chart to identify the people who will be responsible for the sections or pages you plan to create if you are working in a group.

ADD A TIMELINE

Now that you have a storyboard and a work flow chart, add a site plan timeline.

❋ Make a calendar and list the targeted dates for completion of each part of your site.

❋ Place dates or estimated amounts of time, such as one week or one month, next to each part of your storyboard for the site plan. Post it where you can look at it frequently to see if you are on target.

❋ Set an absolute completion date. If you are building a site as part of a college course, your deadlines may be set for you or may be determined on a semester basis. Keep on schedule.

❋ If you discover that you cannot meet your deadlines, consider limiting your site. You can create some sections or inside pages at another time. Work on the most crucial parts.

PLAN HOME PAGE ELEMENTS

Now that you have created your storyboard, work chart and timeline, plan the index of items and navigational structure you will use on your home page. If you have a complex site, you may want to do this step after you have designed all the pages for your site. If your site is fairly simple, you can structure the navigation for your home page at this point.

❋ List all the topics you want on your home page.

❋ Decide if you want a frame or table listing links to interior pages or a pull-down menu. The menu technique is helpful if you have a very complicated site.

Select a Section   Go

✳ Plan the location of your navigation bar.

✳ Plan your masthead or logo, your primary identifier of the site. Use this logo or a variation of it to identify all your internal pages. Make sure your users know they still are in your site when they click to other pages. Brand identity is important.

✳ Plan placement for advertisements if you expect to have them on your site. If you don't consider advertising placement in the initial planning stages, you may have to redesign your pages later.

✳ Consider the kinds of graphics you will use.

✳ Time elements: Do you plan to date your pages to indicate when they were updated?

✳ Copyrights and credits: If the material is copyrighted, indicate that on your home page. If you are creating this as a class project or under contract, you may want to give yourself a credit line on the home page, as well.

✳ Contacts and feedback. You may want e-mail contacts on your home page or linked to it on an "About Us" or "Contents" page. Include an address and phone number for site contacts as well. Many online sites use only e-mail, which can frustrate someone who prefers to contact the site by other means.

✳ Link to any software plug-ins that might be necessary to view your site.

PLAN INTERNAL PAGES

You may want to plan these pages before considering the content of your home page. If you have a commercial site, you should plan a page "About Us." If you have a fairly complex site, you should plan an index or "Contents" page. Here are some steps to take in planning your internal pages.

✳ Decide how many pages you need for the content you want. Your storyboard should indicate this.

✳ Plan layout for each page in your site. You might sketch the layout or create it in a layout program, such as Quark Xpress or Pagemaker, in a fashion similar to laying out a newspaper or magazine page.

✳ Plan content for each page.

✳ Plan links for each page.

✳ Plan a navigation bar for each page with a link back to the home page.

✳ Plan your logo or other way you will identify the page with the site.

Your design will not be viewed the same way by different browsers. Your pages will also look different on Macintosh and PC computers. You should try to test your design on both types of computers and in Netscape Navigator and Microsoft Explorer. Also consider that the majority of Internet users have a 14-inch monitor, a 28.8 modem (which affects loading time), and many users need alternative text form. If you are designing on a larger monitor, view it in a smaller size. Put your cursor on the bottom-right corner of the page and move it to adjust the viewing area of the page. You'll find more information about design in Chapter 11, but here are some general tips.

✳ Design your pages to be 640 pixels wide. That is the size most designers use to accommodate the majority of users.

✳ Find designs of other pages you like and pull down "View Source" under your View menu to see how they were coded.

✳ Build brand-name identity of your site. Put your logo or some identifier of the site on each page.

✳ Keep some consistency of design among several pages in the same site.

✳ Create a template. If you want to have the same format on each page within your site, create a template or model page. After you have designed the page, pull down the File menu to "Save As" and give the template a different name each time you create a new page. Keep the items you want, such as the logo and navigation bar, and just change the rest of the content. Make the navigation consistent on all pages.

C o l o r   Use the consistent color palette of 216 colors that are used by the two major browsers, Netscape and Microsoft Explorer. If you create colors from a palette of thousands of shades, they will be distorted. Browsers will attempt to display an approximation of them, but you may get some strange results. Here are some points to consider:

✳ Does your color scheme reflect the image or mood you are trying to convey? For example, consider the colors of HotWired vs. the colors used by *The New York Times.*

✳ Does your color combination make it easy to read your text? Does the type contrast enough with the background?

✳ If you are using a patterned background, can you read the text over it?

✳ Will your background color make it difficult for the user to print (e.g., black or dark backgrounds with very light type)?

✳ Dark type on a light background is easier to read text than a lot of reverse light type on dark background.

G r a p h i c s   Remember to use gifs or jpegs and be careful to observe copyrights if you are taking graphics from the Web. Do not take any graphics from a Web site unless it offers them for your use. If you are building a commercial site, observe the copyright restrictions. Most graphics sites on the Web offer their images for noncommercial use.

✳ Design for text-only alternative browsers (use the *alt* tag).

✳ Keep images, photos and gifs small for loading speed.

✳ Limit your use of animated gifs.

✳ Limit blinking text, if you use it at all.

✳ Save photos in jpeg format, graphics in gif format.

L a y o u t   Some of the layout techniques for print media products are also applicable to Web sites.

✳ Put your most important or interesting material near the top (just as in a newspaper). Imagine that you are displaying your site as a newspaper is displayed in a street-sales box. Put the best graphics, headlines and information above the fold.

✳ Use block quotes in stories to create space.

✳ Use subheads to break up type.

✳ Keep lines of type short; it's hard to read a long line of type in print and even harder online.

S t o r y   S t r u c t u r e   You'll learn much more about online storytelling in future chapters. But if you are putting stories or large blocks of text on your Web site, consider these tips.

✳ Clicking vs. scrolling: Consider alternatives to scrolling for long text stories. Try breaking up long stories into sidebars or links.

✳ List technique: Sprinkle lists (bulleted items) through your text to break up the lines of type. This print technique works just as well online.

* Space between paragraphs: HTML coding <p> automatically puts a space between paragraphs (equal to hitting Return in Netscape Page Composer). Keep the spaces; it's easier to read text with these spaces.

* Links placement: Don't put hyperlinks in the middle of a story if you want people to keep reading without interruption. A link is like a jump page in a newspaper. The reader may not return to the story.

* Teasers and abstracts: Borrow from broadcast news and use teasers or abstracts before you launch into a large block of text.

* Layer news stories: Provide readers with a headline, an abstract or news brief and the full text.

Experiment. Web design is evolving. Take risks. Now that you have a great plan for your site, create it!

Test your design with a group of friends. Watch how they use the site. This is your "interface" testing—checking how people interact with your design.

* Is there anything that confuses them?

* Are there any buttons or menus that they can't find or access properly?

* Are there pages or features they don't understand or don't want to use?

A Web site is always in progress. At this point, if your user testing shows problems with the site, fix them.

Checklist

Here are some points to check before you upload your site to the Web.

* Are you sure you have abided by copyright restrictions? If you have used graphics from another Web site, make sure they are offered without charge and that you have attributed the sources correctly.

* Are all your links working? Check them regularly.

* Does your site have a distinct personality?

* Do you have information that needs to be updated regularly? Can you maintain your site?

* Do you have an index page that identifies your content and helps readers use your site?

* Have you planned a site that you can create in the time frame you are allotted? Should you scale down your site plan and add sections or pages at a later date?

* Have you provided e-mail links so users of your site can reach you? Have you also provided a phone number and address for the organization? Remember that some visitors to your Web site may want to contact you by phone or old-fashioned "snail" mail.

* Have you provided navigation back to the home page on your internal pages?

Safaris

http://www.mhhe.com/socscience/comm/rich/ch9/

9–1 **Web Site Planning Safari** | Check our Web site for links to sites offering tips for planning and creating Web sites.

9-2 Storyboard Safari

Using an existing media site, such as your college or local newspaper, develop a storyboard for it.

* If you were a consultant to that site, what site planning steps would you suggest to the Web editor to improve the site?
* What steps would you take to create a new section for the site?
* If your college or local newspaper lacks an online site and has few resources, what parts of the print product would you create online first?

9-3 Site Plan Prospectus

Develop a site prospectus using the site planning steps in this chapter. Create a booklet or written site plan before you create your site online. Following the prospectus, create your Web site.

9-4 Project Ideas

Develop a Web storytelling site based on a day in the life of your campus or community. (See Chapter 13 for more information about writing for the Web.)

* Borrow from a concept called *24 Hours in Cyberspace* and do a Web site on 24 hours in the effect of the World Wide Web on your campus. You can write vignettes or combine them with photos and video if you have the equipment.
* Develop a major new project of your choice. How would you present the project on the Web. If you don't want to do the reporting, take an existing project from your campus or local paper (with copyright permission) and interpret it for the Web.
* Develop a Web site for a client. Find a campus organization, a group or class in your school, a nonprofit or charitable organization in your community, or a commercial venture and develop a Web site for this client.
* Advertising students might develop a Web campaign or site for a product.
* Develop a hypothetical media site. Create your ideal newspaper, public relations, magazine or broadcast site.
* Choose an area of new media such as nonlinear writing or design, and develop innovative forms. Do research and conduct online experiments. Build your Web site with models and with links to your resources.

✳ Write an online research paper. How would you present it in nonlinear form? Provide links to resources.

Check our Web site for Safaris 9 for some links to project ideas for inspiration.

9–5 **Resume Posting**	Here's a reminder: If you are seeking free sites where you can post your resume, return to Safaris 6 or access the Web site for this chapter for a direct link. *American Journalism Review, Editor & Publisher,* and several career resources will allow you to post your resume on their sites without charge.

Chapter 10

WEB ADVERTISING

Goals

❋ To learn how to develop a business plan.

❋ To understand the importance of Web advertising to media sites.

❋ To learn terms for advertising on the Web.

❋ To learn methods of measuring Web advertising.

❋ To understand different types of Web advertisements.

❋ To explore ethical dilemmas of advertising for media sites.

Check our Web site for advertising resources.

http://www.mhhe.com/socscience/comm/rich/ch10/

Some highlights of this chapter are:

Hyperleap

Web sites

Des Moines Register:
http://www.dmregister.com
University Daily Kansan:
http://www.kansan.com
Lawrence Journal-World:
http://www.ljworld.com
HotWired:
http://www.hotwired.com
Arizona State University State Press:
http://news.vpsa.asu.edu/spress/spress.html
New York Times book review section (free registration subscription required):
http://www.nytimes.com/books/

Glossary at a Glance

A full glossary is in the appendix and on our Web site.
http://www.mhhe.com/socscience/comm/rich/glossary.html

ADVERTORIALS Advertisements that look like news stories.

BANNER ADS Advertisements stripped across the top or bottom of a Web site like a billboard. Banner ads also may be half size.

BLINK An HTML code that causes text or images to blink like a neon sign.

CACHE The place in your browser that stores sites you have visited previously.

CLICK-THROUGHS Clicking on an advertisement that links to the advertiser's site.

COOKIES A coded piece of information that tracks where you go within a site. When you access a site with a cookie, your browser stores the code. The next time you visit the site, your movements in the site can be tracked by the code assigned to your computer.

CPM Cost per thousand of page impressions.

ENCRYPTION A method of scrambling digital documents on the Internet so that they can be read only by people authorized to receive them. If you send credit card information to a site, you would want the information encrypted.

EYEBALLS Because people view Web sites, measuring eyeballs is an expression for counting views of a Web site. The methods of measurement can vary.

HITS Every item on a page, including graphics, is counted as a hit for advertising purposes. A page with text and five graphics would count as six hits when someone accesses it.

INTERSTITIALS Sometimes called "in your face ads," interstitials pop up in a window for about five seconds on a site while the rest of the site is downloading.

JAVA A programming language that can feature animation, interaction and moving text.

NARROWCASTING Catering to a niche or small group with similar interests.

NICHE A segment or group of people with similar interests. In advertising, catering to a niche would mean marketing to a specific

population targeted for its similarities, such as age, gender or special interest.

PAGE IMPRESSIONS A Web page accessed by a viewer with all elements on the page counted as one impression.

PAGE VIEWS Same as page impressions—counting each page downloaded by a user as one "view."

PARTNERSHIPS Collaboration between the Web site and other organizations or businesses to produce parts of the site. Media organizations often "partner" with database companies to produce guides, classified directories and other features.

SPONSORSHIPS A business or organization that sponsors an ad agrees to pay for the cost and maintenance of a site in return for placing its advertisement on the site.

VISIT The user must interact with the site in some way (by clicking either an ad or a link) to count as a "visit."

DILBERT reprinted with permission of United Feature Syndicate Inc.

Peter Lundquist

It's 8:30 a.m. and Peter Lundquist is a little nervous this morning. He's about to unveil a new Web site he created for *The Des Moines Register.* He doesn't want the members of his audience to use the site; he wants them to sell advertising for it.

Lundquist is meeting with the classified advertising sales representatives to get their feedback on JobCity, Iowa, a Web site to provide employers and job seekers with local, state and national employment opportunities.

"I want you to role play as though you were going to advertise on this site," he says. "Think of yourselves as job recruiters interested in this site."

This is not what Lundquist expected to be doing when he graduated from journalism school as a reporter. But after five years of reporting, he combined the skills he gained from taking computer science classes in college with his journalism training to create the Web site for his local newspaper, the *Lawrence* (Kan.) *Journal-World.* These days, as online services manager for *The Des Moines Register,* Lundquist spends as much time worrying about selling the newspaper's Web products as he does about creating them.

"We can't just be pie in the sky and take huge losses forever," he says. "Our plan is to be profitable within three years."

Many other media Web managers have a similar goal. They don't expect their sites to generate enough advertising dollars to be self-supporting immediately, but they hope the sites will be profitable within a few years. Because most media sites are offered without charge to Internet users, advertising is their main source of revenue. Some sites charge for specific services such as access to archives or special features. But Web users have become accustomed to surfing for free. And charging subscriptions for access to the site isn't a successful option, except for a limited number of Web sites such as *The Wall Street Journal Interactive.*

As a result, media Web publishers have begun to create or target the areas of their sites that generate money—mainly classified advertising, real estate and ads on the most popular Web pages, usually the home page or sports sites.

Classified advertising is the biggest source of revenue for most print newspapers. If Microsoft chairman Bill Gates has his way, it will become another big source of revenue for his company. Microsoft is creating Web sites containing national databases for car sales, job opportunities, and entertainment guides in major cities throughout the county. Other national online directories such as Yahoo! and Yellow Page guides also are eating into advertising turf that print and online newspapers need for survival.

So great is the concern that the Newspaper Association of America issued a study "Classifieds in Crisis," saying that the average 14 percent profit margin of newspaper could fall to 3 percent if classified advertising were cut in half because of online competitors. Deeper cuts could be catastrophic.

"Classified revenue is a pot of gold," Lundquist says. "The consumer doesn't pay for a billboard advertisement. But they'll pay for classifieds."

In the *Register,* if a person buys a classified ad in the print newspaper, the ad will also be listed in the online product without extra charge. Other online newspapers may charge extra for an ad in both products. In the *Register*'s site, JobCity, Iowa, an advertisement for a local job listing also gets listed on a national jobs database, CareerPath, which has a partnership with the *Register* and several other newspapers.

"We see ourselves like a magazine publication instead of a newspaper," Lundquist says. "We're going to develop individual magazines for particular niches, like sections of a newspaper but deeper."

Unlike many other online newspapers that developed Web sites with all or most of the sections that were in their print papers, the *Register* started with a searchable classified advertising site followed by a real estate site. The Home Register site was profitable almost immediately. The company decided to develop sites that would generate the most advertising before adding the news content that the print product features.

In traditional media, advertising accounts for 100 percent of revenue for broadcast television and radio stations, 80 percent for newspapers and 63 percent for magazines, according to the *Morgan Stanley Internet Advertising Report.* In the new online media, advertising is expected to play an even greater role in financing the sites. As a result, people like Lundquist who manage Web sites have to consider the business end of the product from the start.

"There are so many pieces to developing a Web site," Lundquist says. "You need to build in your advertising spots in advance. You have to know where the revenue is coming from for each screen. If you build your site with content in mind and think of advertising as an afterthought, then you have to redo your site."

BUSINESS PLAN

Lundquist says it is important to create a business plan when you start planning a Web site. He suggests these steps:

* Define the audience and the market.

* Break down content page by page, and decide what type of advertising could apply on each page. In other words, how could you entice advertisers to these pages?

* After anticipating advertising opportunities, estimate the overall revenue you can receive. Consider high traffic spots on your site, such as the home page, and less expensive spots on inside pages that you might be able to sell.

* Project how much advertising you could sell each month.

* Build a revenue table.

* Project your costs. How many employees will you need to staff the site? Then you can figure your profits and losses.

* If you have an existing site, anticipate growth of your site, increases in revenue and new costs.

You may not be able to anticipate selling ads on inside pages for a small Web site, but you should plan for advertising on your home page. "That's very different from a newspaper," Lundquist says. "But for an online site, that is where you are going to get traffic."

MARKETING MEASUREMENTS

Just as in more traditional print media, traffic is like circulation. Only online media managers discuss traffic in terms of "eyeballs," the views their Web sites get. But they measure those eyeballs in several ways, called *hits, click-throughs,* and *page impressions* or *page views.* It's a virtual jungle of jargon.

Software can record every time a page gets requested or delivered on the Internet. The more hits or impressions a Web site gets, the more the ad will cost. If you are building a Web site, should you charge by hits or page impressions? For example, if a page has 10 graphics, you will get 10 hits every time someone looks at it," Lundquist explains. "So you could say your page gets 100,000 hits, but it's not really doing that. Page impressions are more realistic."

If all that seems confusing, here are some definitions to help you sort it out.

HITS Every text and graphic element on a Web page is considered a "hit." If you call up a Web page that has a logo, an ad, text, pictures, and graphics, the Web server delivering that page to your computer records every item on the page as a separate file or *hit*. A hit also can be recorded just as a request for a page, even if the page doesn't get delivered or if the user clicks the Stop button. To complicate matters, when you request a Web page, your browser checks first to see if it is stored on your computer because you might have visited it previously. If your computer cache has stored the page you requested, the cache delivers it, so the hit doesn't count on the server containing the page. This form of measurement is now considered misleading to advertisers.

QUALIFIED HITS These are the number of items on a page that are actually delivered, not merely requested. All the text and graphics still are counted as separate hits.

PAGE VIEWS This is the number of times a Web page has been delivered to a user, but each page counts as one "page view," regardless of the number of items on it. For example, if you set CNN as your home page on your browser, every time you log in and call up your browser, the CNN Web page, its graphics, stories, and all its ads count as one page view.

PAGE IMPRESSIONS The most popular term, this is the same as page views. If you request a page that contains an advertisement, this also counts as a page impression or ad impression whether or not you view or click on the ad.

CLICK-THROUGHS If you actually click on an ad, that counts as a "click-through."

VISITS Even a seemingly simple "visit" to a Web site has a complex meaning for advertising. A visit measures your interaction with the Web site. When you call up a Web page and click on anything in it, that is a visit. If you stop requesting other files from the open site during a specified amount of time, usually 30 minutes, and you return to the site via your back button, the server records it as a new visit.

COOKIES Named for no apparent reason, cookies help Web sites keep track of their users. A cookie is a coded piece of data that can be stored on your browser to identify your unique code number. When you access a Web site that sends you a page coded to "set cookies," your browser saves this information. The next time you request pages from the site, it knows that your computer accessed them because of the code number it sent to your computer. The Web server doesn't know who you are or what you like unless you fill out a registration form, as some sites request. *The New York Times,* for example, requires registration. When you access the *Times,* it stores your login and password so the *Times's* Web server knows whether you are registered. The *Times* uses cookies to track usage of its site and to provide its advertisers with summaries of how many people visited the site. However, it doesn't give out any personal information about you. You can set your browser to accept or reject cookies. In Netscape, pull down the Edit menu to "Preferences." Then click on "Advanced" and decide whether you want to be warned about cookies or turn them off. In Internet Explorer, pull down the View menu to "Options" to "Advanced" and do the same.

PRICING PLANS

Now that you know how Web sites measure their users, how do you decide what to charge advertisers? Pricing is unregulated, uneven, and unfathomable in many cases. Each Web site sets its own rates, and they can change at any time.

Fred Mann, general manager of the online *Philadelphia Inquirer* and *Daily News,* says his site charges advertisers based on the cost per thousands of page impressions and where the ads will be placed. "We deliver eyeballs to the advertiser," he says.

And the front page gets a lot more eyeballs than the obituary site. So an advertiser who wants a position on the home page can pay $7,000 a month or about $75,000 a year because the home page gets about 600,000 page views a month. An ad on the obituary page will cost only $250 a month or $2,700 a year because that site receives about 8,000 page views a month.

Like many online media sites, Philadelphia Online also engages in partnerships with database companies in a system called *bartering.* If the online newspaper gets advertisements for sites containing a partner's database, the advertising revenue can be shared on a percentage basis. Because partnerships between media companies and data-compiling companies are growing, bartering is expected to grow as well.

Some of the most common pricing structures are:

CPM (Cost per Thousand of Page Impressions)
The price is based on the amount of traffic the Web site receives for a specific page. Like the Philadelphia Online price structure, the price also depends on placement and size of the ads. Banners on home pages will cost more than a small ad on the same page or ads on inside pages. Many software applications are available to count user traffic. The majority of Web sites charge from $10 to $150 per thousand page impressions.

Most Web sites will charge a specific CPM rate for a certain period of time. However, some media Web operations have a floating rate structure. If the number of page impressions increases, the fee will be changed to reflect a higher rate for more traffic.

Flat Fee
This is a specific fee for placement on a particular page regardless of the number of hits or page impressions. Although heavily trafficked sites can charge higher fees, a flat rate usually is based on weekly, monthly or yearly advertisements. The campus paper, *The University Daily Kansan interactive* (UDKi), also uses this method, charging $500 for a front-page banner ad per semester. But on its basketball site, which draws thousands of viewers during the season, the *Kansan* charges a flat rate of $1,000 per semester on the site's front page.

Targeted Ad Fees
A site that uses registration so it knows something about its users can target ads to those groups. For example, because *The New York Times* requires registration, it has information about its users. It offers advertisers rates based on a variety of measures, including targeted ads to the age group, occupation, income, gender, and geographical area of its users, which it tracks by its cookies. The *Times* also offers advertising rates based on page impressions without targeted elements.

While many Web sites are reluctant to reveal their rates, the *Times* posts its rates on its Web site, as does Philadelphia Online. But if you want to know more about advertising for a Web site, most sites post a media kit or other information for advertisers.

Click-Through Fees   The click-through rate structure is less popular because it generates less traffic and less revenue. Rates are based only on the number of times a user will click on an ad to connect to the advertiser's site. Some advertisers prefer it because it means their ad received some interaction, but studies show that exposure to ads even without click-throughs is generating brand loyalty on the Web.

Sponsorships   A sponsorship is an arrangement where the advertiser pays the site a flat fee to "sponsor" or pay for the costs of a part of the site. The advertiser's logo or ad then is displayed somewhere on the page or attached to the button for the section it is sponsoring. The site usually guarantees the sponsor a minimum number of page impressions. Sponsored ads usually are labeled. On the *Lawrence Journal-World,* the University Book Shop sponsors the newspaper's online basketball site.

TYPES OF ADVERTISEMENTS

Banner Ads   A banner ad is like a cyber-billboard stripped across the top or bottom of the Web page. This is the most common type of advertisement. It is enclosed in a box and links to the advertiser's Web site when you click on it. It can be static, just the ad with text or graphics that stay on the page, or it can contain some form of motion. The blink, a flashing sign, is becoming unpopular. Instead, advertising designers are using more Java-coded animation that changes words and images within the ads every second. Banner ads can be various sizes, but the most widely accepted are half or full size.

The online campus newspaper, *The University Daily Kansan interactive,* has three banner ads on its home page, and these ads made the *Kansan* profitable a year after going online.

THE UNIVERSITY DAILY
Kansan *interactive*

WITH BOOKS FROM THE MT. OREAD BOOKSHOP

KU Study Abroad
Discover Your Options

HOURS:
MON-FRI 8-8
SAT. 8-4:30
SUN. 12:30-4:30

Since 1906
Watkins Health Center

Watch for:
BEAK HEALTHY
October 13
in the Kansan

Cube Ads These are smaller boxed ads in cube shape that can go anywhere on the page, usually on the sides or bottom. This self-promotional cube ad on the Arizona State University's *State Press* newspaper asks you to "click here." If you do, it links to another quarter-banner ad telling you to advertise in the *State Press*.

Click here!

Unlock *Your Potential*

With an ad in the daily *State Press*. Reach the college market today.

STATE PRESS ADVERTISING

L o g o s   The advertiser just places its logo on the page with a link to its site. This type of ad is better for well-known brand names. In some cases, the advertiser can place the logo on the Web page without charge. If a user clicks through and purchases something, the Web site can receive a percentage of sales or other form of payment in a barter arrangement.

B u t t o n   A d s   Like logo ads, these are buttons that feature an advertiser's name. They are often used for software downloads such as Microsoft's Internet Explorer or Netscape's Navigator browsers.

P o p - u p   A d s   These ads appear for about five seconds when a user calls up a page, and the ad banner remains on the page after the page loads.

I n t e r s t i t i a l   o r   I n t e r m e r c i a l   A d s   Similar to pop-up ads, interstitial ads are highly interactive ads that appear on the screen briefly for about five seconds in a separate window with some form of animation, often including audio for music, while the rest of the site loads. Also called *intermercials,* they are patterned after television, but they can entice users to click on them with games. However, you may require special software plug-ins to view the animated features. They are controversial because they can be intrusive. Netscape labels its interstitial window as illustrated:

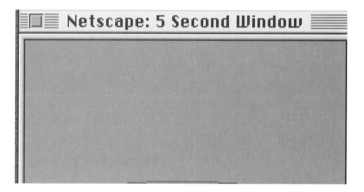

K e y w o r d   A d s   Type a search for beer or cars on Yahoo! and you'll get an ad for beer or cars. Keyword ads are featured mostly in search-engine sites. Advertisers can link an ad to a search for a related text word.

SIZE OF ADS

The instructions you have received for designing home pages and other Web pages apply to advertising sites as well. But the design of banner ads and others to be placed within your Web pages involves the size. When you design your page, you may need to leave space for the type of ad you expect to receive.

Banners and buttons come in different sizes. A full-size banner is usually 468 by 60 pixels, and a half-size banner is 234 by 60 pixels. Although there are no standards, the Internet Advertising Bureau and CASIE (Coalition for Advertising Supported Information and Entertainment, a trade organization representing Internet advertisers) are recommending eight commonly accepted sizes.

* Full banner: 468 by 60 pixels.

* Full banner with vertical navigation bar: 392 by 72 pixels.

* Vertical banner: 120 by 240 pixels.

* Half banner: 234 by 60 pixels.

* Buttons: square button, 125 by 125 pixels; small button, 120 by 90 pixels; smallest button, 120 by 60 pixels.

DESIGN AND CONTENT TIPS

Many media organizations offer to design the Web pages for their advertisers as part of an incentive package. Here are some tips for creating ads:

✻ Limit photos and large graphics on your pages so they load quickly. A slow-loading advertisement is an invitation for users to hit the Stop button.

✻ Always include an e-mail contact, a phone number (preferably an 800-number), and an address. Consumers still are reluctant to purchase goods online, despite growing security from companies like CyberCash, which offer encryption software to protect credit card security. As a result, you need to offer customers options.

✻ Establish your brand identity. Make sure your logo is on every page.

✻ Offer an "About Us" page in your site to explain your company or service.

✻ Provide informative content. Keep it simple. Write short sentences. Don't cram your content on a page.

✻ Make sure your content is readable. Use strong contrast—light type on a dark background, dark type on a light background. Larger type (12 or 14 points) is preferable to type of 10 points or less.

✻ Make your site entertaining. Add games or interactive features if appropriate for your target audience, but avoid requiring consumers to download special software to view your pages. The exception might be if you are offering compelling interactive content such as games that the viewer can't resist.

✻ Provide good navigation. Don't link to pages outside of your site unless your purpose is to provide users with resources.

✻ Add click spots. While most Web users know a hyperlink if it is underlined or in a different color, a lot of users don't know they can click on an ad to link to the advertiser's site. So using "Click here" in an ad is a good idea.

✻ Put yourself in the position of a customer. What do you want and need to know to purchase a product or a service?

✻ Follow design principles in Chapter 11.

ETHICS

Media sites are struggling with such ethical decisions as whether to offer ads under related content like book or restaurant reviews. In traditional media of newspapers and magazines, editors try to adhere to ethical standards that separate content from advertising. But on the Web, the boundaries are less clear.

In general, most media Web editors insist that they will continue to publish reviews and other stories that are not influenced by advertisers. But placement of the ads in proximity to the content makes that distinction confusing to consumers. Some advertisements called "advertorials" even contain editorial content related to the site, which confuses users about the editorial integrity of the information. Advertorials resemble news stories in content and format.

When *The New York Times* created its online book section, it made a deal with Barnes & Noble for advertising on the site. But instead of just merely showing an ad for the bookseller, a button at the bottom of every book review links directly to Barnes & Noble so the user can order the book online.

Some media leaders have criticized it as a serious ethical breach because the newspaper receives advertising money from the bookseller. But in an *Editor & Publisher* online column, *New York Times* Web editor Bernard Gwertzman said the issue was heavily debated and the consensus was that the link provided a useful service to readers. He said that it is clear the *Times* is not selling the book and that there would be no influence on the print reviews of the books, where the online versions originate.

However, such ethical dilemmas surely will continue. Standards to address these ethical concerns were recommended at an ethics conference sponsored by The Poynter Institute for Media Studies and the American Society of Newspaper Editors. The recommendations were as follows:

* Links should be clearly identified as either editorial or commercial.

* The audience should be able to clearly distinguish between editorial content and advertising, including advertorials. Advertising will not dictate news content or presentation.

* Partnerships will not compromise the integrity of the news organization. Partners should be identified if they have a bearing on the content.

* Tracing technologies such as cookies will be used responsibly so they don't intrude or violate the privacy of the reader. If any user information collected from online surveys is to be used by third parties for direct mail or phone solicitations, the readers will be notified in advance.

The Society of Professional Journalists states in its code of ethics that journalists should "distinguish news from advertising and shun hybrids that blur the lines between the two." Although the code does not specifically refer to online journalism, the principles can be used for all media.

The American Society of Magazine Editors also has issued voluntary guidelines of online advertising:

* The publication's home page should display its name and logo to identify who controls the content.

* Online pages should make a clear distinction—through words, design, or placement—between editorial and advertising content.

* Special ad sections should be labeled as advertising along with the sponsor's name.

* Editors shall not create content for special ad sections or other ads.

Now it's time for you to take Peter Lundquist's advice: "As soon as you start a site, think how advertising will fit in."

Take this quiz on paper or online at our Web site; you can check your answers there, too.
http://www.mhhe.com/socscience/comm/ rich/ch10/

10–1 Advertising Quiz

1 A hit counts as
    a. one item on a page.
    b. every item on a page.
    c. a URL for a page.

2 A page view is
    a. a single page delivered to the user with all graphics counted as one view.
    b. a view the user gets of graphics.
    c. a view of an advertisement.

3 Qualified hits are

    a. the number of pages qualified by the Advertising Audit Bureau.

    b. the number of items on a page that are delivered to the user.

    c. the number of items on a page that are requested by a viewer.

4 A visit to a Web page counts as

    a. calling up the page.

    b. looking at the page.

    c. clicking something on the page.

5 Cookies are

    a. codes set in a page to track users.

    b. graphics to entice users into advertisements.

    c. codes required in pages with pornography.

6 Page impressions are

    a. the impressions users have about Web pages.

    b. the number of times pages are delivered to users.

    c. the impressions of graphics on Web pages.

7 CPM means

    a. counting pages in metrics.

    b. cost per thousand of page impressions.

    c. cost per measurement.

8 Click-through fees are

    a. costs based on the number of times users click on ads.

    b. costs based on the number of times users click on text hyperlinks.

    c. costs based on the number of hyperlinks on a page.

9 Banner ads are

    a. always placed on the top of the page.

    b. placed on the top or bottom of the page.

    c. ads that must stretch across the entire top of the page.

10 Interstitial ads are

    a. in the middle of the page.

    b. interactive, animated ads that appear for five seconds.

    c. ads that interrupt the text.

10–2	**Advertising Resources**	Check our Web site for links to advertising resources.
10–3	**Ethics**	Discuss the ethical dilemmas of linking advertising to reviews of restaurants, books, or other relationships of advertising to news.
10–4	**Business Plan**	Create a business plan for your Web site. Include decisions about how you will measure your audience—by hits, page impressions or otherwise—and how you will charge for advertising on your site.
10–5	**Design**	If you are creating a Web site, design your pages with space for advertising. If you don't anticipate receiving advertising, plan self-promotional ads.

Chapter II

WEB SITE DESIGN

Goals

* To understand principles of Web design.

* To learn the importance of design usability.

* To understand principles of color and typography.

* To learn about browser-safe colors.

* To learn about layout.

* To gain tips from Web design experts.

You can leap to the following sections in the chapter:

Hyperleap

Web sites

Lynda Weinman's browser-safe color palette:
http://www.lynda.com/hex.html
Mario Garcia's home page:
http://www.mariogarcia.com
Disney Web site:
http://www.disney.com
Mercedes Benz:
http://www.mercedes.com
JustGo:
http://www.justgo.com
HotWired:
http://www.hotwired.com
New York Times:
http://www.nytimes.com
Chicago Tribune:
http://www.chicago.tribune.com
The Poynter Institute for Media Studies:
http://www.poynter.org

Glossary at a Glance

A full glossary is in the appendix and on our Web site.

http://www.mhhe.com/socscience/comm/rich/
glossary.html

ANTI-ALIASING Low resolution of computer monitors causes some images to have jagged edges, called *aliased* images. Anti-aliasing is a process that smooths the jagged edges by blending tints in the colors.

BROWSER-SAFE COLORS The 216 colors that are recognized by Macintosh and Windows in their color palettes. Each browser reserves another 40 of its own custom colors (in a 256-color palette) that are not common to both platforms. For a list of browser-safe color formulas, check Web designer Lynda Weinman's site at *http://www.lynda.com/hex.html*.

DITHERING The process of adjusting colors that are not in the main color palette of the browser so they approximate the colors you choose. Dithering makes files larger, and the colors that result may not be exactly the same as you wished.

FONT The name of a typeface. Originally it meant the family of different size letters in a particular typeface, but these days *fonts* and *typefaces* are used interchangeably.

GIF Graphic Interchange Format, a compression format for images that reduces the number of bits it takes to load images onto Web pages without losing quality. The gif (preferably pronounced with a hard *g*) format usually is used for graphics, while photographs are processed in another compression format, known as *JPEGs*.

HUE Color gradation as defined by its name such as red or yellow.

INTERFACE By definition, an interconnection between systems or the way different and sometimes incompatible elements communicate. In Web design concepts, it is the way that users can react or communicate with the computer. As a result, a user-friendly interface is a good design goal.

JPEG A compression format, created by the Joint Photographic Experts Group, to reduce the bits needed to view images on the Web. JPEGs (pronounced jay-pegs) are best used on photographic images.

PICAS A unit of measurement used in print media. Six picas equal one inch.

PIXELS A unit of measurement for the dots on the screen that form images and text. The average screen resolution is 72 pixels per inch, compared to the higher resolution of 1,200 to 3,000 dots per inch for printed materials. Ten pixels equal one pica.

RGB Red, green, blue.
SATURATION The intensity of the color; the purer or brighter a color is, the more saturated it is.
SERIF Fonts are created in serif and sans-serif typefaces. Serif typefaces, such as Times Roman, have curves or extra strokes called *serifs* at their tips and endings.
SANS SERIF These typefaces have no serifs such as Helvetica and Geneva, which have straight letters.

Sans-serif typefaces are often used for headlines to contrast with serif typefaces used most frequently in body type.
VALUES The degree of lightness or darkness of colors.

Mario Garcia

You have 20 seconds to make an impression with your Web site. That's all the time you will get before visitors to your site decide to stay or leave, says Mario Garcia, a world-famous media design consultant. "If you are trying to sell information, you must tell me in 20 seconds what is the point of view, the culture of your site, the overall feel," Garcia says. "The point of view should immediately tell you whether you are in a site that is news, entertainment or whether you are fun and for children."

Every design decision you make should be a conscious one, from the colors you choose to the images and typefaces. For example, the Disney site uses a combination of bright cartoon-type colors that would appeal to children. Conversely, the Web site for Mercedes Benz automobiles uses subdued colors that convey a feel of sophistication and money to target a wealthy audience.

Garcia, author of *Redesigning Print for the Web,* says the Mercedes site has a definite point of view that it is selling to a corporate audience for men and women who have a certain status. "Without saying much, in 20 seconds they convey exactly what it is all about."

Studies show that most Web users spend about seven minutes online compared to 20 minutes reading a newspaper, Garcia says. That's another reason for the urgency of hooking them into your site. With a world of information at their fingertips, competition for Web users' time is keen. Content is still the primary draw, but good design enhances the way to convey content.

Principles of good Web design will last longer than the current styles on the Web. "Web sites are being redesigned every four months," Garcia says. One year in the life of a Web site is equivalent to seven years in a newspaper. Some newspapers don't change designs for 10 or 20 years, he says.

Although many online newspaper sites mirror their print designs, that will change. "Whereas the print media have a history of design, there is no legacy for the Web," Garcia says. "So you can bring fresh ideas without dealing with a syndrome of the way things are supposed to be done. In seven years there will be a whole generation of people who never worked in print. So that will be the real revolution."

One of the problems the Web has created is that its global reach is fostering copycat Web design. "We all see what everyone else is doing," he says. "From coast to coast in this country newspaper Web sites all look the same. This is beginning to happen on a global scale."

For example, Garcia says, someone at an online newspaper in Argentina clicks into the Web site for the *San Jose Mercury News,* likes what he or she sees, and copies the design. In the south of Argentina, there is a wonderful landscape, but the Web site for an online newspaper there doesn't reflect that, he says.

"Why should you make a Web site with the color and texture of southern California," Garcia says. "I am beginning to see Web sites in countries that do not at all resemble that country. People should be able to smell your location to see who you are."

THREE ELEMENTS OF WEB DESIGN

Web design is based on three things: point of view, texture and appropriateness, Garcia explains.

1 The point of view, previously discussed, gives the immediate impression of the mood or content your site is trying to convey.

2 Texture also conveys a message about your site by the combination of typography, color and story structure you use. The blend of visual, content and aesthetic elements provides a sense of identity for your site. For example, Garcia says, when you are reading *Time* magazine or *Newsweek* online, you are aware of the identity of those magazines. "The whole idea of maintaining a sense of identity on the screen is very important. People who surf the Web and go from one site to another begin to lose touch with where they are because so many sites look alike. You should make sure that your site reflects the individuality of your product."

3 Appropriateness is the use of design to reflect the content of your site. "If you are trying to sell paint, I should see paint and colors the moment I open this Web site," Garcia says.

THE IMPORTANCE OF CONTENT

Although the design should convey your message, the quality of text on your site is becoming increasingly important. "Words tend to be more effective to make you click than icons," Garcia says. "This is one of the ironies of the medium. In spite of the fact that the Web is the ultimate communications tool because it can offer motion, sound, images and text, the people who use it want a lot of information. This one is taking us back to words. We are going to need the best word people in the world. Writing is back."

Garcia says many sites are beautiful, but they have too little information. "Ninety percent of your efforts should be put into the information," he says. "The basic formula for doing a good Web site or for any design is understanding the nature of the information. *The Wall Street Journal* is not very visual, but it is very successful. They understand the nature of information."

John Caserta

CREATING
A BRAND
IDENTITY

John Caserta also believes that content dictates design. "Design is the communication of information in a clear way," says Caserta, design director for the Internet *Chicago Tribune.* He spent more than six months redesigning the site for the online *Tribune.* Caserta says he began his redesign by asking himself some questions about the objectives of the *Tribune* site: "Who are we; why do we exist; what do we mean to people?"

Those questions narrow down design, he says. "The *Tribune* has a certain look, color and mood. He says he wanted to create a brand identity so users would know they were in the *Tribune* site. On the other hand, he wanted to make it clear that the Internet *Tribune* was not a print product. He decided on a single-screen home page so users would not have to scroll.

"Scrolling is a carryover from the print environment," Caserta says. "Ideally, what we're looking at is how to take advantage of what a monitor is."

Caserta suggests that you create a template for your inner pages so the site will have some unity of design. "If you are trying to create a large site, you need to keep the same labels and organization and the same family of fonts," he says. "Color is also important. The colors you choose reinforce and create a brand identity."

Before you create a home page and template that will give your site unity, consider a theme for your site. How will the design reflect the content? If you plan your site with a theme in mind, your design will be more compatible with your content.

Bill Skeet

USABILITY

Good organization and navigation are the cornerstones of making a Web site easy to use. Bill Skeet, chief designer for Knight-Ridder New Media, considers usability the most important part of design.

"Web designers should start with the question: 'How do you use content in a meaningful way to people?' The main driving factor in site design should be utility," he says. "If it isn't useful and easy to use, it doesn't matter how attractive it is."

Skeet originated the concept of three clicks to content, meaning users should not have to click through more than three screens from the home page to get to the content they want. Now, he says one click to content is even better. Users are impatient and want to find information quickly from the home page.

"Design isn't what it used to be," says Skeet, who designs online products for newspapers in the Knight-Ridder chain. "There's an aspect that deals with attractiveness, but now you start with content and data structure. How you organize the data affects how you design the site."

He cites the JustGo Web site he and designer Andrew DeVigal created for Knight-Ridder online newspapers in several cities. The site is an entertainment database offering users listings of movies, concerts, restaurants, and theater performances in each city, with interactive maps that give users directions from their addresses to the locations of the events.

The massive JustGo database, developed in a partnership with Zip2 company, created enormous design challenges, Skeet says. In the San Francisco Bay area alone, the database lists more than 5,000 restaurants. The main challenge was to make the site easy for users to navigate.

"One of the major changes in design is coming from user studies," Skeet says. "In the past designers just created sites; now they test them."

He and fellow designer DeVigal started with focus groups to ask people what kind of content they would be interested in receiving on the JustGo site. Users wanted movies and dining first and then information about performing arts. "Our focus groups said people just wanted to get the information and get out [of the site]," Skeet said. "They just wanted utility."

After DeVigal and Skeet designed the site, they again tested it with focus groups to see if the site was easy to use. "We were behind a mirror watching people use the site. We wondered why they weren't clicking on the buttons. Some things seem so obvious to designers, but they are not to users. One of the biggest things we learned was to label things clearly and make them obvious."

DeVigal also stresses the importance of testing your site design. "I test the difference between browsers and platforms [Macintosh and Windows]," DeVigal says. "Then I go to a bigger screen and start stretching it to make sure it's still stable. Test, test, test."

Skeet designs on a 20-inch monitor but tests it on a 14-inch screen, the size most users own. He says he became a newspaper designer because he loves to solve problems. "I think that's what a designer is—a problem solver. Design is just about critical thinking. And thinking is the first step in Web design." Skeet offers these steps:

※ Figure out what you want to do and who the audience is. Write a mission statement. What is your objective for the product? Have a measurable objective that you can test at the end of your design to see if you were successful, he says. Your audience also determines design. For example, if you have an audience of senior citizens, make bigger buttons because they have problems with motor control because of arthritis or other diseases, Skeet explains.

※ Create a list of content.

※ Prioritize and categorize it. Prepare a flow chart (similar to the storyboard discussed in Chapter 9). "You have to look at the architecture and the foundation structure of the blueprint before you decide what kind of wallpaper to put up," Skeet says.

※ Establish an interface for navigation. The interface, which is the way people are going to use your site, consists of the navigation tools such as buttons and links or menus and other tools to provide usability. Make your site easy to use, Skeet says. "How many of you have been frustrated by a VCR? You say

'The hell with it.' If nothing happens when a user clicks a button, he feels stupid. Make a button look like a button. Navigation in a site should be consistent so users don't get lost and confused."

Every page in your site should have consistent navigation. Because users may not scroll through a site, make sure your navigation bar is at the top or on the side of your site. If your site requires scrolling, you may want to put navigation bars at the top and bottom of your pages.

✳ Create a prototype for the site. Make it look good.

✳ Test, evaluate and evolve. "You're not going to build the final version the first time."

TYPOGRAPHY

Now that you understand the concepts of site design, how do you decide what typefaces and colors to use? Consistent use of the same typefaces and colors creates brand identity from one page to another within a Web site, says Ron Reason, an expert in typography and director of visual journalism programs for The Poynter Institute for Media Studies. "Your type decisions send a message to the reader about what's important," he says. "Limit your fonts to two typefaces. The 1,000 fonts available are distracting you from conveying information."

Web designers should think about typographic contrasts, the relationships created by different typefaces and the relationships between one element and another within a site, including white space and photos, Reason says. You need to consider how type works together with logos, headers and display type, which are the artistic typefaces that might be used as graphic elements for headlines to "display" stories. Icons combined with display type can create busy pages and may be unnecessary, he says.

Print products make a clear distinction between advertising and editorial content, Reason says. But on the Web, advertisements may appear on the side, above, or in the middle of editorial content. Because the typefaces used in advertisements may be different from the display type and fonts used in content, the chance of creating "visual chaos" is greater, Reason says. The Web also creates competition among many sites for the users' attention, increasing the need for brand identity within a site.

Reason says Web designers should avoid changing the colors of individual words or phrases within text. "When you shift to a different color, you risk making associations for the reader that it is a link."

Another problem Web designers face with body type is a lack of control. Users can set their browser preferences to deliver typefaces they choose, so the typeface designed in HTML may not be the one the user sees. However, most designers recommend that you create body type in the default typeface of Times Roman or Times New Roman. Headlines, which can be created and saved as gifs, may be in a different typeface.

Types of Typefaces   The term *font* originally was used to mean a family of different size letters in a particular typeface, but these days *fonts* and *typefaces* are used interchangeably. Fonts are created in serif and sans-serif typefaces. Serif typefaces, such as Times Roman, have curves or extra strokes, called *serifs* at their tips and endings. Sans-serif typefaces, such as Helvetica and Geneva, are straight—without serifs. Sans-serif typefaces are often used for headlines to contrast with serif typefaces used most frequently in body type.

On the Web both typefaces work well, and many sites are using sans-serif fonts for body type as well. They are easy to read on the Web especially because screen resolution makes readability on the Web more difficult than in print. For example, HotWired often uses sans-serif typefaces in large 14 or 18 point sizes for body type against its bright-colored backgrounds. *The New York Times* consistently uses a serif typeface for its body type. Both sites have distinct brand identity by their use of typography and color.

Reason says that regardless of the font you choose, you can create interesting design with only one typeface by using some of these contrasts.

* Size: big and small. Letters in large sizes, such as 36 points, can contrast with others in 12 or 14 points.

* Positive and negative: black type against a white or light background (positive); white or light colored type against a dark background (negative).

* Upper and lowercase contrasts.

* Light and dark, using boldface and regular type or gray versus solid black letters.

* Plain text and italics. However, be careful about using too much text in italics. It's hard to read, especially on the Web.

* Weight: Letters given heavy weight can contrast with letters that are narrower.

Here are some examples of contrasts adapted from materials by Ron Reason:

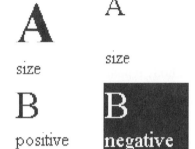

If you had to describe yourself in a color, what color would you choose? What color is happiness? Sadness? What colors would you use to describe autumn, spring, summer and winter? As with other design elements, color should be a conscious decision. It can portray a mood or an impression for your Web site.

"We respond to color in a physiological way," says Pegie Stark Adam, a Poynter Institute associate, who is an expert in color theory and design. "Some colors make you feel good and others not so good. People respond to color whether they're aware of it or not."

Contrast is as important in the use of color as it is in typography. Dark colors contrast with light ones, warm colors (reds, yellows) contrast with cool ones (blues, greens). All colors come from three primary colors: red, yellow and blue.

Adam conducts this experiment, which you can take on our Web site. Stare at a blob of red on a screen for one minute and then close your eyes tightly. With your eyes closed, you will see a blue or purple vision. Your body gave you another color, a color of balance. In this case the balance color was blue or purple, the complement to red. The complement is the opposite color on a color wheel.

When you use strong contrasts of warm and dark colors, such as the warm red next to its cool and darker complementary blue color, the cool color will recede and the warm one will come forward on your Web site. When you place dark colors next to light ones, the contrasts will give the effect of dimension on your pages.

"Our eyes are always trying to look for something that's different," Adam says. "If everything is the same size and color, the page flattens out. One color item needs to be bigger and bolder for the eyes to focus on."

If you are using a colored background, compensate for readability by making your type larger. Color also can be used as punctuation in a page, pulling the eyes through the page, Adam says. An example is *The New York Times* site, where red bullets next to the section labels are used to draw you through the page.

The use of gray on a Web site or a printed page is neutral. Gray is equal proportions of red, yellow and blue. If you go to the color wheel or color bars on your Web editor and move your arrow to the middle until you get 50 percent for each of the three color bars (red, green, blue), you will produce gray. But if you put gray against a background of blue or yellow or red, it will appear to be different shades of gray even if it is not. The shade of gray will change according to the color that surrounds it, Adam explains. Other colors also shift depending on the colors around them.

BROWSER-SAFE COLORS

Web designers advise using "browser-safe" colors. Netscape and Microsoft Internet Explorer feature 216 colors that are "safe," meaning they will show up on your Web site in the same hues that you created them. If you use colors in the Netscape Communicator cube, you will get safe colors. When you create a new color combination, the browser tries to adjust by "dithering," meaning it creates the color to the closest match it can. But that may not show up as the exact color you intended. Dithering also makes your files larger, taking longer to load. That's why designers say stick with colors that browsers can view accurately.

How do you know what those colors are? The expert in this area is Lynda Weinman, who created a chart of browser-safe colors that is widely used.

Weinman, author of several books on Web design, provides a chart of her color-safe palette on her Web site:
http://www.lynda.com/hex.html.

It may look confusing at first. Once you understand that all colors on a Web browser are mathematical combinations, you'll understand her chart. Weinman's palette offers the safe mathematical computations to create colors. If you want to make sure you are using safe colors, download or print Weinman's palette and check it against the color combinations you are creating. She gives permission for you to copy it freely. While you are in her site, check the test pages to see what a difference browser-safe colors make:
http://www.lynda.com/dwg/flatdither.html.

For example, the hue of a bright blue is a combination of Red:000, Green:000, and Blue:255 in Weinman's palette. Now try it. Open a blank page in Netscape Composer. Pull down the Format menu to "Page Properties," and click on a background or other color. Then click on "Other" to open custom colors in your color wheel so you can see the mathematical formulas.

If you can't get the safe color by moving your palette arrow in Windows or bars in Macintosh, type in the combinations under "Red," "Green" and "Blue." On Macintosh, you'll need to use the color wheel and type or adjust to "Blue 255" to get this hue. Windows offers more choices. But you should also be aware of these colors if you are creating a graphic in Photoshop or other graphic program.

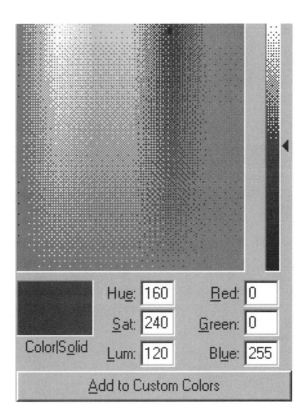

LAYOUT

The same principle of contrast is needed in laying out your Web pages. You need a dominant element for the eyes to focus on as a point of entry, whether it is a graphic or a headline. Mario Garcia says that in focus groups he has conducted, most people scan a Web site first from top to bottom and then from left to right.

Just as in newspaper designs, Web designers suggest that the most important information be placed in the first screen if you plan to have a page that scrolls. Then you can place your information in grids or tables. The number of columns, often from two to four, depends on your content.

A very common design for an online newspaper involves a navigation table or border on the top or side of your screen. You also can place your navigation links at the bottom if you have a top navigation bar, as *The New York Times* does. The important concept is to make sure you have navigation links in the same place from one page to another so the user doesn't get confused.

Here are some calculations that will help you design your Web site:

* In newspapers or magazines, column width is measured in picas. On a Web site, space is measured in pixels, the number of dots on the screen that make up images and text. Ten pixels equal one pica.

* The most common size monitor is 640 pixels wide by 480 long. Most designers plan their pages not to exceed that width so the text won't scroll horizontally off the screen. The tables you design for one page should total 640 pixels in width.

* The average newspaper column is 12 picas wide. That's 120 pixels. A rule of thumb is that a column of print type should not exceed 20 or 22 picas because it is hard to read. Eye movements become difficult going far to the right and back to the left. But many Web sites allow their text to run the full width of the screen. If you convert 640 pixels to picas, that would mean you are asking readers to read the equivalent of a newspaper column that is 64 picas wide! That's three times the recommended width.

* Limit your text to 350 pixels in a table for readability. Plan your other tables and elements accordingly to total the 640 pixels for a screen. Even though Web editors also allow you to measure tables in percentages, pixels will give you a more accurate measurement and more control. Just set the width of tables; you don't need to set the height in most cases.

* Limit your graphics to less than 20 KB (kilobytes), according to Mario Garcia, so they will not take too long to load. You can check the size of your graphics by calling up your directory in your computer. All files should be listed by name, size, type and date.

* Make sure you have created your images as gifs or jpegs with a program such as Photoshop or Graphic Image Converter. If you take your images from a copyright-free Web site, they will be in either format automatically. Also make sure you have labeled your images with a *.gif* or *.jpeg* suffix (that's a dot before *gif* or *jpeg*). But don't just label images if they haven't been created in those formats, because they will not show up on the Web.

* The average screen resolution is 72 pixels per inch, lower than the resolution of 1,200 to 3,000 dots per inch for printed materials.

CLICKING VS. SCROLLING

Should you create a page that requires the user to scroll, or should you chunk the information into several pages so the readers click? The results of many studies are mixed. But most studies say Web users are scanners, not readers (see Chapter 13). The Web designers interviewed in this chapter recommend that your home page should be limited to one screen. But once readers get into a story they want to read, if the content interests them, they will scroll. How far will they scroll? That's hard to measure.

Jakob Nielsen, a distinguished engineer at Sun Microsystems, conducts readability studies, and he says only 10 percent of users scroll beyond information visible on a screen when a page loads. He says that's why all critical content and navigation should be at the top of the page (or visible on the side) in the first screen. He also says if it takes longer than 10 seconds for your page to load, users lose interest.

Clearly, shorter is better on the Web. But if the site demands a long text on one screen, consider subheads and internal links so the readers can still scan or quickly get to the subhead topics of interest to them. This issue is discussed more completely in Chapter 13.

Here are some points to remember:

Checklist

* Is your navigation clear and consistent on every page in your Web site? Do you have links back to the home page and to other pages within your site?

* Have you used text links or buttons with text to help users navigate rather than icons or obscure buttons for navigation links?

* Does your typeface contrast strongly with your background?

* Have you limited your typefaces to two fonts?

* Does every page in your site have a logo or a brand identification with your site?

* Does your site have a theme that gives it unity?

* Does your page layout have a focal point on the page as a point of entry for users' eyes?

* Have you used browser-safe colors?

* Do your colors reflect the mood and content of your site?

* Does your home page convey an impression of your content and site in 20 seconds?

* Is your content strong enough to make people want to use your site?

* Have you included an address and phone number on your Web site in addition to e-mail, possibly on an "About Us" page, so visitors to your site can contact you by phone or regular mail?

* Have you avoided underlining words or highlighting them in a different color for emphasis so that users don't get confused and think they are links?

* Have your tested your site on users, especially friends or other people who are not sophisticated Web surfers?

Safaris

http://www.mhhe.com/socscience/comm/
rich/ch11/

11–1   **Site Design
Analysis**

Conduct a comparative study of designs of online sites in your field. For newspapers, broadcast sites and magazines, start with the *American Journalism Review* site (*www.ajr.org*) and click on newspapers or magazines. Check sites in different parts of the United States and in different countries for comparisons. Access at least a dozen or more sites and evaluate their designs on the following criteria:

* Do you get a first impression in 20 seconds that reveals what the site is about?
* Does the site have a theme that gives it unity?
* Does the design reflect the location of the media organization if that is relevant?
* Is the design appropriate for the type of content?
* Do the colors match the mood and purpose of the site?
* Are the colors consistent or coordinated throughout the site?
* Is the navigation throughout the site easy to use?
* Does the site download quickly?
* Is the layout of the site clear or cluttered?
* Is the contrast of typeface and background strong enough so the text is easy to read?
* Are the typefaces limited to one or two fonts or is there a mixture of too many typefaces?
* Is anything distinctive about the design of the site or does it resemble many others?

11–2   **Color Safari**

On a piece of scrap paper, write your instant response to the following questions:

  a. What color would you use to describe yourself?
  b. Write a color to describe the following moods: happy, sad, excited, bored, stressed.

c. What color combinations would you use on a Web site for the seasons: summer, winter, autumn, spring?

d. Take the complementary color test based on an exercise created by Pegie Stark Adam of The Poynter Institute: Click into our Web site for this chapter and call up the red screen. Stare at it for a full minute, blinking as little as possible. Then close your eyes very tightly. What color do you see? If you have looked at the red site long enough, you should see the opposite color of the color wheel: blue or purple. This is your body's physiological attempt to create balance.

e. Check out how gray takes on the colors that surround it on our Web site safari for this chapter.

11–3 **Graphic Resources**

Click into our Web site for this chapter for a variety of graphic resources and tools.

11–4 **Design Your Own Site**

If you started creating a Web site based on information in Chapter 9, now you can finish designing it. Create your hierarchy or storyboard of Web pages to design the structure of your site. Decide whether you will use a navigation bar at the top, along the side, or bars at the top and bottom.

Part 3

Applying Journalism Skills

Chapter *12*

ONLINE
REPORTING
AND RESEARCH

Goals

* To learn trends in online reporting.

* To understand how databases, timeliness and competition affect online reporting.

* To learn about inaccuracy in online sources.

* To learn the merits and disadvantages of e-mail reporting.

* To learn how to attribute online sources.

* To gain tips for online reporting.

Hyperleap

Leap to the Reporting Safari at the end of the chapter or online if you want to check your knowledge before you read the chapter. You can also check the Virtual Media Source Book at our online site to acquire great resources for journalists.

Safaris:

http://www.mhhe.com/socscience/comm/ rich/ch12/

Source Book:

http://www.mhhe.com/socscience/comm/rich/ sourcebook.html/

Web sites

Internet *Chicago Tribune*:
> http://www.chicago.tribune.com

People-finding search engines:
> Four11: www.four11.com
> WhoWhere: www.whowhere.com
> Switchboard: www.switchboard.com

reporter.org:
> www.reporter.org/beat

DejaNews, a search engine for newsgroups:
> www.dejanews.com

Profnet:
> www.profnet.com

U.S. Census online:
> www.census.gov

Wolfgram Memorial Library:
> http://www.science.widener.edu/~withers/news.htm

Hundreds of other sources are listed in the Virtual Media Source Book in our online site for this chapter.
> http://www.mhhe.com/socscience/comm/rich/ch12/

Glossary at a Glance

These terms are also mentioned in previous chapters. A full glossary is in the appendix and on our Web site.

http://www.mhhe.com/socscience/comm/rich/glossary.html

USENET Online discussion groups open to anyone if the Internet service provider offers them.

FAQ Frequently asked questions.
LISTSERV Online discussion groups to which you subscribe.
LURK Read messages on a discussion group without posting or responding to messages.
NEWSGROUPS Public discussion groups in the Usenet category.
NETIQUETTE Good manners for communicating in e-mail and discussion groups.
PHOTOBUBBLE A 360-degree angle picture taken by a special camera that can scan a site and patch two 180-degree shots for a full view.

Malia Zoghlin

When Malia Zoghlin went to Hong Kong as an online reporter for the Internet *Chicago Tribune,* she carried a lot of weight on her shoulders—a video camera, a special photobubble camera, a regular camera and a tape recorder. To add to all that equipment, she carried a reporter's old-fashioned tools—a notebook and pencils. And she was carrying some additional weight.

"I was four months pregnant!" she said. "I had a backpack and a shoulder bag. It was heavy. But the hardest thing was trying to decide which piece of equipment I was going to use for different parts of the story."

That is the kind of multimedia equipment Zoghlin and other online reporters use these days when they produce stories for the Internet *Chicago Tribune.* Although other online media sites are adding staff members who report exclusively for their Internet editions, the *Tribune* was one of the first Web newspapers to have its own reporting staff. In most cases, newspapers use reporters' stories from the print editions or reporters write for both print and online editions.

Zoghlin expected to go to Asia to help another *Tribune* reporter cover a story about the mood of Hong Kong a month before the nation was to change from British to Chinese rule. When she arrived, she discovered that her colleague had been called back to Beijing and she was on her own.

The other difficulty she faced was making sure she had all the video, pictures and taped interviews for the package before she returned to Chicago. "I needed to be sure I had every last thing," she said. "There would be no second chance. I needed to check my tape. I needed to educate people I was talking to about how this was going to be used. That was hard when you're dealing with people who have never seen this equipment."

Although Zoghlin does reporting for the online *Tribune,* she also produces stories—her own and those reported by other staff members. Production of a Web package includes planning and writing the story, converting it to HTML, adding the photos, video and audio clips and designing the story sites.

Coming from a background as a broadcast reporter for a public television station in Hawaii, Zoghlin was comfortable handling a video camera and a tape recorder. The photobubble camera is a new addition to her repertoire. It is a special camera that takes 360-degree angle pictures, giving viewers the feeling of being at the scene. But she has reservations about one person doing it all well.

"I'm still of the belief that people have their strengths for certain things," she said. "Hopefully, you can hand the multimedia producing over to someone else."

NEED FOR MULTIMEDIA

Fortunately for her, she can turn for help to Paul J. Pustelnik, multimedia editor for the Internet *Chicago Tribune.* He believes multimedia elements will become essential to online reporting.

"It's becoming as though readers are expecting it," he said. "Online there are so many neat things other sites are introducing, you almost have to provide multimedia. We're giving our readers their own ability to see how they want to use a story. A lot of our e-mail shows that readers respond more to multimedia. Advertisers like seeing it, too. They want to sponsor something that is high tech."

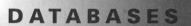

DATABASES

In addition to multimedia, databases are being used in online news sites so readers can search information that relates to their needs. For example, the Internet *Tribune* presented a database of homicide statistics from the Chicago Police Department in one of its packages. Reporters compiled statistics and wrote stories about neighborhoods with the highest crime rates. The *Tribune* added search engines and maps so users could check the crimes in their own neighborhoods.

The online joint Web site for *The Philadelphia Inquirer* and *Philadelphia Daily News* also uses databases extensively for news packages, including a similar homicide package that allows people to search the crimes in their neighborhoods.

These types of Web packages are changing the way reporters need to gather information. Because very few newspapers have separate online reporting staffs, the job of gathering information for a print and online product increasingly will fall to the print reporters. Because Web sites have no space limitations, print reporters are expected to gather more information such as databases and full-text versions of speeches or complete lists of winners in local contests for science fairs or spelling bees.

As you will see in the chapter on storytelling, Web users want stories in layers. That means you need to gather much more information than a print product would use. Some people may want to read only headlines and briefs, while other Web users want the full text or a searchable database.

TIMELINESS

Online media deadlines are changing the scope of reporting. The practice of producing a story for one edition of a newspaper or two news broadcasts a day is giving way to continual news coverage. Several sites, such as MSNBC and CNN, call themselves a 24-by-7 operation, meaning they break news stories 24 hours a day, seven days a week.

"People who go online expect news to be current," says Andy Beers, executive director of news at MSNBC, a Web site that is a joint venture of Microsoft Corporation and NBC. "You have to produce constantly updated information, in some cases sooner and in ways that are very different from television. In television you have to wait to find what you want. If you go to the Internet, you can find what you want when you want it. That's the basic premise of online."

But that premise places a burden on reporters to find updated information and new angles to their stories. It also requires reporters to gather background that might be presented as timelines in a person's life or sequences of an event and other information that might offer more understanding of a story.

Although Web producers may provide links and interactive questions for a reporter's story, as online products continue to grow, the roles of a reporter may continue to grow as well. At a small operation, many of the reporting, writing and researching duties may be the responsibility of a reporter. At a major news site like CNN, these responsibilities are divided among many people.

ANATOMY OF A CNN STORY

Jeff Garrard, executive producer of CNN Interactive, says the demands of a current news site require teamwork. Most CNN stories are produced by a writer, producer and multimedia specialist. "Our first order of business is to be a multimedia news site," Garrard says. "We work on a tripod basis of technology, editorial and design."

As executive producer, Garrard oversees daily operations in the newsroom of 60 staff members who produce the CNN Interactive site. As many as 10 people can be involved before the story is posted online. CNN Interactive has three shifts of writers and editors, called *producers,* every day to create online stories.

* The producer searches through CNN's database of network news and consults with a senior producer to plan the day's news coverage in order of importance. The stories then are listed on an old-fashioned white board, like a chalkboard. "A white board never crashes," Garrard quips. Each person involved in creating the story puts a check on the white board when his or her role is completed.

* A writer and associate producer are assigned to each story. The writer sifts through wires and video feeds and writes the story. The associate producer finds the multimedia elements, creates the audio and video elements and consults with a multimedia designer.

* A Web editor scours the Internet for appropriate links.

* An editorial assistant searches through Lexis–Nexis for further background information.

* A copy editor checks the story for style, spelling and accuracy.

* The associate producer then lays out the page on paper.

* A Web editor takes the story and codes it in HTML for the Web.

* A producer and senior producer check the story for accuracy.

* A Webmaster double checks the story to make sure it works in different browsers.

* If a story includes feedback from readers, an online coordinator gathers the feedback.

This process takes place on hundreds of stories throughout the day as the site is constantly updated to be competitive in the world of online news.

COMPETITION

When newspapers began producing online versions, many editors became concerned that breaking a story online would compete with their print editions and deter readers from buying the newspaper.

The Dallas Morning News changed that. A month before the trial was to begin in 1997 for Timothy McVeigh, the newspaper published a story in its online version saying McVeigh had confessed to his lawyer that he had bombed the federal building in Oklahoma City where 168 people were killed in 1995. The story was published online seven hours before the newspaper's print edition could appear. When the online newspaper published this confession, the issue of breaking the story online garnered more attention than the ethical concerns about publishing a confession that could affect the jury selection and might violate lawyer-client confidentiality. McVeigh later was convicted of murder and conspiracy and sentenced to death.

Editors for *The Dallas Morning News* said the Web site gave the newspaper a chance to be immediate. It also gave the paper a chance to publish the story before McVeigh's lawyers could get a court order preventing publication, a concern the newspaper's editors had. But it had a profound impact on the media, marking a turning point when a newspaper used its online site to break news before the print cycle.

The Newspaper Association of America gave *The Dallas Morning News* an award for excellence in recognition of its online accomplishment. When he accepted the award, the newspaper's editor, Ralph Langer, said that the newspaper couldn't scoop itself. The online paper was as much of a core product as the print, he said. He also stressed that the Web site gave the newspaper a chance to be immediate, just as CNN is in breaking major news stories.

A few months later when McVeigh was convicted by the jury, almost every major newspaper and broadcast Web site published the verdict online immediately with no concerns about waiting for print publications or regular broadcast news shows.

The urgency to be timely online was so great that ABC News even declared McVeigh guilty an hour before the jury did. The online broadcast site had prepared the news story in advance, but mistakenly revealed it too early and apologized 30 minutes later.

Still the message was clear. Online news had come of age. Timeliness had overridden competition with media's print or regular broadcast counterparts.

INACCURACY

A rush to publish online isn't the only cause of inaccuracy, however. How can you trust the information you get from the Internet? The Web is full of inaccurate information because anyone can post messages to newsgroups and forward e-mail messages around the world. Online newspapers, magazines and broadcast sites claim their information can be trusted because they conform to the journalistic standard of accuracy, and they have established a reputation for credibility in their traditional media counterparts.

Reporters must filter through much faulty information while they are gathering the news. For example, a highly creative "graduation speech" that author Kurt Vonnegut supposedly delivered at MIT was forwarded by e-mail around the world. The author claimed most graduation speeches are filled with unreliable advice but the advice to "wear sunscreen" was proven to be beneficial by scientists. The author further advised graduates to sing, floss, and "don't worry about the future."

But Vonnegut didn't deliver the speech. Nor did he write it. Mary Schmich did. She's a columnist for the *Chicago Tribune*. She had written it in a column as a spoof on graduation speeches. In a subsequent column she explained how she tried to track down the source of the e-mail hoax but gave up when she realized that tracking the origin of a message through cyberspace was like finding the origin of every star in the sky.

You never can tell what will happen to an e-mail message. Nor can you always tell who is a valid source for material on the Internet. The journalistic value of checking your sources is just as important with information from the Internet as it is in reporting for traditional media.

QUOTING FROM NEWSGROUPS OR E-MAIL

Many people post information on newsgroups that is useful to reporters in compiling a news story. Even if you know the person by reputation or familiarity in a newsgroup, should you use his or her comments in a news story?

You may have the legal right to use information posted in a public forum, and even that is uncertain, as you will see in the chapter on legal and ethical issues. More certain is the ethical responsibility you have to notify the person that you want to use the comments. The same holds true for e-mail messages you receive.

When someone posts a message to a newsgroup or sends you an e-mail message, the intent is for discussion or personal communication, not for publication. You should contact the person by e-mail, phone or letter requesting permission to use the comments for publication. In many cases people don't even use their real names in newsgroups. Quoting people with pseudonyms is worse than using an anonymous source. In this case the source is as anonymous to the reporter as to the audience.

E-MAIL AS A REPORTING TOOL

E-mail and newsgroups can be effective reporting tools. The Online-News listserv discussion group, which has a membership of thousands of journalists and experts in online media, often receives messages requesting information for columns, research or news stories its members are writing. This is an instant way of gathering information from sources you might never even consider. Even if you just read messages in a journalism-related newsgroup, you can identify sources you want to contact personally.

But discussion groups can be abused by students, a fact that many professionals on these listservs resent. Jay Black, a renowned ethics professor at the University of South Florida, says he receives scores of e-mail requests from students who want him to provide information for their ethics term papers. He says it would take all his time just to answer their requests.

Despite their usefulness, e-mail and discussion groups are not a substitute for traditional interviewing methods. Almost all the interviews for this book were conducted in face-to-face reporting or by telephone. However, the author set up the interviews by e-mail correspondence with the sources. In one case, when the author sent a list of 10 questions to a source for an e-mail interview, the source responded by asking her to call him. The lesson is this: If you are going to gather information by e-mail, limit your questions—preferably to one or two.

The greatest advantage of e-mail is that you can contact people easily when they are not available by phone. They may not check their e-mail regularly, but if they do, the chances of getting a response are very good. When you create an address book of sources, you should always ask for e-mail addresses and regular mail addresses. Ask your sources to respond to your messages with their full name, title and phone number. Sign your full name, affiliation, and give your telephone number at the end of your e-mail message. Your return e-mail automatically is inserted, but it doesn't hurt to add that to your signature.

The greatest disadvantage of e-mail reporting is the lack of spontaneity for follow-up questions, which often yield the best information. Another disadvantage is the inability to observe your source in action. If you want to write a story with any descriptive color and flair, you won't be able to describe your source or the setting just by reading words from an e-mail or discussion group message. Cyber-reporting has limitations.

ATTRIBUTION AND PERMISSIONS

When you obtain information from a discussion group or Web site, get the exact name of the site, just as you would if you were interviewing a source in person or by telephone. In this case, the Web site is your source. Cite it by its name and URL. Do not say, "according to the Internet." That's like saying, "according to information in the world."

Check sites for copyright information. Do not take quotes, graphics or other information from copyrighted Web sites without seeking permission. In addition, don't forward copyrighted cartoons and news articles via e-mail to friends on the Web. That's still a violation of copyright. However, you may cite URLs in messages and your stories.

RESEARCH

The research you can do online is staggering. The U.S. federal government maintains almost 5,000 Web sites with access to federal documents, e-mail accounts of employees and job sites. Almost every town and city in the United States is gaining a presence on the Web, and information from scores of international sites also is becoming more prevalent. The type of information you can get ranges from directories to find people to documents.

For example:

* You're trying to contact a source but you don't have his or her e-mail address or phone number. Try people search finders, such as Four11, **http://www.four11.com;** WhoWhere, **http://www.whowhere.com;** Switchboard, **http://www.switchboard.com;** or any directories on search engines.

* You want some ideas and sources for a beat; you can find scores of them on reporter.org, **http://www.reporter.org/beat.**

* You want to search Usenet newsgroups for any messages on a topic you are researching: Try DejaNews, **http://www.dejanews.com.** See Chapter 5 for more information about newsgroups.

* You're looking for an expert, such as a college professor, to comment on a story you are writing. Profnet is an organization of more than 4,000 public information officers who will find you an expert, usually from a university, who will contact you in a day or two via **http://www.profnet.com.**

* You want the demographic data for a marketing project you are doing in an advertising class or campaign. Check the U.S. Census online for a searchable database that will give you instant information at **http://www.census.gov.**

These are just a handful of sources you can use to find information for news stories or anything else you are interested in learning. You'll find hundreds more in our online site under the Virtual Media Source Book and when you take the Reporting Safari at the end of the chapter.

THREE RESEARCH/ REPORTING STEPS

Nora M. Paul, director of the library at The Poynter Institute of Media Research, is an authority on computer-assisted reporting and online research. She suggests going through these steps before you do your reporting for an online story.

1 Think through story angles:

* Who is involved or affected by the story?

* Who in the story might need to be profiled?

* What terms need to be defined?

* What recent background needs to be explained?

* When will the next phase of this story occur?

* How can readers help or get help?

2 Focus your research needs:

* Who would know about this topic?

* What kind of link are you seeking?

* What is the best source for this type of link?

3 Evaluate resources:

* Who put the site together?

* Who was the site designed for?

* When was the information last updated?

* Where did the information come from?

* Why is this link going to help?

* How many links do you need?

* How will readers use this information?

REPORTING TIPS

* **Don't trust technology.** Print out your notes. Computers crash.

* **Print out information from Web sites.** Web sites change daily, and information you retrieved from a Web page can disappear, especially in online newspaper sites.

* **Plan ahead.** Research on the Internet can be time-consuming, and e-mail requests may not be answered in time for your deadline.

* **Use the Internet as a starting point, not a stopping point.** Check the Internet for Web sites of organizations in your community or elsewhere before you start reporting. You may find sources and information that can lead to good reporting questions for follow-up interviews by telephone or in person. Old-fashioned reporting is still in vogue, and it's very effective.

* **Get e-mail addresses of your sources.** Build an address book of contacts: full names and titles of sources, phone numbers, mail addresses and e-mail addresses.

* **Identify yourself and your sources in e-mail.** Make sure you sign your name and give your affiliation and your phone number at the end of your e-mail address so your source knows how to respond to you. You should create a signature file in your e-mail program that will insert this information automatically.

* **Limit questions in e-mail interviews.** Sources do not respond well to long lists of questions or surveys. E-mail interviews work best with one or two questions.

* **Check all information from the Internet for accuracy.**

* **Save bookmarks on a disk.** Build a bookmark file of useful sites, but save them on a floppy disk. Better yet, save them on two floppy disks in case one gets damaged. Internet servers can experience problems that cause data losses. Organize your bookmarks in folders. (See Chapter 3 for instructions.)

* **Take a tape recorder and disks to interviews and events.** Robin Palley, Web editor for the online *Philadelphia Inquirer* and *Philadelphia Daily News,* says reporters should always think about offering more information online. She suggests that reporters ask if databases are available on disk or if they can get the full text of a speech, the complete list of contest winners,

and other information that would not fit in a print newspaper. Taped comments may provide audio sound bites for online delivery.

✱ **Check posting dates on Web sites if they are available.** Information you retrieve may be outdated.

✱ **Use several search engines.** If you don't find the information you want in one search engine, check a few others.

✱ **Don't plagiarize.** Attribute any information you take from a Web site or discussion group. Almost all information posted on the Web is protected by U.S. copyright laws, especially if you are taking it from an online publication. Copying information from an online source without attribution is the same as plagiarizing from a print source.

✱ **Don't cite e-mail messages without permission.** E-mail correspondence usually is private and not meant for publication without the sender's knowledge.

✱ **Use discussion groups to gain ideas, not facts.** Don't trust anonymous messages from discussion groups. If you want to quote a message from a discussion group in a story, ask the person's permission. That's the ethical approach. Check it out for factual accuracy. Everyone is an author on the Internet, but not everyone has the journalistic commitment to accuracy.

✱ **Cite your online sources.** Attribute your information from a Web site by the name of author (if available), the site, and the URL. (See Chapter 13 or the Style Guide in the Appendix for citation styles in research papers.)

✱ **Think ahead.** Online news needs constant updating. When you cover a story, consider the next step and the information that will need to be updated.

Before you use information from a Web page, you should consider if the information on the site is credible and accurate. The Wolfgram Memorial Library of Widener University in Chester, Pa., has produced a checklist of questions to ask about the Web Page. You can link to it on our Web site for this chapter or access it at **http://www.science.widener.edu/~withers/ news.htm.** Here are some highlights.

✳ **Authority:** Is it clear who is sponsoring the page? Is a phone number or postal address offered so you can verify the site?

✳ **Accuracy:** Are sources of factual information clearly listed?

✳ **Objectivity:** Is the informational content clearly separated from advertising and opinion?

✳ **Currency:** Is there a date or time to show when the page was last updated?

✳ **Coverage:** Is the Web coverage more extensive than the print coverage if this is a newspaper site?

http://www.mhhe.com/socscience/comm/ rich/ch12/

12–1	**Virtual Media Source Book**	Create a source book of Web sites you want to keep in your files, much like you would an address book or a desk Rolodex file. Check the Virtual Media Source Book on our Web site to get started; then add your own favorite resources. You can bookmark the sites you like and then save your bookmarks to a disk or file in your computer. For directions, see Chapter 3.
12–2	**Reporting Safari**	Take this safari online at our Web site and click into the clues. Or you can take it by following this paper trail, but you'll have to do the hard work of finding the sources.

1 You are writing a story about how much debt college students incur for their education. You want some national statistics. Clue: Find The National Center for Educational Statistics and check the FAQ (frequently asked questions). Check out other sites in Fedstats to learn how many federal statistics you can get.

2 You are having trouble getting information from a source, and you want to check out your rights granted under the Freedom of Information Act. Clues: Check the Freedom of Information Center (FOI) at the University of Missouri or the FOI Center maintained by the Society of Professional Journalists.

3 You are writing a story about sexually transmitted diseases, particularly the growth of herpes among college students. You want a good medical definition and some statistics about the disease and incidence among age groups. Clues: A lot of bad medical information is on the Web. But you can trust information from the New England Journal of Medicine. You'll find it on Medline, the National Library of Medicine, which has 9 million medical documents. For excellent medical information on sexually transmitted diseases and other subjects, also check the U.S. government's National Institutes of Health and the Centers for Disease Control, which also have statistical information.

4 You are working on a story about growth in your community and you want to get population statistics from the last U.S. Census. Advertising majors looking for marketing information also can use this site for all sorts of demographic data. Clue: Go to the U.S. Census Bureau site, type in the name of your town and get the statistics you want.

5 It's election time in your state, and you want to know how much money candidates for Congress from your state spent. You also need related information about government in your state. Clue: You can find campaign contributions and much more at the Federal Election Commission site. American University's campaign finance site will give you information on candidates for office in your state. For all other kinds of government information for your state, check out Yahoo!'s state government directory.

6 You are studying media law, and you have to learn about the Supreme Court decision on the Communications Decency Act. Clue: Find the opinion and all sorts of legal resources at Findlaw.

7 The weather has changed drastically, and your editor wants a weather story. You decide it would be interesting to contrast your weather with the temperature in Fairbanks, Alaska, and in Hawaii. You also need a forecast for your city. Clue: You'll find forecast for your local area, state, national and international weather at The Weather Channel or CNN's weather site.

8 You are working on a story about campus crime, and you want to compare statistics for your college or university with others. Clues: You can start your search at the Security on Campus Inc. site. You'll find all sorts of information about college crime. If you don't find what you want there, head over to the Academic Crime Statistics Link guide and a related National Crime Statistics Link Guide, all of which you'll want to bookmark if you're on a police beat.

9 While you were in the campus crime sites, you noticed some interesting stories and statistics about binge drinking on campuses. You've decided to do a story about the subject, and you would like to contact a professor or medical expert in this field. Clue: Contact Profnet, a network of public information officers who will find you an expert at www.profnet.com.

10 You've got a project and you're not sure what resources you will need. But no journalist should pass up the chance to visit the Library of Congress, especially when you don't have to go to Washington to do it. Check out resources for Latin American studies, blind and disabled people, and access historical or other documents. Enjoy your visit to the Library of Congress. Clue: Search for the Library of Congress, and while you're there, you should bookmark the Thomas Web site just in case you ever need some legislative information about bills or historical documents.

11 Bonus search: A plane has crashed in your community, and you want to know more about the accident and incident record for this type of aircraft. Clues: This search may take you a little more time, but the Federal Aviation Administration will give you access to its database of aviation safety data. You can speed up your search if you know the type of aircraft, the carrier and the airport where the incident occurred. If you want to see how many other air safety incidents occurred in a particular area, just type in the city.

12–3 People Safari

This is a repeat from Chapter 3 in case you skipped that chapter.

Search for your e-mail address or your residential address and phone number using any of the following people-finder Web searchers. If you don't find yourself with one of these search directories, try another.

* Bigfoot: **www.bigfoot.com**
* WhoWhere: **www.whowhere.com**
* Four11: **www.four11.com**
* Switchboard: **www.switchboard.com**

12–4 Deadline Web Reporting Weather Disaster

You have a class period of two or three hours or two class sessions to do this assignment, depending on your instructor's preferences and the length of your class periods. It is best to work in teams of two or three people if you are on deadline. Although this assignment can be done as homework, it is more fun to do it under deadline pressure.

Tasks: Assemble research for a breaking news story about a weather disaster. You choose whether you will report about a flood, earthquake, hurricane, natural fires or other weather-related news story. Choose the type of disaster that might occur in your area.

Although the main purpose of this story is for reporting and research on the Internet, if you are familiar with a Web editor at this point in the course, create a news page online.

Gather all the research you will use on your news page for your weather story. Then write a brief story or introduction of about five or six paragraphs to a story for your Web site if you are creating one.

Suggestions: Your research should include links to:

* related weather resources.
* national weather centers devoted to your type of disaster.
* rescue agencies.
* possibly timelines and history of previous weather disasters of this type.
* agencies or organizations in your state that offer help.
* a good site for constantly updated weather news.
* online visuals (maps, photographs, graphics).
  Check attribution and copyright restrictions. If you don't publish these sites on the Web, copyright permission won't be an issue, but you should attribute your sources in any case.
* Check our Web site for some links. The URL is listed under Safari.

12–5	**Be a Virtual Reporter**	Have some fun. Create a story as a virtual reporter. Tampa Bay Online, the Internet product of the *Tampa Tribune,* makes it easy and fun. Select your beat and start creating your story: Access the site directly from our Web page or from the online newspaper. Virtual Reporter: **http://tampabayonline.net/interact/reporter/home.htm**
12–6	**Test Your Editorial Judgment**	Test your news judgment against producers at CNN. What stories would you choose to put on the CNN site, and which ones would you feature prominently? Play the game, "You be the Producer!" on the CNN Web site. You can click directly to it from our Web safaris page for this chapter or from the following address. You be the Producer!: **http://www.cnn.com/EVENTS/1996/anniversary/how.things. work/producer.game/index.html**

Chapter 13

WRITING FOR
THE WEB

Goals

* To learn how to use layers.

* To learn the difference between linear and nonlinear writing.

* To study the affect of clicking vs. scrolling on writing.

* To learn about inverted pyramid and narrative structures.

* To learn how people read online.

* To learn how to write enticing teasers.

* To learn a process for writing online.

* To learn tips for writing online.

This chapter is written in nonlinear form as it might be presented on a Web site. Each section is related to the main topic of online writing but could be read as a separate chunk. On a Web site you could link to any of the subtopics. In this print version, you could take a hyperleap to the sections on these pages.

Hyperleap

MSNBC:
> http://www.msnbc.com

Jakob Nielsen's Alertbox column about how people read online:
> http://www.useit.com/alertbox/9703b.html

Home page for Janet Murray, MIT professor of nonlinear and interactive narrative writing:
> http://web.mit.edu/jhmurray/www/

MIT's News in the Future Consortium:
> http://nif.www.media.mit.edu/abs.html

Michele Evard's MIT experiment on how children view news:
> http://mevard.www.media.mit.edu/people/mevard/papers/what-is-news.html

Electronic citation stylebook by Nancy Crane and Xia Lu:
> http://www.uvm.edu/~ncrane/estyles

MLA Style Citations of Electronic Sources:
> http://www.mla.org/set_stl.htm

A full glossary is in the appendix and on our Web site.

http://www.mhhe.com/socscience/comm/rich/glossary.html

LEXIAS Chunks of information presented in separate, self-contained units of a nonlinear story. They are like small chapters of a larger work.

LINEAR Information offered in a preordained sequential order such as a newspaper story printed in lines of text from beginning to end or a television news broadcast.

NODES Another term for separate chunks or self-contained pieces of a nonlinear story.

NONLINEAR Information that can be read or viewed in any order such as hyperlinks on a Web document.

NUT GRAPH A paragraph in a news story that gives the main idea of the story.

REPURPOSING Reusing information online from another medium such as print. It is essentially the same information used for a different purpose—online distribution.

SHOVELWARE A pejorative term for dumping information online without changing the format or content. A newspaper story presented online exactly as it appeared in print is called *shovelware,* similar to "repurposing."

Andy Beers

MSNBC

When Andy Beers reflects about the first year of MSNBC, he considers how online storytelling has changed.

"I think if I were going to pick the biggest mistake we made, we spent too much time putting text on screen," says Beers, executive producer of MSNBC news. "We spent too much time trying to reinvent the newspaper online. What you are starting to see more is the evolution of the medium as a unique way of telling a story. There is a unique way of allowing people to control information. This is what is really changing."

With such rapid changes in online media, how should journalists write for this evolving form of delivering information? Leaders in online media are wrestling with ways of structuring stories and the effect of clicking or scrolling on writing for the Web. But most of them agree that journalists must rethink the way they present stories online and that they must write in layers.

"Layering information is the idea that people want to be able to find different links or different levels of information on a particular story," Beers says. "When you start to get into layers, you end up with an overwhelming amount of information. People don't have a lot more time, but they do have particular interests. They want to have available a very short take on the news, but they want to scroll down on stories they are interested in. This creates a very different way of how we write the stories."

Almost all media sites structure their stories in layers that feature a headline, an abstract of one or two lines to summarize the story, the full story, and links to related resources or other parts of the package. MSNBC, CNN, *USA Today,* and several other online news sites also offer a brief version of the story—a few paragraphs summarizing the story for people who don't want to read the full version. Online media sites increasingly are offering video, audio and other multimedia elements as parts of their layers.

MSNBC layers its stories with a headline, an abstract and a lead in larger type with a link to the full story below as in this story by the site's columnist Joan Connell:

> **Headline layer:** On the Internet plagiarism is easy
> **Summary layer:** Online world tempts scholar wannabes with papers, essays and 'research'
> **Lead layer in larger type:** Term papers are finding their way on the Internet mill, prompting states to pass strict laws to prevent academic material from being sold or shared on the Net.
>
> Complete story ▼

The downward arrow offers you a quick click to the full story below the first screen on the same Web page. Links to other stories and multimedia elements usually are featured on the side of the page.

Writing these layers to entice readers is no easy task. Web managers say they need journalists with skills of writing intriguing headlines and summaries that will make people click into the stories. While those skills aren't limited to online media, they are crucial to creating readable Web sites because readers have more choices online than in a newspaper or magazine.

To that end, MSNBC has hired hundreds of journalists to work at its 286-acre campus in Redmond, Wash., where 22,000 employees produce other products for Microsoft Corp. MSNBC is a joint venture of Microsoft, NBC-TV and cable CNBC, based in Fort Lee, N.J. To help produce the MSNBC Web site, which began in July 1996, the company hired 200 journalists.

Almost 80 percent of the writing staff comes from a print background, says Beers, who oversees the international and national news content. Many staff members had to learn how to use audio and video for the story presentation. Everyone is required to know a certain amount of HTML, he adds.

That type of multimedia training also is becoming more crucial for students in college journalism programs. Skills in one area, such as broadcast or print, no longer are enough for writing stories in the new medium.

Beers says software is changing the way we tell stories online because of the multimedia capabilities. Pictures, audio, video and text create different ways of telling a story, Beers says. Readers can enter a story in various places and ways; they can read it, hear sound clips or see portions on video.

"The lesson we have to learn is how to use the medium in a new way that really adds value," he says. "The reality of this medium is that it will not succeed unless there is something about it that helps people. Writing for the Web is an ongoing learning process. The reality is that at some level it is a guessing game.

"In the past almost all online newspaper articles were from wire services," he says. "We're starting to see more and more original journalism. That's a real change. I think when you look back at the last few years, you'll see that online news sites in many ways were starting to learn how to use the new medium."

SHOVELWARE

When newspapers first developed their online media sites, most of them used shovelware—the same content online as in the print newspaper. While many online newspapers still use the same content, also called *repurposing,* others are trying to get away from shovelware, which usually is referred to in a negative way.

Elizabeth Osder, content development editor for the online *New York Times,* defends shovelware. She says people who want the content of *The New York Times* want that same information online.

"All too often we forget the reader," she says. "A good site should be useful to people, and it should serve its audience. I don't think there is anything wrong with a Web site that is straight shovelware. It can be useful."

LINEAR VS. NONLINEAR

If a site uses shovelware, the stories most likely are going to be in linear form—information written in an order from beginning to end, like a straight line, as in newspaper and magazine stories. Linear form offers no choice in the way people can read the story except to reject or stop reading. A television broadcast also is linear; the viewer must receive it in the order it is given.

Nonlinear storytelling breaks the story into several parts, with links to other Web pages or multimedia elements, so readers may read the story in any order they choose. It is more akin to a package of stories with sidebars or a story broken into several chunks that are related but self-contained.

For example, if you choose to read this chapter in a nonlinear fashion, you could go to the beginning of the chapter under Hyperleap, where the topics in this chapter are listed. You then could skip to any of the sections and read that information instead of reading from beginning to end. If this chapter were on the Web, each subhead might be a link to a separate page containing a chunk of the story. The subheads also could be linked to topics (as they are in this chapter) within one story that you could scroll. But designing a story in chunks requires restructuring the way you write.

Leah Gentry, editorial director for the online *Los Angeles Times,* calls the Web a "user-driven experience" that lends itself to nonlinear storytelling. She says writers should "deconstruct" the story, taking it apart and figuring out how it could be told in pieces, then reconstruct the story from the point of view of storytelling.

"Divide your story into its component pieces," Gentry says. "Look for similarities and relationships between the pieces. Group those that are similar. Then reconstruct it. A storyboard is a good tool for reconstructing stories. The storyboard diagrams the relationships between the pieces. Mostly, I scribble on paper. It doesn't have to be fancy. It becomes a blueprint for your site, and a blueprint is a wonderful thing to have."

The same method of storyboarding that you used to plan your Web site pages in Chapter 9 will work in planning parts of a nonlinear story. For example, suppose you are covering a trial. In a linear presentation, you would write the whole story as one element with a lead, the action, comments from various people, and a conclusion. In a nonlinear presentation, you might write a short overview of the main news and break the testimony of different people into separate chunks, with links to background, history of the trial, a timeline, profiles and other elements related to the main topic.

The Chicago Tribune took that nonlinear approach in the coverage of the trial in Denver, Colo., of Timothy McVeigh, the man convicted of bombing the federal building in Oklahoma City, where 168 people died. After the verdict, the *Tribune* presented this story in nonlinear form with links to the following Web pages:

> THE TRIAL
> <u>McVeigh says death penalty unlikely to be overturned</u> (the main story of the day)
> On to <u>archived coverage</u>.
> TIMELINE
> <u>Photos, archive stories, and video detailing events leading up to the trial</u>.
> PLAYERS
> <u>Photos and biographies of the defendant, attorneys and judge</u>
> COURTHOUSE
> <u>A detailed look at the Denver federal courthouse and inside the revamped courtroom</u>.

Such nonlinear presentation with links is not unusual for major stories. More unusual is nonlinear structure of a single story divided into chunks. That approach is taken more frequently in fiction sites. HotWired uses this method of dividing columnist Jon Katz's stories into screen-size chunks, usually a few paragraphs totaling about 21 lines per screen. Each screen has a watermark number behind the text to let you know which screen you are reading. The column also is offered in a text-only scrollable version for printing out or reading plain text.

While most online newspaper sites are presenting stories with links to other Web pages in their own or other sites, CNN sometimes uses the nonlinear structure of internal links at the top of a story to take readers to sections within a scrollable story, as in this example:

> **Headline:** The Lemon Awards: Winners would rather lose
> **Links to topics within the story:** In this story:
>
> *　Sprint wins for 'free calls' ad
>
> *　Awards 'carry a serious message'
>
> **Lead:**
> WASHINGTON (CNN)—A coalition of consumer watchdog groups held an awards ceremony Thursday where the winners would rather lose.
> 　Statuettes, each holding aloft a single fresh lemon, were awarded for trying to sell products through "misleading, unfair and irresponsible" advertising campaigns.
> 　Nine of them were presented. Among the unlucky recipients were such companies as Sprint, Cadillac and R. J. Reynolds Tobacco Co.

CLICKING VS. SCROLLING

How much will readers scroll and how many screens will they click?

Nonlinear presentation of stories requires clicking links instead of scrolling through one long story. Although you can structure a story in chunks with links at the top connecting to sections within the story, as mentioned in the CNN illustration, more often nonlinear storytelling is offered with links to separate Web pages.

Which is preferable? Several studies favor clicking. But informal testing with students in an online journalism class proved inconclusive. About half of the 40 students said they preferred to scroll because they didn't want to wait for another Web page to download. Others said they preferred to click because they lost their place in a story when it scrolled to another screen.

Jakob Nielsen, distinguished engineer for Sun Microsystems, conducts studies on Web usability, including clicking vs. scrolling preferences. In his first studies in 1994, only 10 percent of Web users wanted to scroll pages, especially on home pages where links were not visible in the first screen. In subsequent studies three years later, he reported that users were more willing to scroll pages, a factor he attributed to consumers' increasing experience using the Web.

Other studies report similar findings. Almost all Web experts advocate clicking in favor of scrolling, but if users are truly interested in the content, they will scroll to read it. That doesn't mean you should write long stories that require scrolling through many screens, but it does indicate that a story that spans several screens is an acceptable, but not preferable, style of writing.

Clicking through several screens offers Web managers the economic advantages of providing advertisements on each new page. But technology poses problems for readers either way. If readers click, they have to wait for pages to download. On the other hand, resolution of type on computer monitors makes reading more difficult. Readability is 25 percent slower online, Nielsen says. Other eye movement studies say it is as much as 40 percent slower.

"As a result, people don't want to read a lot of text from computer screens: You should write 50 percent less text and not just 25 percent less, since it's not only a matter of reading speed but also a matter of feeling good," Nielsen writes in Alertbox, one of his bimonthly columns.

How do users read online? Nielsen's conclusion: "They don't." He says online readers scan. They rarely read Web pages word by word. In a 1997 study, Nielsen says 79 percent of the users in his tests scanned pages compared to 16 percent who read word for word. Although they may scroll a home page to seek links, they don't like to scroll long pages, he says. His studies show that users prefer text to be short and to the point.

He recommends structuring stories in nonlinear fashion with links to related topics called *nodes,* as suggested previously. He does not recommend taking one long linear-structured story and splitting it into multiple pages just to break up the type because that creates downloading problems and slows reading.

Another study Nielsen conducted with researcher John Morkes revealed these conclusions about the way readers want online information to be written:

* Write concise text, preferably on one screen.

* Use simple, straightforward language; avoid adjectives and marketing hype.

* Use summaries and inverted pyramid style.

INVERTED PYRAMID VS. NARRATIVE STYLE

The inverted pyramid, the most common newswriting style, gives the conclusion or main idea at the top of the story, and the rest of the story is supporting information presented in descending order of importance. Stories written in inverted pyramid style are ideal for readers who scan and want information quickly. But will users want to read the whole story if all the important information is in the first few paragraphs?

Probably not. An eye-tracking study by The Poynter Institute of Media Studies to test the way readers read print newspapers in early 1990s revealed that the majority of readers are scanners, and less than 12 percent of them read a story thoroughly. In a subsequent Poynter Institute study testing readers' preferences in story structures, the inverted pyramid structure did not fare well for readability to the end of the story. However, most online users are seeking information quickly instead of reading, so the inverted pyramid has much merit online if not much thorough readability.

As in any type of newswriting, the content should dictate the style. If you are writing a news story that lends itself to a direct lead such as breaking news, the inverted pyramid method may be preferable. If a story lends itself to a feature approach such as a profile, a storytelling approach can be used.

Here is an example of traditional inverted pyramid structure with the main idea in the lead from *The Spokesman Review* in Spokane, Wash.

> **Headline:** Upset motorist soaks driver with toxic spray
> **Summary:** Victim decontaminated, recovers; crews treating her also become ill
> **Lead:** A traffic argument Sunday escalated into what a firefighter called "road rage" when one driver soaked another with a burning, choking, toxic spray.
> Dawn Santos, 23, was rushed to Sacred Heart Medical Center's decontamination room. Two ambulance crew members and three nurses also had trouble breathing after being exposed to Santos. Everyone was treated and had recovered by Sunday evening.
> [The story continues telling how the incident occurred.]
> —Ward Sanderson

An inverted pyramid story can still have a creative lead as in this example, also from *The Spokesman Review:*

> **Headline:** WSU professor, police feuding
> **Summary:** Journalism class assignment leads to lawsuit, questions about open records
> **Lead:** It started innocently enough, as homework.
> But a routine assignment for a Washington State University journalism class has resulted in a professor feuding with the city police chief, an internal police investigation and a lawsuit.
> "Pullman police are already looked at negatively by most students, and after my visit, I can understand why," said Amber Ternan, who said she was treated rudely when she asked to see police records for her assignment.
> Ternan and 22 other students in David Demers' Beginning Reporting class were directed in September to visit the Pullman Police Department, read the daily log and use other department records to write a basic crime story.
> But students were told the records would not be available for five days.
> When they did get the records, the department withheld information on 31 incidents in the first week of October.
> [The story continues to explain the incident and the backup.]
> Last week, Demers filed a lawsuit in Whitman County Superior Court accusing the Pullman Police Department of withholding information on incidents such as drunken driving, automobile accidents, thefts and an unattended death.
> The police claim most of those cases are under investigation, and, therefore, the records are not considered open under state law.
> —Eric Sorensen

At the end of the story the online newspaper offers readers a chance to voice their opinions with this question: "What are your thoughts on WSU professor, police feuding?"

Nut Graphs   If the lead does not reveal the main idea of the story, you need a focus paragraph, called a *nut graph,* that tells the reader what the story is about. In print writing, this focus paragraph should be in the first few paragraphs of the story, but that is even more crucial in online writing because readers have more choices and are more impatient to get to the point. The structure of an anecdotal lead that tells a story or focuses on a person and is followed by a nut graph often is referred to as *The Wall Street Journal* formula, because that newspaper originated this format in its main front-page feature stories.

Here is an example of this story form with an anecdotal lead followed by a nut graph. It is from a story written for the Web in a package developed by MSNBC about online gambling:

> **Headline:** Wagering on Web is risky business
> **Subhead:** Legal gray areas bedevil bettors, entrepreneurs
> **Anecdotal lead:** Bruno Paniccia wandered into a legal "Twilight Zone" in April when, at the recommendation of friend, he sent $500 to an Internet sportsbook operating from the Caribbean and started winning big.
> 　　But the 25-year-old insurance claims evaluator from Chatsworth, Calif., received a rude awakening after he built his bankroll to more than $5,000 during an unprecedented hot streak. His "cyberbookie" refused to pay him, saying it could not meet its obligations because the FBI had raided the U.S. offices of its parent company and frozen its bank accounts.
> 　　"Legally, I didn't feel like I was doing anything wrong," a dismayed Paniccia said. "To my understanding, it was not illegal to bet over the Internet as long as it was with an offshore. I mean, I listen to sports radio and all you hear is just ads about 'Call this number and you can have an offshore betting [account] and it's completely legal.' "
> **Nut graph:** His was a painful introduction to the strange and chancy world of Internet gambling, which exists because there are no laws specifically prohibiting it.
> **Backup nut graph:** Despite its fledgling status, Internet gambling is generating increasing concern among legislators, regulators and gambling opponents, who see grave consequences arising from games of chance invading the home.
>
> —Mike Brunker

The package is accompanied by an interactive slot machine you can play to learn how wagering works in online gambling. If MSNBC keeps this package online, you can link to it on our Web site for this chapter, which will be updated regularly.

A NARRATIVE EXPERIMENT

Despite studies that claim people don't read stories online, good writing can provide good online reading. Roy Peter Clark proved that in an online narrative writing experiment. Clark, an associate director and senior scholar at The Poynter Institute for Media Studies, wrote a 29-part news series of short stories in narrative form—each less than 1,000 words—called "Three Little Words." Each chapter was published daily in print and online in the *St. Petersburg Times.* The series was about a woman coping with her husband's death from AIDS. In Chapter One the main character recalls how her husband lay in a hospital and told her three little words: "Not 'I love you.' But 'I have AIDS.' "

It ends, as do most of the chapters, with a cliffhanger:

> Number one: her husband would die. Number two: their relationship was a lie.
> But now the third revelation hit her so hard that she heard herself speaking the three little words aloud: "What about me?"

The series is no longer online, but Clark wrote a subsequent one called "Sadie's Ring: A Journey of the Spirit," in the same manner about his heritage. Both series contained no hyperlinks. Their popularity came from the power of the storytelling form—compelling narrative in brief stories that could be read in less than 15 minutes. Clark says in an article describing his experiment that almost 10,000 callers used the *Times* audiotext service to keep up with the series. Some days readers were trying to access the new chapters online at 2 a.m. just to read the next installment. "I've learned that people will come back day after day to follow a good story," he wrote.

This experiment reinforces what most online media editors are saying: Good content is still the most important part of online writing. Clark's series resembled fiction writing more than news. Many other online experiments are being conducted in hypertext fiction writing, which can serve as models for online news stories.

ONLINE WRITING EXPERIMENTS

Janet Murray, author of *Hamlet on the Holodeck: The Future of Narrative in Cyberspace,* describes hypertext storytelling as a series of chunks of information, called *lexias,* that can be linked in nonsequential order to allow readers to enter a story many ways. She compares the potential of computer storytelling to the holodeck from *Star Trek,* an empty black cube with white gridlines on which a computer can project simulations. In hypertext literature the author can project the story like a hologram for readers to follow many paths of plots and characterizations.

Murray, a research scientist in the Center for Educational Computing Initiatives at the Massachusetts Institute of Technology, teaches an interactive fiction writing course called Nonlinear and Interactive Narrative. She asks students to create a story with at least three distinct paths through a narrative Web using games or hypertext. Characters may interact with each other in many ways. Writers can create stories as digital labyrinths.

Murray cites an example of a tragic story about a young man's suicide. She suggests that the story could be written like a stream-of-consciousness novel in the form of an animated web. Using flashbacks, each unit of the story could reveal thoughts that went through the man's mind before his suicide. One thought might link to another but not in a specific order. Like the ramblings of the mind, the character could remember happy and sad moments—each revealing the frames of mind that eventually led to his suicide.

Borrowing from this hypertext structure, you could develop a major news story, such as a murder, in a series of lexias describing the different characters, the plot, motives and other background incidents that led to the crime. Although such stories often are told in print newspapers, they are not structured in nonlinear form.

Several other experiments with online fiction and newspaper writing are being conducted at the MIT Media Laboratory. The News in the Future consortium, a project of the MIT Media Lab, is exploring ways that computers can help people, especially children, learn when they engage in news-related activities.

Children may provide the clues for online newswriting in the future. They are learning to use the Internet in elementary school, so within a few years children may be reading most of their news online. But the majority of Web sites geared to children in newspapers these days involve just games.

An MIT study by Michele Evard for News in the Future explored children's conceptions and uses of news. Every one of the 38 fifth grade students she interviewed was interested in some aspect of news, with sports the most common topic. Most of the children in her study watched news on TV or read about it in newspapers.

Evard asked the children to define news. One boy said: "It's stuff that happens, that affects everyone's lives . . . sort of. Stuff that's important enough that they have, that they want people to know about it, so they like, write it or show it on TV, write it in the newspaper cause they want people to know about it."

If that definition were applied to most of the news stories in print or online, how many would comply with the expectation that it's stuff "that affects everyone's lives . . . stuff that's important enough that they want people to know about it"?

INTERACTION

Interaction is the key to writing online stories that affect people's lives. It is the element that differentiates the Web from other media. Here are some suggestions for adding interactive elements to your online stories.

* **Calculators and forms:** Suppose you are writing a story about taxes in your community. An interactive calculator or form that lets readers figure how the tax rate affects them could provide a valuable component to the story.

* **Discussion questions:** Soliciting readers' opinions at the end of a story with a discussion question is another way of engaging readers interactively.

* **Polls:** Although not scientific, polls can involve readers in the news. CNN uses them frequently on controversial issues.

* **Quizzes:** News quizzes or multiple choice tests may not seem like fun to college students, but readers enjoy them. CNN offers a daily news quiz on its main index.

* **FAQ:** The use of frequently asked questions is another technique to provide a lot of information in an easy form that is also somewhat interactive.

❋ **Games:** Many people enjoy participating in online games. The online *Philadelphia Inquirer* offers games related to some of its news stories. MSNBC's slot machine is an interactive game that also provides insight about the package on gambling. Advertising sites also use games to involve readers.

❋ **Discussion groups:** You can build community—a concept of bringing together people with common interests—through newsgroups and chat discussions linked to your stories, especially if they are about specific topics, such as health, Web design, or other topics of interest to your readers. HotWired and the *Chicago Tribune* offer these discussion groups linked to some of their columns.

TEASERS

Before you can get people to interact with your story, you have to entice them to read it. That means journalists need to write summary teasers that will make readers click into the story. But most of the summaries are written as dull inverted pyramids that tell enough about the story, leaving little reason to click further unless readers are very interested in the topic. If writers borrowed from the broadcast format of teasers that make you stay tuned or narrative cliffhangers to entice readers into a full version, perhaps they would click into the full story more often.

Consider this example from the online *New York Times:*

> **Headline:** Privacy Devalued in Information Economy
> **Summary:** As the free-flowing exchange and exploitation of information is being celebrated as the main engine of economic prosperity in the digital age, individual privacy is looking more and more like an endangered natural resource.

The headline and abstract give little clue to the compelling story that awaits. A woman filled out a marketing survey detailing her preferences in toothpaste and other products. It was read by a prison inmate whose job in prison was to input the data into a database. He knew all about her, including her vital statistics and favorite products. He began to write her letters describing his sexual desire for her. The anecdotal lead began:

> It was past midnight when Beverly Dennis came home, weary from her second-shift factory job, and found a letter with a Texas postmark among

the bills and circulars in the day's mail. As she read it in her small house in Massillon, Ohio, alone in the dark stare of the sliding glass doors, her curiosity turned to fear.

The letter was from a stranger who seemed to know all about her, from her birthday to the names of her favorite magazines, from the fact that she was divorced to the kind of soap she used in the shower. And he had woven these details of her private life into 12 handwritten pages of intimately threatening sexual fantasy.

[Several paragraphs follow to the nut graph.]

Nut graph: The explanation that eventually emerged deepened Ms. Dennis's sense of violation—and places her experience at the heart of a far-reaching national debate over legal protection for privacy in a world where personal information is ever easier to mine and market.

Imagine how much more enticing the story might have been to readers if the summary teaser had been written with some of that suspense.

This example from *The Philadelphia Inquirer* is more enticing:

> **Headline:** Murder on the Main Line
> **Summary:** Stefanie Rabinowitz was found dead in her bathtub on April 29. Her husband, Craig Rabinowitz, turned himself in on May 5. What came next were tales of a double life, juggled finances, and exotic dancers and hookers. Then the story got really strange. . . .

Which story would you want to read based on the headline and summary?

Another problem with the headlines and summaries is repetition. Most online newspapers use the lead of the story as the summary. So readers have to read the headline and promotional summary, which is the same as the lead, and then read the headline, summary and lead again when they click into the story. While it may help the reader to know that the headline, summary and lead are the same on the story as in the promotion, it can also bore the reader. When you are competing for readers' time with a world of choices instead of a just another newspaper, why ask the reader to read the same thing two or three times?

Consider this headline, summary and lead from the online *St. Petersburg Times:*

> **Headline:** At Some Florida Prisons, Shoe Can Be a Passkey
> **Summary:** In Florida, getting out of a prison cell could be as easy as banging a shoe on a lock.
> **Lead:** In Florida, getting out of a prison cell could be as easy as banging a shoe on a lock.
> Department of Corrections Secretary Harry Singletary told a Senate Committee Monday that inmates at one prison have opened cell doors by hitting them with a shoe.

Here's a better alternative, also from the *St. Petersburg Times:*

> **Headline:** Alligator Chases Man Home
> **Summary:** When an East Lake man left his condo for work, he didn't expect to find an alligator waiting outside.

Lead: Lyle Brown had an 8-foot-7, 300-pound excuse for being three hours late for work Monday.

When Brown walked out of his condominium to go to work about 6:30 a.m., he didn't notice the big alligator loitering in the parking lot.

Until the alligator hissed.

"My heart just dropped," Brown said.

Brown ran. The gator charged after him.

Here is an alternative teaser that might even add more mystery to the story:

When Lyle Brown stepped outside his condominium Monday, a 300-pound alligator confronted him in his parking lot. Brown ran. The alligator charged after him. . . .

Here's a teaser summary with a bit of mystery, which unfortunately is repeated in the lead from the *Philadelphia Daily News*:

Headline: Manayunk man faces DUI, homicide counts
Summary: A Manayunk man is hospitalized today with severe head injuries, but that might not be his worst problem.
Lead: A Manayunk man is hospitalized today with severe head injuries, but that might not be his worst problem.

Charles Brugger, 22, faces a long list of serious criminal charges—including two counts of murder—after his car slammed the rear of a stopped vehicle on Roosevelt Boulevard late Wednesday night. He was drunk behind the wheel, police said.

Question leads, considered a bad technique in news stories, can be enticing in summary teasers and in online news stories to make the reader continue. For example:

What are the top 10 mistakes in creating a Web site? Discover what to avoid and how you can improve your site with our tips.

Not all headlines and summaries should be written as feature teasers. Summary subheads in inverted pyramid style can be very effective on Web stories, especially for readers who are scanners. They are particularly suitable for breaking news and basic news stories.

A study the author conducted for The Poynter Institute for Media Studies revealed that content was the most important determinant for whether people would click into Web stories, and the style of headlines or subheads did not matter.

More than half of the 52 journalism students in the study said they preferred hard-news summary subheads when they are scanning Web sites for information. While most of the students said they skim leads if they repeat the information in the headlines and subheads, 52 percent said the repetition did not affect whether they would read the whole story. About 30 percent said repetition bored them, and 18 percent said repetitious leads and subheads helped their comprehension on Web stories.

ONLINE WRITING PROCESS

Writing for the Web requires critical thinking. Alan Richman, a writer for *Gentlemen's Quarterly* and former writing coach for *The Boston Globe,* once said: "Before you turn on your computer, turn on another piece of equipment— your mind." That should be the first step in your process for writing online stories.

Online news sites producing packages for the Web, such as CNN, MSNBC or the *Chicago Tribune,* use a team approach of planning with a writer, an editor, often called a *producer,* and in some cases a multimedia specialist and a Web designer. Whether you are working alone or with a team, you need a writing process.

* **Define the focus.** What is the purpose or main idea of your story? Write a brief sentence to explain the focus of your story.

* **Gather all your material.**

* **Plan visual and multimedia elements.** Do you need maps, photos or graphics? Consider only elements that are crucial to the story. Discard graphic elements that will add to download time but not to understanding the story.

* **Write a headline and teaser for your story.** Sell your story. Ask yourself how you will make readers care enough to click into your story. This process will help you plan your lead.

* **Write a brief of less than 21 lines for your story.** Even if you don't use briefs, this process will help you identify the information you must include. It will also help you envision how your story could be written in one screen.

* **Write a paragraph explaining how the story will affect your readers.** This paragraph will help you plan interactive elements even if you don't include it in your story.

* **Plan interactive elements.** Will you have a discussion question, a quiz, a game, or a poll? Jot down ideas for a discussion question or quiz. They will help you plan the content of your story.

✳ **Outline the content.** What are the main topics or parts of the story? Write subheads to define the topics. Ask yourself some guiding questions:

   ✳ What do you want people to remember from your story?

   ✳ What are the key points you must make?

   ✳ How can people best use your information?

   ✳ How can people relate the information to themselves?

   ✳ What other resources, such as links, do you need to include to help people understand and make decisions about the news? Add only links that are relevant.

   ✳ What sense of community can you build into your story (discussion questions, chats, newsgroups)?

   ✳ Are any ethical or legal issues involved? Have you contacted sources with opposing points of view? Have you checked the accuracy? Have you considered whether links will take readers to offensive sites? (See Chapter 14 for a discussion of legal and ethical issues.)

✳ **Deconstruct the story.** Now that you have the main topics, decide whether you will use the subtopics as internal links to a story that scrolls or external links to other chunks of the story in related Web pages.

✳ **Create a storyboard.** Plan pages for each section of the story that will be a separate chunk.

✳ **Write the story.**

✳ **Rewrite the story.** Cut every extra word. If you had to limit your story to three screens, what information could you delete?

ONLINE WRITING TIPS

* Write short sentences. Reading online is difficult.

* Use simple words. Eliminate connectors such as *however, therefore, in addition,* and so on. Usability studies show that online readers slow down over multisyllabic words and connecting expressions used in print.

* Write short paragraphs.

* Use subheads in your story.

* Use lists. Bulleted items help readers move through your story in print and online.

* Place links on the side, before or after your story. Avoid embedded links in sentences. They disrupt the text and tend to confuse readers, according to usability studies.

* Limit your links to relevant information. Don't offer links just to show that you found a lot of resources. Journalists need to synthesize information for readers.

* Use text links, not icons.

* Break out backgrounds with timelines or bulleted lists when the story or main source has a history that would help the reader understand the issue.

* Write FAQs (frequently asked questions) for yourself as a guide to information that you want readers to understand from your story.

* Provide graphic elements only if they enhance understanding of the story. Limit your use of large photographs or graphics that will take a long time to download.

* Offer a text-only version, especially if you have a graphics-intensive site.

STYLE TIPS

The Associated Press Stylebook, used by most media organizations, has very limited style rules for online terms. Here are a few AP style tips:

✳ Capitalize *Web* and *World Wide Web.*

✳ Capitalize *Internet.*

✳ *Online* is one word (no hyphen) in all cases when referring to the computer connection term.

✳ Capitalize *URL,* the acronym for Universal Resource Locator, in a story. The *Wired* style guide says *Uniform Resource Locator* is the preferred term. The *AP Stylebook* says URLs should be self-contained paragraphs at the end of the story. It does not specify italicizing them as does the *Wired* style guide (see the next section). Note that the author has boldfaced them in this textbook. Your Web sites are listed in the beginning of the chapter and occasionally within the text so you can access them as you read the information to enhance your learning experience. In a news story, placement of these links on the side or at the end of the story is a better alternative to encourage reading the whole story.

✳ Capitalize the acronym *HTML* for HyperText Markup Language.

✳ Capitalize the acronym *HTTP* for HyperText Transfer Protocol.

✳ Use *e-mail* as a shortened form of electronic mail. When needed, spell out *tilde* for the symbol ~.

✳ Capitalize but do not use quotation marks around software titles such as Microsoft Word or Windows.

✳ Use quotation marks around the name of computer games, "Myst."

✳ The word *media* is plural. The media *are* producing Web sites.

Another style guide that is widely used is *Wired Style: Principles of English Usage in the Digital Age.* This guide offers additional tips:

✳ Italicize e-mail addresses and surround them with parentheses or brackets, as in (*crich@ukans.edu*). Never break an e-mail address into two lines if it doesn't fit on one line.

* Italicize URLs in text: *www.hotwired.com*. For Web sites, it is not necessary to include an *http://* because all Web browsers will add it automatically. (Citation manuals for research papers do not italicize the URL and do include the *http://* tag as explained later in this chapter.)

* If a URL ends a sentence, add the period.

* If a URL is longer than a sentence, don't break it with a hyphen. The hyphen will confuse readers and may be mistaken as part of the Internet address.

* Do not capitalize e-mail addresses or URLs even in headlines if they are lower case addresses.

* Although *Wired*'s style guide says *media* can be used with a singular verb, stick to AP style and use a plural verb. *Wired* suggests being more specific: broadcast medium, print medium, the Internet.

* *New media* can be used with a singular verb: New media is his area of expertise.

CITATIONS

For citations in research papers, the *MLA Handbook for Writers of Research Papers* by the Modern Language Association often is the preferred reference, especially in English departments. Several variations of MLA online guidelines exist on the Web in university sites. If your university has issued guidelines for Web citations, use them. Note the hanging indentation style in the examples: first line flush left and subsequent lines indented. Here are guidelines for citing electronic sources, based on the *MLA* Web site; not all of these items may be available on a Web site:

* Name of author(s) or editor if given, book title underlined or in italics, or article in quotation marks, and publication information.

* Title of Web site underlined or in italics. If site has no title, such as HomePage, describe site without underlining.

* Date of the material if offered on the Web site. (Certain sites date their information or post the last updated version.)

✳ Name of discussion list if citing a post to a forum.

✳ Name of organization sponsoring the site.

✳ Date you accessed the site. (This is different from the date listed on the site, which may change daily.) Sites change or disappear frequently, so including the date you accessed the information helps the reader know that this was the version available at that time.

✳ Web site address in angle brackets <URL>.

Here are some examples.

✳ **Citation for works only on the Web:**
Paul, Nora. "Computer Assisted Reporting: Frequently Asked Questions," April 7, 1995, *Poynter Online.* Poynter Institute for Media Studies, Date accessed.
   <http://www.poynter.org/car/cg_carsem1.htm>.

This is an example of a document created exclusively for a Web site, the John F. Kennedy School of Government, Harvard University.
Callahan, Christopher. "The Internet as a Reporting Tool," Feb. 1, 1996, *John F. Kennedy School of Government, Harvard University.* Date accessed.
   <http://ksgwww.harvard.edu/~ksgpress/umdcc.htm>.

✳ **Citations for works with printed and electronic sources:** Start with the basic print citation rules—author, title of article, title of book or journal, volume number or edition, place of publication, publisher, date, page numbers if using a portion of a whole work. Then add the electronic medium information and the Internet address, as in this example:
Paul, Nora. *Computer Assisted Research: A guide to tapping online information.* 3rd ed., St. Petersburg, Fla.: Poynter Institute for Media Studies, 1997. *Poynter Online.* Date accessed.
   <http://www.poynter.org/car/cg_chome.htm>.

✳ **Journal, newsletter or newspaper with printed and electronic source:**
Hyman, Valerie. "What Newspaper Writers Can Learn from TV," *Workbench: The Bulletin of the National Writers' Workshop.* Vol 1, 1994, pp. 6–7. *Poynter Online.* Poynter Institute for Media Studies. Date accessed.
   <http://www.poynter.org/research/bj.htm>.

✳ **Citation from e-mail:** List name of writer, description of the document, such as e-mail to author, date of document or posting.
Student, John. "Need help on HTML." E-mail to the author. 10 Dec. 1998.

✳ **Citation from a discussion group post:** List name of author, title of document, date posted, description (Online posting), date of access, name of location where information was posted such as a newsgroup or forum, name of network (Usenet or AOL).
Student, Joe. "Re: Journalism jobs." 10 Sept. 1998. Online posting. Date accessed. Alt. Journalism: Students, Usenet.

Several variations of the MLA guidelines exist on the Internet.

＊ Nancy Crane and Xia Li have adapted the guidelines for MLA and for the American Psychological Association in *Electronic styles: A Handbook for citing electronic information.* They recommend putting the word *Online* in parentheses and adding the term *Available* before the Internet address. Available:

    http://www.uvm.edu/~ncrane/estyles

＊ Another source is offered by Janice R. Walker at the University of South Florida:

"MLA–Style Citations of Electronic Sources," 17 Dec. 1997. Online. Internet.

    http://www.cas.usf.edu/english/walker/mla.html

＊ MLA style Web site.

    http://www.mla.org/

Click into our Web site if you want to take this quiz online.
http://www.mhhe.com/socscience/comm/ rich/ch13/

13–1 Style Quiz

Test your knowledge of style for Web terms by applying AP style and choosing the correct answer. You can check your answers on our Web site.

1   a. In this course you have learned how to create documents for the web.

    b. In this course you have learned how to create documents for the Web.

2 a. You'll find the urls for safaris in this book on the McGraw-Hill web site.

b. You'll find the URLS for safaris in this book on the McGraw-Hill Web site.

c. You'll find the URLs for safaris in this book on the McGraw-Hill Web site.

3 a. The internet was created long before the world wide web.

b. The Internet was created long before the world wide web.

c. The Internet was created long before the World Wide Web.

4 a. The media is experimenting with new ways of writing online.

b. The media are experimenting with new ways of writing on-line.

c. The media are experimenting with new ways of writing online.

5 a. I have installed several software programs for windows, including "Netscape Communicator."

b. I have installed several software programs for "Windows," including "Netscape Communicator."

c. I have installed several software programs for Windows, including Netscape Communicator.

6 a. If you have any problems with this book, please send me an E-mail message.

b. If you have any problems with this book, please send me an electronic mail message.

c. If you have any problems with this book, please send me an e-mail message.

7 a. It is helpful to understand the basic concepts of html, although it is easier to use a web editor.

b. It is helpful to understand the basic concepts of HTML, although it is easier to use a web editor.

c. It is helpful to understand the basic concepts of HTML, although it is easier to use a Web editor.

8 Which of the following citations is correct, according to MLA style, for a document posted only on the Web?

Paul, Nora. "Computer Assisted Reporting: Frequently Asked Questions," April 7, 1995, Poynter Institute for Media Studies. *Poynter Online*. Date accessed. <http://www.poynter.org/car/cg_carsem1.htm>.

Paul, Nora. "Computer Assisted Reporting: Frequently Asked Questions," April 7, 1995, *Poynter Online.* HTTP://www.poynter.org/car/cg_carsem1.htm, (date accessed).

Paul, Nora. "Computer Assisted Reporting: Frequently Asked Questions," *Poynter Online.*

<http://www.poynter.org/car/cg_carsem1.htm>.

13–2 Teaser Safari

Using your community, campus or national newspaper, write headlines and summary teasers for at least three news stories and two feature or sports stories.

13–3 Writing Process Safari

Plan a nonlinear story package. This assignment also is effective in teams. Decide on a focus, brainstorm about the sections, and plan the types of elements you would use in a package on any news story of interest in your community, in the current national news or one of these topics:

* Parking problems at your college or university.
* Underage drinking in your community.
* Plagiarism from the Internet.
* The effect of the Internet on college students.
* The effect of the Internet on the future of newspapers.
* How e-mail has changed business communications.

13–4 Create a Nonlinear Web Story

Write a story and put it on the Web. Original work is preferred, including your own reporting, but you also may take a news story and redesign it for the Web if you have copyright permission. Do not post a story on the Web without permission if you haven't written it.

13–5 Discussion

How visionary can you be? Using a current news story, discuss (or create a prototype) for the way you think it might be presented 10 or 20 years from now on the Web. Take into consideration the way children are learning the Internet now and that they will be the audience for this story.

13–6 Writing Resources

Check our Web site for links to writing and copy editing resources, including a spelling test by Mindy McAdams, a renowned online journalism trainer.

Chapter 14
LEGAL AND ETHICAL ISSUES

Goals

* To learn about legal efforts to restrict information on the Internet.

* To learn about copyright on the Internet.

* To learn about privacy concerns on the Internet.

* To learn about other legal issues for online communication.

* To discuss ethical issues for the Internet.

Hyperleap

Take the interactive approach to this chapter before you read it. Test your knowledge in the 14–1 Safari and then read the chapter. You can also leap to our Web site to link to resources as you read.

http://www.mhhe.com/socscience/comm/ rich/ch14/

Anti-Defamation League:
   http://www.adl.org
American Civil Liberties Union:
   http://www.aclu.org
American Library Association:
   http://www.ala.org
U.S. Copyright Office:
   http://lcweb.loc.gov/copyright
U.S. Copyright Office frequently asked questions:
   http://lcweb.loc.gov/copyright/faq.html
Microsoft Sidewalk Seattle:
   http://seattle.sidewalk.com
Ticketmaster:
   http://www.ticketmaster.com
TotalNews:
   http://www.totalnews.com
New York Times **book review section**:
   http://www.nytimes.com/books/home/
Poynter Institute for Media Studies:
   http://www.poynter.org
Electronic Frontier Foundation:
   http://www.eff.org

A full glossary is in the appendix and in our Web site.

http://www.mhhe.com/socscience/comm/rich/
glossary.html

COOKIES A coded piece of information stored in your browser to identify your computer every time you access a site that sent the code.

BULLETIN BOARDS Online discussion groups available to members who subscribe, in most cases, without charge.

ENCRYPTION Codes that scramble data so that only authorized people can read the information. For example, when you purchase something on the Internet with your credit card, you should send the information to a site that uses encryption.

FORUMS Another term for discussion groups.

NEWSGROUPS Discussion groups that are part of the Usenet system, which allows anyone to post or read messages if the server carries the groups.

SYSOP A system operator.

USENET A worldwide group of electronic discussion lists, part of a network named for "users' network." Unlike discussion groups that require membership, Usenet groups are open to anyone for posting or reading messages as long as the server carries them.

" IT IS UNPLUGGED..."

BILL SCHORR reprinted by permission of United Feature Syndicate, Inc.

LEGAL AND ETHICAL DILEMMAS

You're writing a story about hate groups using the Internet to spread their message. Should your story link to their sites?

You are providing a discussion forum about sports on your campus newspaper site. Should you monitor the discussion so you can delete potentially libelous comments?

You have just read a story in an online newspaper that you think would be of interest to a few friends. Are you violating copyright laws if you send them a copy of the story via e-mail?

You belong to an online discussion group, and you want to quote some of the members' comments in a magazine article or newspaper story you are writing. Because their comments were posted to a public forum, can you do this without violating copyright laws?

You are writing a review of a new book. Should you accept advertising from the store that sells the product and provide a direct link to the store's Web site enabling readers to order the book online?

Journalists constantly face difficult legal and ethical decisions about information they want to publish. Even if you have the legal right to use some information, is it ethically responsible to do so? Just because you could doesn't mean you should. The Internet is posing many new legal and ethical dilemmas for journalists, and the solutions often are murky.

Consider the first dilemma of providing links to Web sites of neo-Nazi militia groups and other organizations promoting hatred against groups of people or violence against governments.

For example, the National Alliance Web site contains the following information:

> We must have no non-Whites in our living space, and we must have open space around us for expansion. . . . What we must have, however, is a thorough rooting out of Semitic and other non-Aryan values and customs everywhere. . . . We will do whatever is necessary to achieve this White living space and to keep it White.

The First Amendment of the U.S. Constitution guarantees the right of free speech. It also is a guiding principle of the media:

> Congress shall make no law respecting an establishment of religion or prohibiting the free exercise thereof; or abridging the freedom of speech, or of the press; or the right of the people peaceably to assemble, and to petition the Government for a redress of grievances.

Although the Internet is a global community and not all nations have similar freedoms guaranteed by law, many of these sites espousing hate exist on U.S. servers. The Anti-Defamation League has issued several reports warning about the proliferation of "high-tech hate" on the Internet.

If you were writing a story about the league's report that decries these sites, you might be doing readers a service by linking to these sites so they can determine for themselves whether the groups' messages on the Web constitute hate and danger. On the other hand, do you want to contribute to spreading the messages on these sites?

These groups have a legal right to exist on the Internet. Although this book usually offers URL citations and actual links on our book's Web site to sites mentioned in each chapter, in this case the messages of hatred were so intense that the author decided not to link to the groups' sites. You may disagree with that decision, but chances are you, too, will face such a choice sometime.

NORTHWESTERN UNIVERSITY PROFESSOR'S SITE

Northwestern University faced a similar dilemma when Arthur R. Butz, an electrical engineering professor there, posted a personal Web site to espouse his view that the Holocaust of World War II never existed. Officials of the Simon Wiesenthal Center in Los Angeles protested that such a site was carried on a university server. The center, named after Nazi death camp survivor Wiesenthal, is dedicated to remembering the Holocaust and fighting bigotry and antisemitism.

In a *New York Times* article, the president of Northwestern University described Butz's theories as "idiotic" and "monstrous," but he supported academic freedom and the professor's right to express it on the university's Internet server. *The New York Times* linked users to Butz's home page and the Wiesenthal Center Web site.

Although Butz doesn't advocate eradication of nonwhite groups, as do some of the other sites mentioned, his Holocaust revisionist theories are just as odious to many people. Would you have provided a link to his home page if you had written the story about this conflict?

Several Internet service providers offer software that allows users to filter out sites that contain hate messages or pornography and other types of information that parents might consider objectionable to children. Who decides what is pornographic or hateful?

COMMUNICATIONS DECENCY ACT

The U.S. government tried to make such decisions in the Communications Decency Act, which sought to regulate indecent material on the Internet. But the U.S. Supreme Court didn't permit it. In its first landmark decision regarding regulation of the Internet, the Supreme Court ruled that the online censorship provisions of the CDA violated the First Amendment. Portions of the Act made it a criminal offense to publish and make indecent material on the Internet available to people under age 18. The Court ruled 7–2 that the Act was too broad. Writing for the majority, Justice John Paul Stevens, wrote:

> As a matter of constitutional tradition, in the absence of evidence to the contrary, we presume that governmental regulation of the content of speech is more likely to interfere with the free exchange of ideas than to encourage it. The interest in encouraging freedom of expression in a democratic society outweighs any theoretical but unproven benefit of censorship.

Stevens cited this example of the problems the Act posed: A parent who allowed her 17-year-old child to read information in college on the Internet about birth control might be incarcerated if the college community considered the material indecent.

Although indecent material in print is protected under the First Amendment, broadcast information on radio and television is subject to regulation because "warnings could not adequately protect the listener from unexpected program content," Stevens wrote. On the Internet, however, users must seek out the information that might be considered unacceptable by some, the Supreme Court ruling said.

The suit against the CDA was filed by the American Civil Liberties Union on Feb. 8, 1996. The U.S. government appealed it to the U.S. Supreme Court after a federal three-judge panel had ruled that portions of the law unconstitutionally restricted free speech. The High Court affirmed the lower court ruling by striking down the censorship provisions of the law in *Reno* v. *ACLU* on June 26, 1997.

However, several states have enacted or proposed legislation to restrict certain types of material on the Internet. In Virginia it is illegal for state employees to use computers at work to view sexually explicit sites on the Internet. Other states have proposed bills or have passed laws limiting online content, usually related to pornography, to children or people under age 17.

Software products can filter out sexually explicit terms and pornography from Web sites. But free speech advocates are concerned that filtering is a form of censorship that still violates the First Amendment and may block many sites that provide useful information. For example, software that searches sites for the words *sex* or *breast* can also block sites providing information about safe sex or breast cancer. Nevertheless, libraries in several states have installed such software on their computers that access the Internet.

The American Library Association has denounced these actions by libraries. It claims that content on the Internet has the same constitutional protections that apply to books on the libraries' shelves.

GLOBAL REGULATIONS

Other countries also are enacting or considering regulation of the Internet. Germany passed a law that online providers could be prosecuted for offering illegal content, such as pornography or neo-Nazi propaganda, if they knowingly carried the material and were reasonably able to prevent its distribution.

At least 20 other countries have some restrictions for Internet use. Most restrict Internet service providers from carrying Web sites with hate speech or pornography. Several countries don't regulate the sites; they regulate the providers.

* Singapore allows only three Internet service providers, and they may not offer sites that contain anti-government information.

* China requires users to register with the government.

* Vietnam and Saudi Arabia permit only one government-controlled Internet service provider.

However, regulation on a global basis is difficult because a site banned in one country can easily be "mirrored," in another country, meaning the site can be copied and posted elsewhere.

ACCESS TO NEWSGROUPS

Several universities, especially public, state-funded ones, have been criticized by people and organizations for carrying Usenet newsgroups that offer sexually explicit material. Unlike listservs, which are discussion forums that require membership, Usenet groups are accessible to anyone who wants to post or read messages as long as the university or other Internet service provider offers them on its servers.

The University of Oklahoma was targeted by an organization in its state that claimed certain Usenet groups in an "alt-sex" category carried pornographic material accessible to people under age 18, in violation of state law. The university initially restricted access to about 100 of these groups. Concerned about the state law, the university then decided to continue offering these newsgroups on a separate server only for people over age 18 who were using them for research or academic endeavors.

Bill Loving, a media law professor in the journalism school, sued his university on the grounds that such restrictions violated First Amendment rights. He lost in a lower state court, and he has filed an appeal to seek full access to all newsgroups. (See Chapter 5 for more discussion of newsgroups.)

DISCUSSION GROUPS AND LIBEL

Issues of free speech on the Internet extend far beyond concerns about pornography. Consider the second dilemma posed in this chapter about monitoring discussion forums on your campus newspaper site, or any Web site, to prevent libel. *Libel* is defined as a published statement that is false and defamatory because it harms someone's reputation. So if someone makes a potentially libelous comment on a Web site you offer, can you be held responsible because you provided the venue?

In 1997 and 1998, two libel suits against America Online were dismissed by judges in federal courts on the grounds that portions of the Communications Decency Act of 1996, which had not been struck down by the Supreme Court, protect an online service provider from liability for content transmitted by its subscribers.

Blumenthal v. Drudge and American Online Inc.

Matt Drudge, an online gossip columnist, had published rumors claiming a White House aide had covered up a past of spousal abuse. The aide, Sidney Blumenthal, sued him and America Online for defamation. Drudge withdrew the column the next day, but Blumenthal sued anyway. In 1998, the case was dismissed against AOL but not against Drudge.

Zeran v. American Online Inc.

Kenneth Zeran, a Seattle man, received death threats after someone posted messages with his telephone number on AOL and falsely claimed that he was selling T-shirts with offensive slogans about victims of the bombing of the federal building in Oklahoma City, where 168 people died. Zeran sued AOL, but a U.S. Circuit Court of Appeals ruled in 1997 that the online service was not responsible for the postings. Two earlier cases sent mixed messages.

Cubby v. CompuServe

In 1991 CompuServe carried an online forum that published Rumorville, a newsletter about the broadcast industry. Cubby Inc., which planned to produce a competing newsletter, claimed it had been libeled in Rumorville. CompuServe claimed it wasn't responsible because it didn't exercise any editorial control over the content of its forums. A New York state court agreed and dismissed the case.

Stratton Oakmont v. Prodigy Unlike CompuServe, Prodigy had marketed its service as one that monitors its bulletin boards to prohibit offensive messages. Stratton Oakmont, a securities investment firm, claimed that comments made by an anonymous user on Prodigy's Money Talk bulletin board were defamatory. A New York trial court ruled that Prodigy could be held liable because the Internet service provider had exercised editorial control over the content.

None of these cases reached the U.S. Supreme Court, so the rulings aren't binding. But these last two cases were considered classic because they were the first of their kind. While some online media sites monitor their bulletin boards, many take a hands-off approach to deleting messages for fear they will be held liable if they exercise editorial control.

ONLINE COPYRIGHT ISSUES

Suppose you read a message in an online discussion group and want to quote it in a story you are writing. Is the message copyrighted by the person who wrote it? Yes. All information published on the Web, including your own Web site or e-mail messages you send, is the copyrighted property of the author.

"Your work is under copyright protection the moment it is created and fixed in a tangible form so that it is perceptible either directly or with the aid of a machine or device," according to the U.S. Copyright Office.

You don't even have to publish it in print or electronically, according to the U.S. Copyright Act of 1976 (Title 17 of the U.S. Code). You also don't have to post a copyright notice on your Web site or on anything you write. When the copyright laws were revised in 1976, the notice no longer was required. But it's still a good idea to use a notice so readers will think twice before copying your material. The proper form for a copyright notice is: Copyright, [the copyright symbol] ©, the year, and your name or the name of the copyright holder. The copyright symbol is optional.

But not all work is protected by copyright laws. Titles, U.S. government documents, and slogans are not covered. However, titles and slogans may have been registered as trademarks, so you still have to be careful about using them without attribution or permission. Other items not covered by the copyright laws include:

✳ Facts, ideas, procedures. You can take an idea, but you can't take the exact words someone used to express the idea.

✳ Short phrases. But copyright laws don't specify how many words constitute "short."

✳ Works consisting entirely of information that is common property and contains no original authorship, such as calendars, lists or tables from public documents.

✳ Information in the public domain. This means the information no longer is protected by copyright if it was published more than 75 years prior to 1963, and if the copyright wasn't renewed. Any work created after 1964 is protected for the life of the author plus 50 years. Works created for hire are protected for 75 years from publication or 100 years from the time the work was created.

In the past a person who copied material or passed software to a friend but didn't profit from it wouldn't be subject to criminal penalties, although he or she could be sued in a civil court. Now it is a crime.

NO ELECTRONIC THEFT ACT

In December 1997 a new law was created making it a criminal offense to infringe on copyrighted material, including software and material on the Internet. The No Electronic Theft Act provides for penalties of imprisonment up to three years and fines of up to $250,000 for copying materials, "including by electronic means." For making one or more copies of information worth at least $1,000 but less than $2,500, the penalties are imprisonment for up to a year and a fine of up to $100,000. Copies of material worth more than $2,500 could lead to the higher penalties.

The law targets software piracy but isn't limited to that. Software and entertainment companies supported the new law because they sought protection from electronic copying of their products. But researchers protested, saying the law would make it a criminal offense for them to post their own research on the Web if their materials were published by a journal or other academic publication because they would be copying copyrighted material.

Copyright laws are being revised to regulate use of materials on the Internet and strengthen penalties for copying software and other online documents. The Digital Millennium Copyright Act provides for penalties of up to $1 million and 10 years in jail for people who violate copyright of online materials for financial gain.

You'll find many answers to questions about copyright in the Frequently Asked Questions and the laws posted on the U.S. Copyright Office's Web site listed in the beginning of the chapter.

You won't find direct answers to questions about the legality of quoting from newsgroups. Many legal sites on the Web discuss "implied license," meaning that people who post messages to a Web discussion group are giving implied consent for their messages to be reposted. Implied license generally restricts the posting to the same discussion group or at least the same Internet server.

It is not clear whether you can forward these messages to other discussion lists. Some listservs set rules that forbid reproducing any messages without the writer's consent. Legally it may be acceptable, but ethically journalists should notify people if they are going to use their comments.

Personal e-mail messages rarely are intended for redistribution by forwarding to other people or discussion groups without permission of the author. As a result, the ethical thing to do before publishing someone's e-mail posting to you or to a discussion forum is to seek permission.

Can you send a copy of a cartoon or a story you read on the Web to a friend or other people on a discussion list? No. That information is copyrighted, whether it says so or not. Many graphic sites on the Web allow you to use their images on personal pages, not commercial ones. But unless a Web site specifically states that you can distribute its information freely, you probably are violating copyright. Almost all media sites list a copyright notice, but even if they don't, they are protected by U.S. copyright laws. If you want to send a Web article to someone via e-mail, take the safe route: Send the URL in your message.

PLAYBOY V. FRENA

George Frena, the operator of a bulletin board, didn't take the safe route. He provided 170 pictures from *Playboy* and *Playmate* magazines over his bulletin board, Tech Warehouse, which features adult material. Although he claimed he didn't post the pictures himself, he allowed subscribers to upload them. A federal trial court in Florida wasn't concerned who posted the pictures; the court held Frena responsible for them because he was the system operator.

Playboy Enterprises Inc. sued Frena on the grounds of copyright violation and trademark infringement because Frena had used the company's trademarks in the pictures. The court agreed, and Frena had to remove the pictures. But Frena claimed posting the pictures was "fair use."

FAIR USE

What is fair use and what can you copy without violating copyright? Much of the material you copy as students for academic purposes might constitute fair use, depending on several factors. That's not the same as plagiarizing material by passing it off as your own. You are allowed to copy or quote from copyright protected materials, but you must meet certain standards under a fair use doctrine.

A committee of 93 organizations, The Conference on Fair Use, met in the early 1990s to discuss this issue and its relationship to new media, but its guidelines never were adopted. As a result, the fair use guidelines of the Copyright Act still are being applied to the Internet and multimedia materials. Four major factors are considered:

1 The purpose of the use, usually whether it is commercial or for nonprofit educational reasons. Uses for criticism, comment, news reporting, teaching and scholarship are favored.

② **The nature of the copyrighted work. Published works are favored over unpublished ones.**

③ **The amount of the work to be copied. The copyright law does not specify amounts, but generally a small portion or excerpt of the work is deemed more fair use than an entire article.**

④ **The effect copying will have on the market for the original work. In other words, if you copy an entire book, you may be depriving the publisher of sales or the author of royalties. That's probably not considered fair use.**

If you copy a Web page and claim it as yours or post it in your site, even if it is for educational purposes, you could be violating "fair use." Use links instead.

However, if you create a resource Web page that is a compilation of links to several sites, the individual links aren't copyrighted but the whole page is. It's like a directory. You can copy a link, but not the whole resource page.

LINKING TO WEB SITES

Even linking can be litigious. Microsoft discovered that when Ticketmaster sued the company for linking to the ticket broker's site without permission. Microsoft's Sidewalk Seattle, a Web site listing entertainment in the area, linked to Ticketmaster's site so readers could order tickets for concerts and events.

Ticketmaster officials weren't as upset about the link to their site as the way Microsoft offered the link. Instead of linking to Ticketmaster's home page, which contained the company's most high-paid advertisements, Microsoft linked directly to inside pages where the tickets could be purchased for the specific concerts promoted on Sidewalk Seattle. That allowed readers to bypass the home page ads. As a partial resolution, Ticketmaster blocked entry to its inside pages and forced readers to enter by its front door.

TotalNews Inc. raised a different legal issue when it linked to 1,350 news media sites. TotalNews, a directory of news sites, is designed with frames, which carry the company's advertisements. When TotalNews brought the content of the other news sites into its own frame, its advertisers remained in the frame over the content of the other news sites. That did not please the major news operations, which had their own advertisers to please.

So CNN, the *Washington Post,* Times Mirror Co., Reuters, and Time Inc. sued TotalNews for copyright and trademark violations. The case was settled out of court when TotalNews agreed to stop using a frame with its own advertising to display the other media sites' content.

The case raises the issue of whether you can import other sites' contents into a Web site frame of your own page. But because it was settled out of court, it doesn't clearly provide a legal precedent. The news clearinghouse didn't copy other Web sites' material. It just linked to them. But such issues are sure to resurface.

In general, it's safer to provide links that take readers to other Web sites so you don't risk violating intellectual property rights or upsetting their advertisers. At this point, it seems reasonable to conclude that linking to another site is not going to violate copyright.

LINKING TO ADVERTISING

A more ethical dilemma is involved in deciding whether to provide links to advertisers, such as booksellers, directly under or next to a book review. Such was the issue created when *The New York Times* decided to provide readers of its online book reviews direct links to Barnes & Noble's Web site, where they could order the books online.

At first glance, it appears to be a useful reader service. But journalists have always been concerned about keeping the lines between advertising and editorial content separate. Do these close-linked advertising arrangements on the Web compromise editorial integrity? *The New York Times* doesn't think so. Editors there maintain that their book reviews will continue to be honest, and more are negative than are positive. However, the *Times* is receiving money from Barnes & Noble to post the ad and link to the bookseller's site.

The same issue can be applied to business stories about automobiles with links to car dealerships, restaurant reviews with links to the restaurants, and so on. The close relationships are endless.

PRIVACY

The privacy of online users is a legal and an ethical issue. Many news and advertising sites use cookies, which are coded pieces of information stored in a user's browser to identify the user the next time he or she accesses the site. Browsers such as Netscape and Microsoft Internet Explorer offer users the option of being warned or rejecting cookies. In most cases, they are used by media sites to track users' preferences.

Although cookies cannot identify a user by name unless the site requires registration, many online readers are concerned that their privacy is being invaded. Media sites usually limit the tracking to their own sites. However, it is possible for a cookie to track a user outside of the site, and that is what concerns many people.

The Electronic Frontier Foundation, a nonprofit civil liberties organization, suggests that online users demand to know what kinds of information their favorite Web sites are collecting about them and what they will do with the data.

ENCRYPTION

Another privacy issue involves encryption, the ability to use data-scrambling codes to jumble text so it can be understood only by authorized people. If you bank online or buy something on the Internet and pay by credit card, you would want the site to encrypt the information you send so your credit card information is not accessible to unauthorized people. Encryption offers the user some degree of privacy. Some e-mail programs also offer encryption codes that protect people's privacy in sending messages or documents via e-mail.

The legal battle over encryption involves the U.S. government's attempt to pass legislation allowing law enforcement authorities such as the FBI to have access to encryption codes used by companies on the Internet. U.S. officials have sought to impose a voluntary system whereby software companies that produce encryption products would provide law enforcement authorities decoding ability, called a *key recovery system.* The government says its purpose is to gain access to coded communications of suspected criminals and terrorists.

But civil liberties groups such as the American Civil Liberties Union are fighting such attempts. The ACLU claims on its Web page that restrictions on cryptography will curtail freedom of speech by denying users of computers, cell phones and other devices the right to communicate privately. "In fact, the ACLU believes that privacy, anonymity and security in the digital world depend on encryption," according to information on its Web site.

The U.S. government also bans export of encryption software to other countries. If you access a U.S. Web site with encryption software, it will require you to fill a form stating that you are a U.S. citizen before you can download the product.

NEW MEDIA ETHICS

The Poynter Institute for Media Studies and the American Society of Newspaper Editors, explored many of these issues in a conference to discuss journalism ethics in the new media. A goal of the conference was to develop protocols, which are processes for decision making, that journalists could use to develop their own guidelines to deal with ethical dilemmas in online issues. Here are some of the group's recommendations:

Content Reliability   Notify online users if materials posted on the news Web site were created elsewhere and may not have been edited or reviewed to meet the news site's standards for reliability. Warn users when they are leaving the news Web site that they may be entering a site that does not embrace the same content reliability.

Database Information   Keep data updated and accurate. Reveal the authorship, ownership, scope, validity and limitations of the data posted to the news site.

Linking   Links should be clearly identified as either editorial or commercial. Before linking to a potentially offensive site, explore alternatives such as added storytelling or take steps to warn users of the content.

Potentially Offensive or Harmful Content

Discussion in the newsroom should be required when content contains vulgarity or harmful material such as racial, ethnic, cultural, religious, sexist or homophobic stereotypes. The discussion should involve reporters, editors and other people representing diversity of cultures.

Journalistic Integrity and Commercial Pressures

The audience should be able to distinguish clearly between editorial content and advertising. Tracking technologies such as cookies should be used responsibly so they don't violate the privacy of the reader. If user information is going to be used by third parties for direct-mail or phone solicitations, the readers should be notified in advance.

Robert M. Steele, assistant
dean of The Poynter
Institute for Media Studies

Many of the legal and ethical dilemmas that are emerging are unique to new media. But Robert M. Steele, assistant dean and director of ethics at The Poynter Institute for Media Studies, says the foundations of ethical reasoning can still be applied.

"I'm still of the belief that we need to start with the principles," he says. "We're still talking about privacy, fairness and accuracy. Recognize that the territory we're traveling is different. It's probably not unlike physicians turning to their principles when they are doing genetic research or experimental procedures."

Some of the different territory in online journalism involves time pressures of constant deadlines and the need to instantaneously turn around information. "Because of that, there is less time to reflect on consequences," Steele says. "You often have people doing multiple tasks under great pressure."

As a result, Steele says, it's even more important to weigh consequences and alternatives early in the reporting, writing and editing process. "Ask a couple more questions at the front end," he says.

Other ethical problems are created because many of the people working online are new to journalism, and the online staff usually is limited. He says corporations must deal with issues of training. "We would not accept a medical facility that is putting untrained or under-prepared workers in a family member's case," he says. "Those who are using the Web should not accept poor performance either."

Steele says ethical reasoning should start with protocols, a process for making decisions. "We need to use critical thinking skills that involve common sense and moral reasoning." For example, he says journalists should consider these questions:

* Which people do you call first on deadline?

* How do you frame a story so it enhances fairness?

* How do you decide about sensitive information?

"I don't believe those issues are inherently different," Steele says. "The time demands are different. The implications are different. The extended exposure creates a potential for problems. The reach and harm are greater compared to traditional news."

Another ethical dilemma imposed by new media is the lack of authenticity. For example, he says, if you mail a newspaper clip to a friend, you can be assured it's from a newspaper and that it hasn't been forged. "But the Web does not have the physical indicators that allow us to say if this is a fraud," Steele says. "One message on the Web looks like another and can easily be altered. We have to force ourselves to constantly take a pause and ask, 'What happens with this information?'"

Links also impose new ethical dilemmas. Steele says it is not enough to post a disclaimer that you are not responsible for information on a linked site. "That's saying 'I claim no responsibility.' I don't believe that is legitimate."

He says an explanation saying readers should be prepared for offensive language or photographs on a linked site is preferable. For example, he says we should explain that this link will take you to a site that proposes to give information about a drug for AIDS. But we should tell readers to keep in mind that this site is the creation of a drug company or similar explanation.

"We need to add our journalistic interpretation," Steele says. "Without it we will do a disservice to the public. We need to tell what's important and valid."

Is there one major guideline for ethical reasoning on the Web? Steele says we should paste one word on every journalist's computer: *Think*.

Safaris

14—1 Legal Safari

1 In the Communications Decency Act, the United States government was trying to

    a. overrule the First Amendment.

    b. impose criminal penalties for publishing indecent material on the Internet.

    c. require software to filter out indecent material on the Internet.

2 The U.S. Supreme Court struck down the censorship provisions of the Communications Decency Act because

    a. indecent material is too hard to define.

    b. regulation of free speech would violate the First Amendment.

    c. indecent material already is prohibited in broadcast.

3 The United States is the only country that has attempted to regulate content on the Internet. True or False?

4 In *Cubby* v. *CompuServe,* the court ruled that

    a. CompuServe was liable for material on its bulletin boards because it monitored the information.

    b. CompuServe wasn't liable for material on its bulletin boards because it didn't monitor the information.

    c. CompuServe was responsible for material on its bulletin boards because it was the Internet service provider.

5 In *Stratton Oakmont* v. *Prodigy,* the court ruled that

    a. Prodigy was liable for material on its bulletin boards because it monitored the information.

    b. Prodigy wasn't liable for material on its bulletin boards because it didn't monitor the information.

    c. Prodigy was responsible for material on its bulletin boards because it was the Internet service provider.

6 If you write an e-mail message or publish a Web page on the Internet in the United States, it is protected by U.S. copyright laws whether or not you register it with the U.S. Copyright Office. True or False?

7 If you want your material to be protected by U.S. copyright laws, you must post a copyright symbol on the work. True or False?

8 Facts, titles and ideas are protected by U.S. copyright laws. True or False?

9 Fair use means you have the right to copy any information as long as you are using it for academic purposes. True or False?

10 The U.S. government has attempted to pass legislation to gain access to encryption codes so that
    a. the IRS can monitor all your financial transactions on the Internet.
    b. the FBI will have access to the codes.
    c. no private companies will be able to sell encryption software.

Check your answers on our Web site.

14-2 | **Legal and Ethics Resources**

Check our Web page at the URL listed under Safaris for this chapter.

14-3 | **Ethics Safari**

1 Develop a list of five to 10 ethical guidelines that you think you need to help you deal with online media issues. Use your guidelines to decide some of the following ethical dilemmas.

    a. Boston University sued eight companies that were selling term papers over the Internet for wire fraud, mail fraud and racketeering on the grounds that they were violating a Massachusetts law that prohibits the sale of term papers. You are writing a news story about this. Will you link to the sites that offer term papers? Why or why not?

    b. A local nude bar that has been advertising in the print edition of your college newspaper for several years now has a Web site featuring nude women dancing. The bar wants to run an advertisement on your college newspaper's online version with a click-through ad to its own Web site. It has threatened to withdraw its lucrative advertising from your print edition if you don't. You provide click-through ads for several other advertisers. But in this case, many students, feminists and other groups in your community oppose the use of a university publication for promoting nude dancing. Will you accept the ad?

c. A competing newspaper or television station has a report on its Web site quoting a source about some crucial information you need for the same story, but you could not reach the source. However, this source has commented on the issue in a discussion group to which you belong. You are not sure if the source's comments are true. You are on deadline and cannot reach the source or wait for an e-mail response to verify the information. Should you use the source's comments in the discussion group in your story?

d. Megan's Law, a federal law created in 1996, requires communities to be notified about convicted sex offenders living in their neighborhoods. As a result, you are now able to get the names of sex offenders who have been released from prison and are living in your community. Will you publish their names on your newspaper or broadcast station's Web page? If you do, you will alert people in your community that these people are living in their midst, but you will also alert the world because your Web publication is accessible globally. If you don't, are you being negligent in warning the community if the sex offenders repeat their crimes? Would you publish their names in a print product but not in an Internet site?

STYLE GUIDE

Here are some style tips from the *Associated Press Stylebook, Wired Style: Principles of English Usage in the Digital Age* and for citations from the Modern Language Association. These style tips also are in Chapter 13 on writing.

Style Tips from the The Associated Press Stylebook

* Capitalize *Web* and *World Wide Web*.

* Capitalize *Internet*.

* *Online* is one word (no hyphen) in all cases when referring to the computer connection term.

* Capitalize *URL*, the acronym for Universal Resource Locator, in a story. The *Wired* style guide says *Uniform Resource Locator* is the preferred term. The *AP Stylebook* says URLs should be self-contained paragraphs at the end of the story. It does not specify italicizing them as does the *Wired* style guide (see the next section). Note that the author has boldfaced them in this textbook. Your Web sites are listed in the beginning of the chapter and sometimes within the text so you can access them as you read the information to enhance your learning experience. In a news story, placement of these links on the side or at the end of the story is a better alternative to encourage reading the whole story.

* Capitalize the acronym *HTML*, for HyperText Markup Language.

* Capitalize the acronym *HTTP*, for HyperText Transfer Protocol.

* Use *e-mail* as a shortened form of electronic mail. When needed, spell out *tilde* for the symbol ~.

* Capitalize but do not use quotation marks around software titles, such as Microsoft Word or Windows.

* Use quotation marks around the name of computer games, "Myst."

* The word *media* is plural. The media *are* producing Web sites.

Style Tips from Wired Style: Principles of English Usage in the Digital Age

✳ Italicize e-mail addresses and surround them with parentheses or brackets, as in (*crich@ukans.edu*). Never break an e-mail address into two lines if it doesn't fit on one line.

✳ Italicize URLs in text: *www.hotwired.com.* For Web sites, it is not necessary to include an *http://* because all Web browsers will add it automatically. (Citation manuals for research papers do not italicize the URL and do include the *http://* tag as explained later in this appendix.)

✳ If a URL ends a sentence, add the period.

✳ If a URL is longer than a sentence, don't break it with a hyphen. The hyphen will confuse readers and may be mistaken as part of the Internet address.

✳ Do not capitalize e-mail addresses or URLs even in headlines if they are lower case addresses.

✳ Although *Wired*'s style guide says *media* can be used with a singular verb, stick to AP style and use a plural verb. Wired suggests being more specific: broadcast medium, print medium, the Internet.

✳ *New media* can be used with a singular verb: New media is his area of expertise.

Citations

For citations in research papers, the *MLA Handbook for Writers of Research Papers* by the Modern Language Association often is the preferred reference, especially in English departments. Several variations of MLA online guidelines exist on the Web in university sites. If your university has issued guidelines for Web citations, use them. Note the hanging indentation style in the examples: first line flush left and subsequent lines indented.

Here are the guidelines for citing electronic sources, based on the MLA Web site; not all of these items may be available on a Web site.

✳ Name of author(s) or editor if given, book title underlined or in italics, or article in quotation marks, and publication information.

✳ Title of Web site or project underlined or in italics. If site has no title, such as Home Page, describe the site without underlining.

✳ Date of the material if offered on the Web site. (Certain sites date their information or post the last updated version.)

✳   Name of discussion list if citing a post to a forum.

✳   Name of organization sponsoring the Web site.

✳   Date you accessed the site. (This is different from the date listed on the site, which may change daily.) Sites change or disappear frequently, so including the date you accessed the information helps the reader know that this was the version available at that time.

✳   Web site address in angle brackets <URL>.

Here are some examples:

Citation for Works Only on the Web

Paul, Nora. "Computer Assisted Reporting: Frequently Asked Questions," April 7, 1995, *Poynter Online.* Poynter Institute for Media Studies. Date accessed. <http://www.poynter.org/car/cg_carsem1.htm>.

This is an example of a document created exclusively for a Web site, the John F. Kennedy School of Government, Harvard University:
Callahan, Christopher. "The Internet as a Reporting Tool," Feb. 1, 1996, *John F. Kennedy School of Government, Harvard University.* Date accessed. <http://ksgwww.harvard.edu/~ksgpress/umdcc.htm>.

Citations for Works with Printed and Electronic Sources

Start with the basic print citation rules—author, title of article, title of book or journal, volume number or edition, place of publication, publisher, date, page numbers if using a portion of a whole work. Then add the electronic medium information and the Internet address, as in this example:
Paul, Nora. *Computer Assisted Research: A guide to tapping online information.* 3rd ed., St. Petersburg, Fla.: Poynter Institute for Media Studies, 1997. *Poynter Online.* Date accessed. <http://www.poynter.org/car/cg_chome.htm>.

Journal, Newsletter or Newspaper with Printed and Electronic Source

Hyman, Valerie. "What Newspaper Writers Can Learn from TV," *Workbench: The Bulletin of the National Writers' Workshop.* Vol 1, 1994, pp. 6–7. *Poynter Online.* Poynter Institute for Media Studies. Date accessed. <http://www.poynter.org/research/bj.htm>.

Citation from e-mail

List name of writer, description of the document such as e-mail to author, date of document or posting:
Student, John. "Need help on HTML." E-mail to the author. 10 Dec. 1998.

Citation from a Discussion Group Post

List name of author, title of document, date posted, description (Online posting), name of location where information was posted, such as a newsgroup or forum, name of network (Usenet or AOL), date of access.

Student, Joe. "Re: Journalism jobs." 10 Sept. 1998. Online posting. Alt. Journalism:
   Students, Usenet. Date accessed.
Several variations of the MLA guidelines exist on the Internet.
Nancy Crane and Xia Li have adapted the guidelines for MLA and for the
American Psychological Association in *Electronic styles: A Handbook for citing
electronic information*. They recommend putting the word *Online* in parentheses and
adding the term *Available* before the Internet address.
Available: **http://www.uvm.edu/~ncrane/estyles**
            Another source is offered by Janice R. Walker at the University of South
Florida:
"MLA-Style Citations of Electronic Sources," 17 Dec. 1997.
www.cas.usf.edu/english/walker/mla.html
MLA style Web site:
http://www.mla.org/

THE VIRTUAL MEDIA SOURCEBOOK

These Web sites are subject to change and may not be available as listed in this print version of your textbook. They also are available as direct links on our Web site, which will be checked and updated periodically to eliminate obsolete links and add new sources. Many of these sources are listed in the individual chapters where they are relevant; others have been added here.

All these Internet addresses start with http://, which is inserted automatically by browsers, so it is not listed as part of these addresses except in cases where the addresses might seem confusing.

You can find the source book online at our Web site:
http://www.mhhe.com./socscience/comm/rich/sourcebook.html

Government Sources

* Fedworld (a searchable guide to federal governmental agencies, personnel and government Internet servers):
  www.fedworld.gov

* U.S. Bureau of the Census:
  www.census.gov

* Statistical Abstract of the United States:
  www.census.gov/statab/www/

* THOMAS: (Legislative information on the Internet):
  http://thomas.loc.gov

* Library of Congress:
  http://lcweb.loc.gov/homepage/lchp.html

* The White House:
  www.whitehouse.gov

* Central Intelligence Agency:
  www.odci.gov

* American University's Campaign Finance Site (Complete state-by-state records of campaign finances of state and federal legislators):
  www.soc.american.edu/campfin

❋ The Washington Post Federal Internet Guide (a well-organized set of resources to federal agencies and documents):
www.washingtonpost.com/wp-srv/politics/govt/fedguide/ fedguide.htm

Legal and Ethical Resources

❋ The Electronic Frontier Foundation:
www.eff.org

❋ Findlaw Index:
www.findlaw.com

❋ FOIA Resource Center (maintained by the Society of Professional Journalists):
www.spj.org/foia/index.htm

❋ Freedom of Information Center:
www.missouri.edu/~foiwww/

❋ Cyberspace Law for Non-lawyers: (a complete course in easy terms):
www.ssrn.com/update/lsn/cyberspace/csl_lessons.html

❋ Libel and defamation (definitions for non-lawyers):
www.ssrn.com/update/lsn/cyberspace/lessons/libe01.html

❋ Cyberspace Law Institute:
www.cli.org

Copyright Sources

❋ The Copyright Website:
www.benedict.com

❋ United States Copyright Office:
http://lcweb.loc.gov/copyright

❋ U.S. Copyright FAQ:
http://lcweb.loc.gov/copyright/faq.html

❋ Copyright Basics:
http://lcweb.loc.gov/copyright/circs/circ1.html

❋ Intellectual Property in the Information Age:
www.seas.upenn.edu/~cpage/cis590/

❋ Copyright Crash Course (by Georgia Harper, office of the General Counsel, University of Texas System):
www.utsystem.edu/ogc/intellectualproperty/cprtindx.htm#top

❋ Copyright & Fair Use (Stanford University Web site):
http://fairuse.stanford.edu

Ethics Sources

* Journalism Ethics:
  www.journalism.sfsu.edu/www/ethics.html

* The Ethics Web: Ethics on the Net: (good resources page):
  http://199.233.193.1/cybereng/ethics/

* Ethics on the WWW (a comprehensive collection maintained by Professor Paul Lester at the University of California, Fullerton):
  http://commfaculty.fullerton.edu/lester/ethics/ethics_list.html

Media Organizations and Institutes

* Poynter Institute for Media Studies:
  http://www.poynter.org

* Freedom Forum:
  www.freedomforum.org

* Investigative Reporters and Editors (includes a database of thousands of investigative stories):
  www.ire.org

* Society of Professional Journalists:
  http://spj.org

* Society of Environmental Journalists:
  www.sej.org

* American Society of Newspaper Editors:
  www.asne.org

* Newspaper Association of America:
  www.naa.org

* Journalism & Women Symposium:
  www.jaws.org

* Asian American Journalists Association:
  www.aaja.org

* The National Association of Black Journalists:
  www.nabj.org

* Center for Investigative Reporting:
  www.muckraker.org

* Education Writers Association:
  www.ewa.org

Media Resources for Reporting, Research and Writing

Research

⁕ The World Wide Web Virtual Library: journalism (A huge compilation of reference sites by John Makulowich):
www.cais.com/makulow/vlj.html

⁕ American Journalism Review Resources:
www.newslink.org/spec.html

⁕ American Journalism Review:
www.ajr.org

⁕ Deja News (a good search engine for newsgroups):
www.dejanews.com

⁕ Switchboard (a people finder):
www.switchboard.com

⁕ Whowhere (another good people finder and business resource with phone numbers and e-mail addresses):
www.whowhere.com

⁕ Four11 (Yet another good people-finder with e-mail addresses):
www.four11.com

Reporting

⁕ Profnet (This is a service that will find academic experts in various fields to answer your questions—for working journalists only):
www.profnet.com

⁕ The Reporters Network:
www.reporters.net

⁕ The Reporters Desktop (an excellent collection of resources by *Seattle Times* reporter Duff Wilson):
www.seanet.com/~duff/

⁕ reporter.org (terrific resources for reporters, including links by beat):
www.reporter.org
www.reporter.org/beat

⁕ Facsnet: (excellent resources for journalists):
www.facsnet.org

⁕ Deadline Online.com: (another outstanding collection of resources for journalists by Washington reporter Alan Schlein):
www.deadlineonline.com/

Writing and Editing

* Computer-Mediated Communication Magazine (CMC), special issue on Digital Journalism:
  www.december.com./cmc/mag/1997/jul/toc.html

* "Writing for the Web," column by Jakob Nielsen, distinguished engineer for Sun Microsystems:
  www.useit.com/papers/webwriting

* "How to Write for the Web," study by John Morkes and Jakob Nielsen for Sun Microsystems:
  www.useit.com/papers/webwriting/writing.html

* The American Copy Editors Society:
  www.copydesk.org

* Copy Editing for Magazines, by Mindy McAdams, online writing and design consultant:
  www.well.com/user/mmcadams/copy.editing.html

* "A Spelling Test," Mindy McAdams' spelling test of 50 commonly misspelled words:
  www.sentex.net/~mmcadams/spelling.html

* Inkspot: a comprehensive source for writers:
  www.inkspot.com

* Copyeditor (good links for copy editors):
  www.copyeditor.com

* World Wide Web Citation Formats:
  www.uncc.edu/lis/library/reference/human/webcite.htm

* Electronic Citation Style Manuals:
  www.lib.siu.edu/swen/eciting.htm

* Electronic citation stylebook by Nancy Crane and Xia Lu:
  http://www.uvm.edu/~ncrane/estyles

Broadcast

* WWW Virtual Library, Broadcasters:
  www.comlab.ox.ac.uk/archive/publishers/broadcast.html

* MSNBC:
  www.msnbc.com

* CNN:
  www.cnn.com

* Parrot Media, resources for TV stations, cable, radio and advertising:
  www.parrotmedia.com

❋ Broadcast Education Association:
www.beaweb.org

❋ theAntenna: good information about online broadcast media:
www.theantenna.com

❋ Radio-Television News Directors Association:
www.rtnda.org

Public Relations

❋ PR Central:
www.prcentral.com/index.htm

❋ International Association of Business Communicators:
www.iabc.com/homepage.htm

❋ Directory of Public Relations Agencies and Resources on the WWW:
www.webcom.com/impulse/prlist.html

Advertising

❋ Ad Council:
www.adcouncil.org

❋ Advertising Age:
www.adage.com

❋ The Advertising Research Foundation:
www.arfsite.org

❋ University of Texas advertising site—This is one of the most comprehensive sites with links to hundreds of advertising resources including these two:

http://advertising.utexas.edu/research/Topics.html

web@advertising (a very complete site by graduate students at the University of Texas):

http://uts.cc.utexas.edu/~echo/cover.html

❋ Advertising on the Internet: a tutorial
http://uts.cc.utexas.edu/~ccho/intad.html

❋ Internet Advertising Bureau:
www.iab.net

✳ Newspaper Association of America (contains much marketing and advertising information related to newspapers):
www.naa.org

✳ Audit Bureau of Verification Services:
www.accessabvs.com

Jobs

✳ TV Jobs Employment Bulletin Board:
www.tvjobs.com/bulletin.htm

✳ Online Career Center:
www.occ.com/

✳ Editor & Publisher Interactive Classifieds:
http://epclassifieds.com/EPM/home.html

✳ American Journalism Review's journalism awards and fellowships:
www.ajr.org/ajraw.html

✳ Joblink (a site on American Journalism Review created by Eric Meyer, owner of the Newslink Web service):
www.newslink.org/joblink.html

✳ Gannett Co. (jobs and internships in the Gannett media organization):
www.gannett.com/job/job.htm

✳ JobsPage (jobs and internships in the Knight-Ridder media chain):
www.freep.com/jobspage

✳ National Diversity Job Bank (a site intended to recruit members of minority groups and women but not limited to these groups):
www.newsjobs.com/

✳ Marketing Jobs Online (marketing, sales and advertising jobs plus marketing resources):
www.marketingjobs.com

✳ Broadcast jobs in theAntenna:
www.theAntenna.com

✳ Advertising jobs in Advertising Age:
www.adage.com/job_bank/index.html

✳ Yahoo's employment classifieds and career site:
www.yahoo.com/Business/Employment

* Monster Board Job Bank:
  www.monster.com

* College Grad Job Hunter:
  www.collegegrad.com

* Jobtrak (a job listing service for college students):
  www.jobtrak.com

* Nationjob Online Jobs Database:
  www.nationjob.com

* Careerpath—employment listed in many of the nation's newspapers
  but not limited to media jobs:
  www.careerpath.com

Web Design

* HotWired WebMonkey Tutorials:
  www.hotwired.com/webmonkey/teachingtool

* A Beginner's Guide to HTML:
  **www.ncsa.uiuc.edu/General/Internet/WWW/
  HTMLPrimer.html**

* Bare Bones Guide to HTML:
  www.werbach.com

* The Web Developer's Virtual Library:
  www.wdvl.com

* CNet's Web authoring and design resources:
  www.cnet.com/Content/Builder

* Graphics from Yahoo (links to scores of sites offering free or
  shareware graphics):
  www.yahoo.com/computers_and_internet/graphics

* Barry's Clip Art Server:
  www.barrysclipart.com

* Randy D. Ralph's Icon Bazaar (links to hundreds of icons and other
  sites for free Web graphics):
  www.iconbazaar.com

Web Tools

* Graphic Construction Set for Windows:
  www.mindworkshop.com/alchemy/gifcon.html

* Graphic Converter for Macintosh:
  www.goldinc.com/Lemke/gc.html

* Cnet's graphic designing graphics software:
  **www.cnet.com/Content/Builder/Graphics/Design/
  ss3e.html**

* Web Site Garage: a site that analyzes your Web site
  www.websitegarage.com

* Doctor HTML: a site offering free checkups for your Web site
  www2.imagiware.com/RxHTML/

More sites will be added to our online Web site and outdated links will be fixed
or eliminated regularly.

CREDITS

Netscape images throughout the book: Copyright 1997 Netscape Communications Corp. All rights reserved. Used with permission. The electronic files or pages may not be reprinted or copied without the express written permission of Netscape.

Microsoft Internet Explorer images: All images from Microsoft's Internet Explorer browser have been reprinted by permission from the Microsoft Corporation.

Interviews with sources in each chapter were conducted in person unless otherwise noted. Photographs of sources were used with their permission.

The following material was taken from research or these sources.

Chapter 1

Comments from Leah Gentry, Flora Garcia, Dan Patrinos, Mitch Lazar, and Meredith Artley made at sessions during the 1997 convention in Chicago, Ill., of the Association for Educators of Journalism and Mass Communications.

Chapter 2

Interview with Lou Montulli, a member of the original Netscape team, conducted by telephone.

Chapter 6

Comments from Mary Kay Blake: Yovovich, B. G., "Stiff Competition for Web Journalists," *Editor & Publisher Interactive,* Feb. 28, 1997.

Comments by Meredith Artley and Mitch Lazar made at the 1997 convention in Chicago, Ill., of the Association for Educators of Journalism and Mass Communications.

Chapter 12

Column by Mary Schmich about the graduation speech allegedly delivered by Kurt Vonnegut: Schmich, Mary. "Vonnegut? Schmich? Who can tell in cyberspace?" Internet *Chicago Tribune,* Aug. 2, 1997, accessed Aug. 2, 1997. <www.chicago.tribune.news/current/schmich/htm>. No longer available.

Chapter 13

Connell, Joan, "On the Internet plagiarism is easy," MSNBC. Accessed Dec. 4, 1997. <www.msnbc.com/news/91747.asp>. No longer available.

"McVeigh says death penalty unlikely to be overturned," and other trial coverage: Internet *Chicago Tribune,* Web-posted Aug. 18, 1997, accessed Jan. 5, 1998. <www.chicago.tribune.com/news/okcity/okcity.htm>. No longer available.

"The Lemon Awards: Winners would rather lose," CNN Interactive, Dec. 4, 1997, accessed Dec. 4, 1997. <www.cnn.com/US/9712/04/lemon.awards/>.

Nielsen, Jakob. "Be succinct! (Writing for the Web)," posted March 15, 1997, accessed Dec. 10, 1997. <www.useit.com/alertbox/9703b.html>.

Morkes, John and Nielsen, Jakob. "Concise, Scannable, and Objective: How to Write for the Web," Sun Microsystems, accessed Dec. 10, 1997. <www.useit.com/papers/webwriting/writing.html>.

Sanderson, Ward, "Upset Motorist soaks driver with toxic spray," The Spokesman Review, Dec. 15, 1997. Previously available online at <www.VirtuallyNW.com>. Copyright 1997. Reprinted with permission of *The Spokesman-Review.*

Sorensen, Eric. "WSU professor, police feuding," The Spokesman Review, Nov. 20, 1997. Previously available online at <www.VirtuallyNW.com>. Copyright 1997. Reprinted with permission of *The Spokesman Review.*

Brunker, Mike. "Wagering on the Web is risky business," MSNBC, Online. Internet, accessed Dec. 1, 1997. <www.msnbc.com/NEWS/130414.asp>.

Clark, Roy Peter. "Three Little Words: What I learned," Poynter resource file, The Poynter Institute, accessed Dec. 10, 1997. <www.poynter.org/research/nm/nm_clark.htm>.

Murray, Janet. *Hamlet on the Holodeck: The Future of Narrative in Cyperspace,* New York: The Free Press, a division of Simon & Schuster, Inc., Copyright 1997 Janet Horowitz Murray. All rights reserved.

Evard, Michele, "What is 'News'? Children's Conceptions and Uses of News," MIT Media Lab, accessed Dec. 10, 1997. <http://mevard.www.media.mit.edu/people/mevard/papers/what-is-news.html>.

Bernstein, Nina. "Lives on File: Privacy Devalued in Information Economy," *New York Times,* June 12, 1997. Accessed June 12, 1997. Previously available online.

Teaser to "Murder on the Main Line," Philadelphia Online. <www3.phillynews.com/packages/mainline/index.htm>.

Miller, T. Christian, "At some Florida prisons, shoe can be a passkey," *St. Petersburg Times,* Sept. 16, 1997.

Headrick, Christina, "Alligator chases man home," *St. Petersburg Times,* Sept. 16, 1997.

O'Dowd, Joe, "Manayunk man faces DUI, homicide accounts," Philadelphia Online, *Philadelphia Daily News,* Dec. 5, 1997. No longer available online without charge.

Chapter 14

Mandels, Pamela, "Professor Puts Holocaust Theories Online, Prompting Accusations at Northwestern," *New York Times,* Jan. 10, 1997. Previously available online.

GLOSSARY

ADVERTORIALS: Advertisements that look like news stories.

ANCHOR: The word, phrase or image you connect to with an internal link, one within the same Web page you are viewing or creating.

ANIMATED GIFS: Images with motion.

ANTI-ALIASING: Low resolution of computer monitors causes some images to have jagged edges, called *aliased images*. Anti-aliasing is a process that smooths the jagged edges by blending tints in the colors.

ASCII: American Standard Code for Information Interchange, a worldwide standard system for code numbers that computers use to represent letters and numbers. For writing purposes, when you save or write a document in ASCII format, it is plain text that can be read by any word processing program. It does not retain any formatting, such as boldface type, sizes or special fonts.

BANNER ADS: Advertisements stripped across the top or bottom of a Web site like a billboard. Banner ads also may be half size.

BIT, BYTE: A bit is the smallest unit of data transmitted on computers. A byte is a string of eight bits, the unit of data needed to store one character. For example, a byte to make the letter *A* requires the eight digits 01000001.

BLINK: An HTML code that causes text or images to blink like a neon sign.

BOOKMARK: A function in a browser that saves addresses of Internet sites. In

Microsoft Internet Explorer, this feature is called *Favorites.*

BROWSER: A software program that allows you to explore documents on the Internet. Netscape Navigator and Microsoft Internet Explorer are the two most popular browsers, but many others are offered by Internet providers.

BROWSER-SAFE COLORS: The 216 colors recognized by Macintosh and Windows in their color palettes. Each browser reserves another 40 of its own custom colors (in a 256-color palette) that are not common to both platforms. For a list of browser-safe color formulas, check Web designer Lynda Weinman's site at *http://www.lynda.com/hex.html.*

BULLETIN BOARDS: Discussion groups to which you subscribe, most without charge, and post or reply to messages.

CACHE: The place in your browser that stores the location of Web sites you have previously visited.

CGI: Common Gateway Interface, a program that takes data from the Web and allows interaction by interpreting the data and responding to it. Forms often are written in CGI scripts.

CHAT: A discussion via e-mail among people who are online at the same time in a specified location, often called a *chat room,* on a Web site. Think of it as a computer conference call, but the participants speak to each other by typing messages, although audio and video chat software is available. These simultaneous e-mail discussions often are called *real-time chats* and resemble a computer conference call.

CLICK-THROUGHS: Clicking on an advertisement that links to the advertiser's site.

CLIENT: An application on a computer that requests information from another computer that has software to "serve" to you. The computer that delivers the information is the "server."

COMMUNITY: Online communities are groups of people who share a common interest. Discussion groups, chats and other interactive forums help build online communities.

COOKIES: A coded piece of information that tracks where you go within a site. When you access a site with a cookie, your browser stores the code. The next time you visit the site, your movements in the site can be tracked by the code assigned to your computer. Because of privacy concerns, browsers like Internet Explorer and Netscape issue warnings when cookies are installed in a Web site and allow users to turn off the cookie mechanism in the browser. Cookies are helpful to managers of Web sites, particularly in the media and advertising, to determine readers' preferences.

CPM: Cost per thousand of page impressions, which are the number of times a Web page is accessed.

CRAWLER: An indexing program that scans documents on the Internet for key words.

CYBERSPACE: A term coined by science fiction writer William Gibson in his book, *Neuromancer,* to describe a simulated realm on a computer where people experience "virtual reality" by interacting with technology that makes their actions seem real.

DITHERING: The process of adjusting colors that are not in the main color palette of the browser to approximate the colors you choose. Dithering makes files larger, and the colors that result may not be exactly the same as you wished.

DNS: Domain Name Server (or Domain Name System), a standard system of addressing World Wide Web sites; also a synonym for an Internet address.

DOMAIN: The unique name given to an Internet address, including the type of site such as *edu* for educational, *gov* for governmental, *org* for organization, or *com* for commercial.

DOWNLOADING: Retrieving a document from the Web.

DYNAMIC HTML: A form of HTML that enhances design possibilities by allowing text or images on a Web page to change colors or movements. For example, with dynamic HTML a headline could move across the screen or text could change color when you move your mouse over it. This allows design in layers.

ENCRYPTION: Codes that scramble data so that only authorized people can read the information. If you are sending your credit card to an online source, you would want an encrypted site.

EXTERNAL LINKS: Links to other Web pages.

EYEBALLS: An expression used in advertising, such as *measuring eyeballs,* for counting visitors to Web sites because they view them.

FAQ: Frequently asked questions.

FLAME: Responding to another person's message with an abusive or sarcastic reply.

FONT: The name of a typeface. Originally it meant the family of different size letters in a particular typeface, but these days *fonts* and *typefaces* are used interchangeably.

FORUMS: Another term for discussion groups on a particular issue.

FRAMES: Like picture frames that enclose paintings, Web frames are containers for Web documents. A site with frames can have two or more documents on the same screen, each within a frame that can have its own scrollbar. However, borderless frames without scrollbars are popular too. Although frames are useful for navigation, they divide screens, making the viewing area smaller.

FREEWARE: Software that you can download or receive without charge.

FTP: File transfer protocol, a system that allows you to transfer files from an Internet site to your own computer. Many computer servers at universities and Internet software providers have repositories that allow you to log in with the password *anonymous* or *guest* so you can transfer files that you want without requiring an account and personal password for the site. Software programs such as Fetch for Macintosh and WsFTP for Windows make the process of transferring files easy.

GIF: Graphic Interchange Format, a compression format for images that reduces the number of bits it takes to load images onto Web pages without losing quality. The gif (pronounced jifs or with a hard g) format is usually used for graphics; photographs are processed in another compression format, known as *jpegs.* Images in this format can be read by all browsers.

GIGABYTE: One billion bytes of data (see *bit, bytes*).

HITS: When a user accesses a Web page, every text and graphic item on the page is called a *hit.* A page with text and five graphics would count as six hits. The term is misleading if used for advertising because one page could contain many hits. The preferred

measurement term is *page impressions* or *page views,* meaning each page accessed is counted as one page impression.

HOME PAGE: The main page of an online site, like a front door to a home.

HOST: The computer that provides the service that connects you to other computers.

HTML: HyperText Markup Language, a coding language for documents on the World Wide Web.

HTTP: HyperText Transfer Protocol, a system of rules that computers on the World Wide Web use to transfer HTML documents. All HTML documents on the World Wide Web start with *http* in lower case; browsers automatically insert this part of an address so you don't need to type it.

HUE: The color gradation as defined by its names, such as red or yellow.

HYPERLEAP: A word the author made up (a journalistic taboo!) to speed your progress through the book. It's meant to be the print equivalent of a hyperlink.

HYPERLINK: Also called a *link* in HTML documents, a hyperlink allows you to click and connect to another document on the World Wide Web. Links in text usually are in a different color from the text and often are underlined. Images also can serve as hyperlinks.

INTERACTIVE: Active participation by users in a Web site.

INTERFACE: By dictionary definition, an interconnection between systems or the way different and sometimes incompatible elements communicate. In Web design concepts, it is the way that users react or communicate with the computer. As a result, a user-friendly interface is a good design goal. File folders on your desktop, for example, are graphical user interfaces, meaning interfaces that provide you with visual cues.

INTERNAL TARGETED LINKS: Links that connect words or images within the same Web document you are viewing or creating, not to another document.

INTERNET: A global collection of computer networks that are connected through cables, phone lines or satellites to share information.

INTERNET EXPLORER: A browser made by Microsoft Corp.

INTERNET RELAY CHAT (IRC): Software that sets up a chat area in a server connected to networks of servers around the world that feature the same software, like a global conference call. IRCs feature channels in which people can log in and communicate with each other simultaneously by typing messages.

INTERSTITIALS: Sometimes called *in your face ads,* interstitials pop up in a window for about five seconds on a site while the rest of the site is downloading.

ISP: Internet service provider.

JAVA: A programming language that can feature animation, interaction and moving text.

JPEG: A compression format, created by the Joint Photographic Experts Group, to reduce the bits needed to view images on the Web so they can load faster. JPEGs (pronounced jay–pegs) are best used on photographic images.

LINEAR: Information offered in a preordained sequential order, such as a newspaper story printed in lines of text from beginning to end or a television news broadcast.

LISTSERVS: Discussion groups that are "served" to your e-mail. You must subscribe to this type of discussion list before you can post messages.

LURKER: Someone who reads messages in discussion groups but does not respond or actively participate by posting messages; he or she "lurks" behind the scenes.

MAILING LIST: Same as a listserv; a discussion group sent to your e-mail account.

MAJORDOMO: An automated software program that manages subscriptions to a listserv-type mailing list.

MEGABYTE: One million bytes of data storage.

NARROWCASTING: Catering to a niche or small group with similar interests.

NETIQUETTE: Etiquette or good manners on a network, particularly when sending e-mail messages to discussion groups.

NETSCAPE NAVIGATOR: A browser made by Netscape Communications Corporation.

NEWSGROUPS: Electronic bulletin boards where users may read and post messages on various topics. The most common are Usenet newsgroups, open to anyone if the server carries these groups.

NICHE: A segment or group of people with similar interests. In advertising, catering to a niche would mean marketing to a specific population targeted for its similarities, such as age, gender, or special interests.

NONLINEAR: Information that can be read or viewed in any order, such as hyperlinks on a Web document.

PAGE IMPRESSIONS: A Web page accessed by a viewer with all elements on the page counted as one impression instead of counting each item separately as in "hits."

PAGE VIEWS: Same as page impressions—counting each page downloaded by a user as one "view."

PARTNER, PARTNERING: A collaborative arrangement often used by media in partnerships with database companies.

PHOTOBUBBLE: A 360-degree angle picture that takes pictures by scanning the site and patching two 180-degree shots for a full view as though you were standing in the middle of the site being photographed.

PICAS: A unit of measurement used in print media. Six picas equal one inch.

PIXELS: A derivative of the words *picture element,* pixels are dots that make up images or characters on computer screens. They are units of measurement for computers. It takes 10 pixels to equal one pica. The most common design for screen-size of a Web page is 640 by 480 pixels. The average screen resolution is 72 pixels per inch, compared to the higher resolution of 1,200 to 3,000 dots per inch for printed materials.

POSTING: Sending a message to a discussion group.

PROTOCOLS: Rules that govern the way information is conveyed on the Internet.

PULL: An expression for browsing, where the user seeks the information by typing Internet addresses or searching.

PUSH: Technology that delivers information the user chooses to his or her computer via headlines scrolling across the screen like a screensaver or by sending documents to the user's e-mail. It is akin to an electronic clipping service or home delivery of a newspaper.

REAL TIME: A software program that allows computer users to simultaneously converse via typed or audio/video messages to each other while they are connected to the Internet as though they were communicating face to face or on the telephone.

REPURPOSING: Reusing information online from another medium such as print. It is essentially the same information used for a different purpose, online distribution.

RGB: Red, green, and blue, the values used to create different colors in computers. The combinations and strengths of the colors determine the hues.

ROBOT: A program or tool that scans documents on the Web in search of information for indexing, errors, or key words.

SANS SERIF: Typefaces with straight letters that have no serifs, the extra curvy strokes on the ends of letters. Helvetica and Geneva are examples of sans-serif typefaces. They often are used in headlines to contrast with serif typefaces, which are common for body type.

SATURATION: The intensity of the color; the purer or brighter a color is, the more saturated it is.

SEARCH ENGINE: A computer program that finds documents on the Internet at the user's request.

SERIF: Fonts are created in serif and sans-serif typefaces. Serif typefaces, such as Times Roman, have curves or extra strokes called *serifs* at their tips and endings.

SERVER: A computer that connects with other computers and delivers or "serves" information through a network.

SHAREWARE: Software you can download from the Internet without charge initially, but you are expected to pay a fee to the developer after a trial period.

SHOVELWARE: A pejorative term for dumping information online without changing the format or content. A newspaper story presented online exactly as it appeared in print is called *shovelware,* similar to *repurposing.*

SMILEYS: Symbols that describe a person's mood when sending e-mail messages, such as happy, sad or jesting.

SNAIL MAIL: Mail sent the old-fashioned way, by the U.S. Postal Service or other countries' postal services.

SPAM: Electronic junk mail.

SPIDER: A program that scans documents on the Internet for key words or indexing.

SPONSORSHIPS: A business or organization that sponsors an ad agrees to pay for the cost and maintenance of a site in return for placing its advertisement on the site.

STORYBOARD: A layout of pages in order they will appear. In Web site design, a storyboard is an outline of your site. A storyboard of the individual pages would show the content and page layout. In a cartoon, a storyboard is a layout showing each frame that will follow in story sequence.

SURF, SURFING: A slang synonym for browsing the Internet.

SYSOP: System operator.

TAGS: HTML codes enclosed in brackets. While other languages require an alphabet, HTML requires tags with codes that make the document readable in a browser.

TARGET: Same as an *anchor,* the word, phrase or image you connect to with an internal link.

TELNET: Terminal Emulation Protocol, the rules or programming that allow one computer to connect to another one at a remote location. The telnet protocol allows you to log into the remote computer system.

THREADS: A discussion of messages on a specific topic.

UNIX: One of the most common operating systems for computers on the Internet. Many university e-mail accounts reside on UNIX operating systems.

UPLOADING: Putting a document onto the Web.

URL: An Internet address, called a *Uniform Resource Locator,* to locate sites on the Internet, much like your street address locates where you live. The *AP Stylebook* refers to it as a *Universal Resource Locator,* but that is not the preferred term.

USENET: A worldwide group of electronic discussion lists, part of a network named for "users' network." Unlike discussion groups that require membership, Usenet groups are open to anyone for posting or reading messages as long as the server carries them. There are about 25,000 Usenet groups on a huge range of topics from scientific subjects to sex.

VALUE: The degree of lightness or darkness of colors.

VISIT: In advertising and marketing terms, a user must interact with the site in some way by clicking either an ad or a link to count as a "visit."

WORLD WIDE WEB: A worldwide system of storing and retrieving Internet documents created in a coded language (HTML) that features hyperlinks and can support graphics and multimedia. It is one part of the Internet and has become the most popular part of it other than e-mail.

WORM: A program that scans documents on the Internet for keywords.

WYSIWYG: "What you see is what you get," used to describe Web authoring tools that allow you to create a Web document that will look the same way when you view it in a browser.

INDEX

About the Author

Carole Rich has spent more than 25 years in journalism as a reporter, editor, and professor. Rich is an associate professor of journalism in the William Allen White School of Journalism and Mass Communications at the University of Kansas. Prior to teaching, she was a reporter for the former *Philadelphia Evening Bulletin,* city editor of the Fort Lauderdale, Fla., *Sun-Sentinel,* and deputy metropolitan editor of the *Hartford* (Conn.) *Courant.*

Rich teaches online journalism at KU and has developed a distance education course in the subject. She also teaches reporting, writing and ethics courses. Rich is the author of *Writing and Reporting News: A Coaching Method,* published by Wadsworth Publishing Co. In 1997–1998, she was awarded a research fellowship by The Poynter Institute of Media Studies to develop new ways of writing online. Rich has been a visiting writing coach at newspapers throughout the United States.